POVERTY AND LEADERSHIP IN THE
LATER ROMAN EMPIRE

THE MENAHEM STERN JERUSALEM LECTURES

sponsored by the Historical Society of Israel
and published for Brandeis University Press by
University Press of New England

Carlo Ginzburg, *History, Rhetoric, and Proof*

Anthony D. Smith, *The Nation in History: Historiographical Debates about Ethnicity and Nationalism*

Peter Brown, *Poverty and Leadership in the Later Roman Empire*

POVERTY and LEADERSHIP in the LATER ROMAN EMPIRE

Peter Brown

THE MENAHEM STERN JERUSALEM LECTURES

Brandeis
University
Press

Historical
Society of
Israel

PUBLISHED BY UNIVERSITY PRESS OF NEW ENGLAND

Hanover and London

Brandeis University Press/ Historical Society of Israel

Published by University Press of New England, Hanover, NH 03755

© 2002 by Historical Society of Israel

Printed in the United States of America

5 4 3 2 1

Library of Congress Cataloging-in-Publication Data

Brown, Peter Robert Lamont.
  Poverty and leadership in the later Roman Empire / Peter Brown.
    p. cm. —(The Menahem Stern Jerusalem lectures)
  Includes bibliographical references.
    ISBN 1-58465-145-8 (cloth : alk. paper)—ISBN 1-58465-146-6 (pbk. :
  alk. paper)
    1. Rome—Politics and government—284-476. 2. Poor—Rome—History.
  3. Church work with the poor—Rome—History. 4. Christianity and
  politics—Rome—History. 5. Church and state—Rome—History. I. Title.
  II. Series.
    JC89 .B72 2001
    937'.08'086942—dc21   2001002533

Contents

Foreword by Miriam Eliav-Feldon   vii

Preface   xi

1. "Lover of the Poor": The Creation of a Public Virtue   1
2. "Governor of the Poor": The Bishops and Their Cities   45
3. "Condescension": Poverty and Solidarity in the

   Eastern Empire   74

       Notes   113

       Index   147

       Index of Authors   155

Foreword

Miriam Eliav-Feldon

It is an honor and a pleasure to welcome Professor Peter Brown to Jerusalem on behalf of the Historical Society of Israel. Almost eleven years have passed since the brutal and senseless murder of Professor Menahem Stern in the Valley of the Cross, just a few hundred meters away from this elegant hall of scholarship where we are gathered today. One could hardly imagine a person less associated with brutality or hatred than the gentle and soft-spoken Professor Stern, who was loved and respected by all, colleagues, students, and acquaintances alike. His sudden and horrifying death left a wound and a pain that is still felt not only by his family and close friends but also by the entire academic community in Israel and by historians of the classical period around the world. The establishment of the Menahem Stern Jerusalem Lectures is, I believe, the most appropriate way of commemorating the life and contribution of such an erudite and influential scholar. As long as lecture halls are filled to capacity by men and women seeking knowledge and wisdom, as we see here tonight, we know that Menahem Stern's legacy is still maintained.

This year, the seventh since the series began, our distinguished guest is Professor Peter Brown, the doyen of Late-Antiquity historians, whose works encompass several fields that were of particular interest to Menahem Stern. A series of lectures by Professor Brown, on the subject of "Poverty and Leadership in Late Antiquity," is undoubtedly a most fitting tribute to Professor Stern's memory.

Opening address to Professor Peter R. L. Brown's Jerusalem Lectures in History in Memory of Menahem Stern, 16 May 2000.

Professor Brown needs no introduction to an audience composed of historians. Also, were I to read to you his *curriculum vitae*, including the list of his publications and of honors he received, there would be little time left for Professor Brown's own lecture. Therefore, I shall only point out a few facts that caught my attention while reading Professor Brown's career description.

Born in Dublin, Peter Brown studied at Oxford where he later became a Fellow of All Souls College, a Lecturer, and a University Reader. Then, after several years in Royal Holloway College at the University of London, Professor Brown taught at Berkeley, and, since 1986, he has been the Rollins Professor of History at Princeton. But, in addition to this brief outline of Professor's Brown distinguished career, please note the titles of his various appointments: at Merton College, Oxford, he was lecturer in *medieval* history; then he was appointed university reader in *late Roman and Byzantine* studies; in London he was professor of *modern* history, while at Berkeley he held the position of professor of *history and classics*. All these indicate, in part, the unresolved problems of periodization and departmentalization even at the best universities, but they are also evidence of Peter Brown's wide range of interests. The same breadth of scholarship is reflected in the titles of his books and articles, covering so many fields, historical periods, and areas of expertise: from the first centuries of the Common Era to the High Middle Ages; besides late Roman history, there is early Christianity, Byzantium, Parthians and Sasanians, and Islam; alongside Christianization and saints, we find art, sexuality, daily life, and much more.

Thus, it is not surprising that every history student, no matter what his field of specialization, is familiar with Professor Brown's works. It is impossible to study any chapter in the history of Christianity without reference to Brown's magnificent *Augustine of Hippo: A Biography*, first published over thirty years ago but yet to be superseded, or to his analysis of the cult of saints. Brown's handling of the passage from late Antiquity to the early Middle Ages constitutes essential reading for every historian concerned with a period of transition (and what period in history isn't a transition of one kind or another?). And, finally, any serious scholarly work in what is termed nowadays "gender studies" relies heavily on Peter Brown's pioneering analysis of western attitudes to women and sexuality in *The Body and Society* as well as in some of his later articles. From my own experience, in my attempts to understand a period of European history that is over a millennium later than the age of Augustine, I know that I have incurred an enormous debt to the scholarly insights and beautiful prose of Professor Peter Brown.

Thus, for my words of welcome tonight, I would take the liberty of borrowing from him once again. Among his many articles there is one entitled "The Saint as Exemplar"; I should like to present to you Professor Peter Brown—the Scholar as an Exemplar, here in Jerusalem.

Preface

For many years I had been deeply indebted to the all-encompassing work of Menahem Stern on the place of Jews and Judaism in the classical world. It was, therefore, a particular honor to receive an invitation to bring a contribution of my own to the series of lectures founded in his memory. The present book is an expanded version of those lectures. I trust that it will do justice to the memory of this great humanist and scholar of the ancient world.

What print alone cannot express, however, was the delight of finding myself in Jerusalem, to have the opportunity to greet Mrs. Stern and to make contact with so many old friends, with so many long-respected colleagues, and to make so many new acquaintances. I learned in every possible way from my encounters with a lively scholarly tradition, spread throughout Israel—in Jerusalem, Tel Aviv, and Haifa. My visits to innumerable sites, in the enthusiastic company of those who had discovered, interpreted, and meditated for so long upon them, opened up for me entire new facets of the world of late antiquity. I trust that this debt will be recognized by attentive readers of my text.

I owe all this, in large part, to the hospitality shown to myself and to my wife by the Israel Historical Society and especially to the constant care shown, on its behalf, at every stage of our visit and in the months that preceded it, by Mrs. Maayan Avineri-Rebhun.

In the final preparation of this manuscript, I have benefited greatly from the advice and encouragement of learned friends: Peter Garnsey, Avshalom Laniado, Richard Lim, Noel Lenski, and Charlotte Roueché. Their comments reminded me, once again, as in those happy weeks among my friends in Israel, of how much scholars need each other.

Princeton University   Peter Brown
September 2000

POVERTY AND LEADERSHIP IN THE LATER ROMAN EMPIRE

1 "Lover of the Poor"

The Creation of a Public Virtue

From "Lover of the City" to "Lover of the Poor"

In these three chapters, I wish to draw attention to the social and religious implications of a revolution in the social imagination that accompanied the rise and establishment of the Christian Church in the Roman empire in the late antique period, that is, between the years 300 and 600 of the Common Era. It is a revolution closely associated with the rise to power of the Christian bishop as an increasingly prominent leader in late Roman society. For the Christian bishop was held by contemporaries to owe his position in no small part to his role as the guardian of the poor. He was the "lover of the poor" *par excellence:* "A bishop who loves the poor, the same is rich, and his city and region shall honor him."[1]

But not only bishops were expected to be "lovers of the poor." To be a "lover of the poor" became a public virtue. It was a virtue expected of Christian emperors. The *humanitas,* the benevolent style of rule associated with a Roman emperor in the classical period, came to include demonstrative concern for the poor. In 451, Valentinian III and Marcian, the emperors of West and East respectively, declared that "it is a feature of our humane rule to look after the interests of the destitute and to ensure that the poor do not go without food."[2] The gravestones of the well-to-do all over the Roman world make plain that, in Christian as well as in Jewish circles, to be a *philoptôchos,* an *amator pauperum,* a "lover of the poor," an *elemosinarius,* a person "devoted to the giving of alms," or a *philentolos,* a "lover of the commandments [of God, to care for the poor]," were qualities singled out for praise in upper-class men and women.[3]

It is well known that, in the matter of care for the poor, Judaism had once been the mentor of the Christian churches. In late antiquity, it continued to be a worthy rival, able (in its own way) to match Christian endeavors in this field.[4] This fact was abundantly clear to the last pagan emperor, Julian the Apostate, when he came to compare the giving habits of his fellow-pagans unfavorably with the charitable deeds of Jews and Christians. Arrived at Ancyra (modern Ankara) on his way to the Persian frontier in 362, Julian wrote to Arsacius, the pagan high priest of the province of Galatia. He informed Arsacius that he was providing from imperial funds no less than 30,000 *modii* (around 200,000 kilos or 220 tons) of grain and 60,000 pints (34,000 liters or 7,500 gallons) of wine each year to the pagan priests and temples of Galatia. These would form the basis of a system of pagan poor relief, modeled on the activities of Jews and Christians:

In every city establish frequent hostels in order that strangers [in fact, the wandering poor] may benefit from our benevolence . . . I order that one-fifth of this be used for the poor who serve the priests, and the remainder distributed by us to strangers and beggars. For it is disgraceful that, when no Jew ever has to beg, and the impious Galilaeans [the Christians] support not only their own poor but ours as well, all men see that our people lack aid from us [that is, from the pagan priesthood].[5]

It is a particular pleasure and honor to find myself, on the occasion of the Menahem Stern Lectures, citing this well-known text in the edition and translation provided by Menahem Stern himself, in the second volume of his magisterial collection of classical texts, *Greek and Latin Authors on Jews and Judaism*. In that volume (which deals with the late classical period) the extensive observations of the emperor Julian on Jewish piety and social practice hold pride of place.

Yet even a contemporary observer as acute as the emperor Julian did not fully realize the extent to which the growth of a Christian system of care for the poor heralded a change in the self-understanding of late classical society as a whole. We moderns, also, tend to take this phenomenon for granted. We regard the widespread practice of "care of the poor" in the later Roman empire as being, in many ways, self-explanatory. We treat it as an entirely natural consequence of the Christianization of the Roman world. It is regarded as the inevitable—and, for most of us, the laudable—result of the final triumph of that *Evangelium der Liebe*

und Hilfleistung, of that "Gospel of Love and Charity" which
Adolf von Harnack viewed as a principal factor in the rise of the
Church, as he described it in his monumental book on *The Mis-
sion and Expansion of Christianity.*[6]

In fact, in devoting so much attention to the care of the poor,
Jews and Christians were not simply doing on a more extensive
scale what pagans had already been doing in a less wholehearted
and well organized manner. Far from it. It takes some effort of the
historical imagination to realize that, around the year 360 C.E.,
"love of the poor" was a relatively novel (and, for many humane
and public-spirited persons, still a largely peripheral) virtue. As for
organized "care of the poor"—this was a practice that cut across
deeply ingrained and still vigorous traditions of public giving,
from which direct charity to the poor was notably absent.

Let us, therefore, begin by stepping back for a moment to take
an overall view of the system of public giving that had existed for
so many centuries before the rise of Christianity. What needs to
be emphasized in this overview is that, for almost a millennium,
first in Greece and then in Rome, a distinctive "style" of public
giving had always been thought to communicate a distinctive
self-image of the community that benefited from this giving. A
great giver was expected to give to a specific group and to no
other: and in the definition of this group, the "poor," as such, had
no place whatsoever.

First, let us look at the givers. From the time of the Greek city
states up to the later Roman empire, it was a fact of life almost too
big to be seen that the most privileged and self-conscious human
groupings in the classical civilization of the Mediterranean—the
cities—were dependent, to a degree that never ceases to surprise
those who study them, for their economic and political success,
on their ability to draw on a seemingly unlimited willingness to
give on the part of their richer and more powerful inhabitants.[7]
An element of spontaneous, often of almost whimsical, generosity by the wealthy few was deliberately written into the life story
of each city and of every political institution. Centuries before
Saint Paul had declared (in a context very different, of course, from
that of civic beneficence) that "God loves the cheerful giver," the
hilaron dotén (2 Cor. 9:7), Greeks and Romans had professed to ad-
mire and to depend upon the interventions of "cheerful givers."
The more "cheerful" the giver the better; because he who gave

"cheerfully" on one occasion could be relied upon to give yet again.[8] As a result, _euergesia_, the urge to "do good" by public benefactions; the wish to be a _euergetés_, a "doer of good," to be a public benefactor; and the desire to be a _philotimos_, to stand out among one's fellows for the extent of one's public generosity: these Greek words became associated with actions that were especially prized by the elites of the classical world and by their inferiors in every city.

As historians of the social and political history of the ancient world, we need harbor no illusions as to the motives of so many of those who were praised as high-minded lovers of their cities. A _euergetés_ might be no altruistic philanthropist, but a rich landowner who had decided that the time was ripe to offer his grain upon the market, thereby reaping for himself both a handsome profit and the additional glory of being known to have saved "his" city from imminent famine.[9] The emphasis on the personal generosity of the emperor Augustus and his successors toward the _plebs_ of Rome, "his" very own city, was a statement that veiled, in acceptable classical form, their overpowering authority as emperors. Ideally, the emperors gave to the _populus romanus_ so as to express love for the citizens of "their" city, not to assert their power over them.[10]

What matters is that, in all such cases, the situation is spoken of in such a way as to imply that the personal agency of the great, in their decision to sacrifice private wealth for the public good, was the factor that, like a coiled spring, set in motion an entire economic or political process. By the year 300, the Roman world was filled with cities whose ruins still intrigue the archaeologist and the historian. The surviving monuments of each of them are a local history, frozen in stone, of a civic community built up slowly but surely over the centuries by continued acts of public generosity. To take a local example from Israel—the Roman ruins of the city of Bet Shean, ancient Scythopolis: "It is hard to envisage the appearance of Roman Scythopolis without the architectural and artistic contributions of private, civic-minded donors who adorned the city with great love and commitment as well as with the expectation of being honored and praised by their fellow-citizens."[11]

Second, the community these public benefactors, the _euergetai_, addressed and helped to define through their generosity was, first and foremost, thought of as a "civic" community. It was always the city that was, in the first instance, the recipient of gifts, or, if not the city, the civic community, the *démos* or the *populus*, of the city.[12] It was never the poor. What one can call a "civic" model of society prevailed. The rich thought of themselves as the "fellow citizens" of a distinctive community—*their* city. It was their city they were expected to love. A rich man was praised for being a *philopatris*, a "lover of his home-city," never for being a *philoptôchos*, a "lover of the poor."

The *euergetés* showed his "love of his city" by lavishing gifts upon it so as to increase the glory of its urban fabric and the comfort and overall vigor of its citizens. These gifts were directed either to the "city" as a whole—in the form of public buildings—or to a clearly designated core of "citizens," a *démos*, a *populus* or *plebs*. This core of "citizens" was thought of, ideally, as persons who were descended from citizens and who had long resided in the city.[13] If some of them were occasionally spoken of as "poor," it was because they were citizens perceived to be in danger of impoverishment, of coming down in the world, not because they already lay at the very bottom of society.[14] There was little room in such a model for the true urban "poor," many of whom would, in fact, have been impoverished immigrants, noncitizens, living on the margins of the community.

This was true even of the extensive arrangements for free food and other forms of support granted by the emperors to the *plebs* of Rome and to some Italian cities in the first century c.e.[15] A large number of those who benefited from the emperor's gifts were often undoubtedly "poor." The *plebs* of Rome included many who were chronically undernourished and vulnerable to disease.[16] They needed "civic" bread so as to relieve their hunger. But they did not receive this bread because they were "poor." They received it because they could produce a *tessera*, a token, that proved (in the manner of a modern passport) that they were "citizens."[17] In Rome and other cities, many well-to-do citizens received identical *tesserae*, tokens; and although they were not at all poor, they received exactly the same amount of grain as did the other, poorer citizens.

"Love of the poor," therefore, did not grow naturally out of the ideals of public beneficence that had dominated the minds and determined the actions of public benefactors in Greek and Roman times. It could only come to the fore as a meaningful public virtue when the ancient, "civic" sense of the community was weakened. In the period of late antiquity, then, Christian and Jewish charity was not simply one accustomed form of generosity among others, practiced with greater zeal than previously but not otherwise remarkable. It was a new departure. It gained a symbolic weight far out of proportion to its actual extent and efficacy. It was frequently represented as a challenge to the classical, pagan image of a "civic" community. For it threw open the horizons of society. In a social world modeled on the structures of the classical city, only fellow-citizens needed to be clearly visible. Their vivid presence in so many cities eclipsed the grey mass of the poor within the city and effectively blocked out the monotonous landscape of the countryside outside. In the new model of society, which would dominate the social imagination of the Christian Middle Ages up to and beyond the age of the Reformation, society was seen as a single, all-embracing whole that included city and countryside alike.

This more comprehensive community was presented now as frankly divided between the rich and the poor, with the rich having a duty to support the poor. It was now the poor (frequently described with gripping pathos) whose silent presence challenged the rich to give, and to give, above all, to them, the poor. The rich, therefore, were encouraged to look through the many intermediate layers of society—their family, their dependents, their fellow citizens—to focus, as in a dramatic close-up, on those who lay at its very bottom. Their relation to the poor acted, as it were, as a symbolic clamp. It bracketed and held in place an entire society. To act as a "lover of the poor" was to make an assertion, heavy with symbolic meaning, of one's acknowledgement of the ultimate cohesion of the entire human community. The drama of public giving, then, was no longer presented as a contribution of the rich to the vigor of their city and of its core of fellow citizens. It involved, rather, a gesture that reached out, by preference, to touch (in the poor) the outermost margins of society.

We owe our impression of the significance of this major change in the social imagination, from its ancient to its medieval form, to three decisive works of scholarship. Already in 1939, Hendrik Bolkestein, in his *Wohltätigkeit und Armenpflege im vorchristlichen Altertum*, had made plain the profound difference between, on the one hand, Greco-Roman notions of public benefactions and, on the other hand, the ideal of the care of the poor by the powerful, an ideal Bolkestein associated with the ancient Near East. In his opinion, this essentially nonclassical, Near Eastern ideal came to the fore only with the rise of Christianity and with the disastrous collapse of the Roman economy in the third century C.E.[18]

The definitive break-through in our awareness of the significance of this change, however, occurred only in the late 1970s, largely in French circles. In 1976, Paul Veyne's thought-provoking study of the outlook and aims of public benefactors in Hellenistic and Roman times, in his *Le Pain et le Cirque* (now available in an abridged English version as *Bread and Circuses*) did full justice to the irreducible particularity of a system of public giving and of a notion of social obligation that anticipated in no way whatsoever the Christian notion of "love of the poor."[19] Finally, in 1977, Evelyne Patlagean, in her *Pauvreté économique et pauvreté sociale à Byzance: 4–7e siècles*—a book that stands out as one of the most vigorous works of social history ever written by a scholar of the later empire—sketched out the manner in which a late Roman society, whose elites were still largely committed, in the fourth century, to a "civic" model of the community, gave way to a society seen in terms of an all-embracing, frankly "economic" model that juxtaposed the "rich" with the "poor" in town and country alike.[20]

The works of Bolkestein, Veyne, and Patlagean make plain that we are dealing with a profound mutation, during the late antique period, in the self-image of ancient society. But, on looking back upon these books, one cannot but be struck by the manner in which the role of Christian charity itself in late antiquity was not so much ignored in them as dwarfed. Christian "care of the poor" was swallowed up in what was presented as a massive change in the structures and ideology of late Roman society as a whole. Christian preaching and Christian organization of poor relief were presented as one symptom only, among so many others, of the ominous collapse of the ancient city. The proud "civic" model of classical times gave way, in the course of the fourth and fifth centuries, not to Christian preaching or to Christian activity among the poor, but to mute and irresistible pressure from below. The cities proved unable to absorb the novel forms of poverty created, in the eastern provinces of the Roman empire in the course of the fourth, fifth, and early sixth centuries, by a steady growth of population. This unforeseen demographic revolution burdened both city and countryside alike with unprecedented numbers of poor persons.

The existing structures of the city and the civic model that had been associated with them collapsed beneath the sheer weight of a desolate human surplus, as the cities filled up with persons who were palpably "poor." They could not be treated as "citizens," but neither could they be ignored, as in the old, more rigid "civic" model of the community.[21] Patlagean's later Roman empire was not simply a society that had become "Christianized." It was a society where the gulf between rich and poor had, at last, been starkly demystified: "poverty [she wrote] could [now] be seen in its full economic nakedness, stripped of the civic veil with which Rome had screened its reality."[22]

The rise to prominence of Christian forms of care of the poor registered this new situation. Christian preaching on love of the poor gave new words with which to speak of a new, less differentiated, post-classical society. But Christian endeavors did not, in themselves, bring about the collapse of the ancient city and of the imagined ordering of society associated with it. As Patlagean has put it: "was that preaching not [rather] a function of the situation itself? [part of] a history that begins with the poor surging in great numbers into a still ancient Christian society whose traditional framework they appeared to be breaking apart."[23]

If I differ from my friends and colleagues, Paul Veyne and Eve-lyne Patlagean, scholars whose work has been a constant source of inspiration and delight to me for well over two decades, I do not do so by denying their overall perspective—the liberating precision with which they have characterized the transition from one model of society to another in the late antique period. It seems to me, on looking back over the past decades, that these works have brilliantly delineated the poles between which late Roman society changed as it lost touch with its ancient roots and came increasingly to resemble a medieval Christian society. But to have characterized an evolution is not the same thing as to have explained it.

Hence, I wish to trace some of the steps by which the leaders of the Christian church, the bishops, actively engaged in forms of the exercise of power that helped to bring about that transition. The bishops and their helpers—lay and clerical alike—are more than symptoms. They were, themselves, agents of change. To put it bluntly: in a sense, it was the Christian bishops who invented the poor. They rose to leadership in late Roman society by bringing the poor into ever sharper focus. They presented their actions as a response to the needs of an entire category of persons (the poor) on whose behalf they claimed to speak. It was these actions that contributed decisively to the change whose overall significance Veyne and Patlagean have described so cogently. Step by step, they soaked significant areas of late antique society in the novel and distinctive dye of a notion of "love of the poor." It is the aim of this book to delineate, however briefly and tentatively, some of the most significant of those steps and the circumstances in which they were taken.

But this is to anticipate. What needs to be stressed, at the outset, is that when we attempt to trace the manner in which one model of society came to eclipse and replace another, we must proceed with caution. We must not allow ourselves to be unduly fascinated by the models themselves. The history of change in a vast society such as the Roman empire in late antiquity is a continuous and messy process. In describing such a process, the clear typological distinctions drawn up by scholars are often the better for being a little smudged. In all ages, models of society exert a great, and frequently unconscious, influence on those who hold them. In reconstructing them, the historian reconstructs nothing less than the invisible boundaries beyond which contemporaries were little inclined to think about their world. This accounts, in the present instance, for the profound lack of interest on the part of public benefactors of the classical age in a "care of the poor" that would have seemed quite natural to Jews and Christians of the late antique and medieval periods. Classical benefactors were not necessarily more hard-hearted. They simply looked out on society and saw, above all, cities and citizens, while Jews and Christians had come to see, rather, rich and poor.

But we must remember that such models of society have a crispness and a clarity of outline about them that are designed to reduce to order the confusion of real life. Nowhere is this more the case than in the classical period. From the days of the classical Greek city onward, the elites had carried in the back of their minds for centuries firm notions of what their community should be like. But these notions were framed in such a way as to screen out less manageable alternatives. To take one crucial example of this process of screening: The most recent demographic studies of Greek and Roman cities, summarized by Peregrine Horden and

Nicholas Purcell in their magnificent re-examination of the ancient Mediterranean, so aptly entitled *The Corrupting Sea*, suggest
that no citizen body could ever have been as stable or as perpetu-
ally tensed against outsiders as the citizens and their benefactors
liked to believe. The classical *démos*, which seems so vibrant an
entity when we read of it in written works and on countless inscriptions set in solid stone, was always, in fact, a fragile and
permeable human grouping. Long before the dramatic changes
that we associate with the last centuries of the Roman empire,
between the fourth and the sixth centuries C.E., the populations of
town and country alike had been as mobile as dunes of shifting
sand.[24]

We should be aware of this long-term situation. Mobility on the
land and uncontrolled immigration into the cities were vividly described by Evelyne Patlagean as being peculiarly rife in the late
antique period. They were held by her to have provided the demographic motor that drove the replacement of a classical by a medieval, Byzantine notion of society. Yet, such phenomena appear to
have been normal also in earlier centuries. The demographic
changes that we associate with late antiquity were, perhaps, less
dramatic and less novel than we have thought. It was not a period
characterized by a sudden breakdown of the old order. There was
never a time, in the ancient Mediterranean, when an extensive
grey mass of human persons did not pile up to press against the
firm but narrow self-image of the classical city. What mattered, in
late antiquity, may not have been the overall increase in destitute
immigrants. Rather, it was the manner in which the Christian
church gave new meaning to an ancient situation. It designated
the marginal groups that had always pressed in upon the city—
awkward persons, and many of them far from poor—as "the poor,"
entitled to protection and to some degree of integration into the
community.

Furthermore, we must remember that the drama of public giving that linked the *euergetés* to the *démos* was associated, primarily, with the Greek world and with parallel urban elites in the
Latin West, especially in Italy and Africa. It condensed a cultural
ideal of remarkable tenacity and of wide diffusion. But not every
well-to-do Roman in every region of the empire of the first, second, and third centuries was invariably open-handed or invariably
conscientious in living up to the ideals of civic generosity upheld

by Greco-Roman culture. It was a cultural ideal subscribed to by many with a certain nonchalance.[25] The acts of civic beneficence that have impressed historians and archaeologists, as they survey the literary and epigraphic evidence for the urban culture of Hellenistic and Roman times, were associated with persons whose temperament or sense of their self-interest led them to stand out as "virtuosi of euergetism."[26] Their actions were carefully itemized in stone with a lavishness of detail and of patriotic sentiment that tends to rivet the attention of scholars. But this voluble record makes us forget the silent majority of those more canny and less ostentatious members of the upper class who gave less to their city when they were living, and who remembered it in their wills by giving only as much as was strictly necessary to maintain the posthumous memory of their name and of that of their family.[27]

Nor should we forget that, in extensive regions of the Roman empire, from Britain to northern Syria, the city itself was less prominent than it was in the Mediterranean heartlands of Greco-Roman urban civilization. One suspects that, in many such areas, the change from a classical, "civic" model of the community to its post-classical, Christian form took place without the sense of rupture and of paradox that was deliberately fostered by Christian preaching and by the Christian organization of poor relief in the ancient cities of the Mediterranean. There the notion of the civic benefactor was still fresh in everyone's mind. Elsewhere, one suspects, people had been less certain as to what the rich should have been doing with their wealth in the first place, and were, perhaps, less surprised and impressed when, as Christians, they started to give to the poor.

What was new, however, even in areas of the Roman world where the "classical" model of civic beneficence in its pure Greek form was not particularly vibrant in the minds of contemporaries, was the appreciable downward shift in the drama of public giving itself. It was the "poor," and not one's fellow citizens, not even one's dependents, who were now supposed to be the object of acts of public giving appropriate to a Christian world.

For this reason, it is important to look, briefly, at the peculiar nature of the image of the poor in Christian texts of the late Roman period. For, suddenly, they are everywhere. We are presented, in Christian literature, with a society whose horizon is ringed with disturbing images of human misery. In Ancyra, where the emperor Julian had written his letter to the high priest Arsacius in 362, the porticoes of the courtyard outside the Christian church were filled with them: "What is wont to happen in all great cities occurred here too: for in the porticoes of the church there was gathered a crowd of people, some unwed, others married, lying there for their daily food. It happened one time in winter that a woman was lying in labor in the church portico at midnight."[28] To the northwest, at Amaseia (Amasya), the bishop, Asterius, described the poor huddling through the winter nights against the warm walls of the public baths.[29] They are the direct ancestors of the beggars of Ottoman times, who were known as *Külhanbeyleri*, "Lords of the Stokehole," seated on the piles of still-warm cinders raked from the stokehole of the furnace that warmed the baths.[30] At Bet Shean, Scythopolis, it is from a Christian source that we learn that the impressive late antique colonnades in the center of the city were the haunt of beggars: it was lying there that saint Sabas encountered an old woman whose sores "had become so malodorous that no one could bear any longer to go near her."[31]

The poor gather also outside the gates of every city. It is at the gate of Amiens that Saint Martin met one of them, shivering in his flimsy rags.[32] Outside Tyre, blind beggars would edge down to the roadside to beg for alms, alerted by the jingling harness of a passing horseman.[33] In Oxyrhynchus, in Egypt, the poor would doss down in the porch of the church on Saturday night so as to be ready for the Sunday distribution of food. A party of passing monks found shelter with them.

And as we lay down, there was a poor man with a single mat, half of it lay beneath him and half was pulled over him. It was bitterly cold. Getting up to pass water, I heard him groaning with the pain of the cold, but comforting himself, saying: "Thanks be to Thee, Lord, how many rich men there are at this time who are in prison, some bearing chains, others with their feet in the stocks, not even able to get up to pass water. And here I am, free as the Emperor himself, to stretch both my legs.[34]

We meet them, also, as they came to weigh on the conscience of a bishop. On one occasion, at the end of our period, a rich layman gave to John, the patriarch of Alexandria (609–619), an expensive bed-cover. The patriarch spent a restless night. His conscience was disturbed. For he had calculated that a bed-cover costing 36 gold pieces, if sold, could have clothed 144 poor persons:

who shall say that "humble John"—for he always called himself that—was lying under a bed-cover costing 36 *nomismata* while Christ's brethren are pinched with cold? How many are there at this minute gritting their teeth because of the cold? How many have only a rough blanket half below and half above them so that they cannot stretch out their legs but lie shivering, rolled up like a ball of thread? . . . How many strangers are there at this hour in the city who have no lodging place, but lie about in the market place, perhaps with the rain falling on them?[35]

Scenes such as this were meant to linger in the heart. They ensure that the study of poverty, in late antiquity as in any other period, is a painful matter. Whether it is in monastic anecdotes of the sixth and seventh centuries or in the mute records of an early modern English village, "A shudder of pain vibrates across the centuries."[36] The historian cannot claim to be untouched by such pain. But it is doubly important, for just that reason, that we look carefully for a moment at what these images tell us and what they do not tell us.

For they are, indeed, surprising for what they do not tell us. They are far from being mere faithful sketches, taken "from the life," of a generalized and enduring condition of the poor of the Mediterranean and the Middle East. They are highly specific images, created by a specific literature, in a specific period. If we compare these images with those current in medieval and early modern Europe and in the Islamic world, they seem to be peculiarly disembodied. We are presented in them with human beings trembling on the edge of physical and social extinction. They are faceless, anonymous, and wraithlike in their helplessness.[37] They are not the *classes dangereuses* of later European literature. The later empire had its fair number of very dangerous classes. But these were barbarian raiding parties and their hangers-on among the local population, brigands, deserters from the army, savage "Bacaudic" revolts in fourth and fifth century Gaul and Spain, and the murderous violence of the circus factions in the cities of the eastern empire in the sixth century.[38] They were not the poor. On occasions, the *afflicta paupertas* of the "impoverished" and resentful rich led to serious uprisings.[39] But only seldom were the "poor," as such, seen as a source of danger. The sharp anxiety expressed in early modern Europe concerning the threat to society posed by the "undeserving" poor is strangely muted in all but a few sources.[40] Nor are there any merry beggars. In late Roman literature there are

only a few faint hints of a folklore associated with beggars, such as
we meet in the rambunctious Arabic poems of the medieval *Banu-
Sasan*.[41] We are plainly being presented, in the overwhelming bulk
of the evidence, which comes from Christian sources, with the
poor defined, above all, as a passive and anonymous group: they
are seen as the recipients of gifts and as the objects of protection.
The poor in these images press in relentlessly upon us. Yet it is
extremely difficult—far more difficult than appears at first sight—
to estimate their actual numbers in late Roman society. Preaching
at Antioch in the 380s, John Chrysostom told his congregation
that they should think of their city as being made up of one-tenth
of rich residents, one-tenth of "the poor who have nothing at all,"
while the remaining 80 percent were of "the middling sort."[42] We
should not dismiss this statement out of hand. It is a good example of the application of what David Cannadine (speaking of the
notions of class in eighteenth- and nineteenth-century England)
has called "vernacular categories of . . . social self-understanding,
which provided people with the necessary and adequate means to
understand their social world."[43] John's proportion of one-tenth
indicates a level of poverty not dissimilar to that of late medieval
European cities and of early modern societies for which we have
fragmentary statistics. The tolerance level of such societies appears to have wavered between accepting 5 percent to 10 percent
of the population as permanently "poor" and in need of relief,
while being prepared to help between 20 percent and 25 percent of
the population for short periods in times of crisis.[44] Such "vernacular categories of social self-understanding" have a tenacious life.
At the end of the nineteenth century, William Booth could still
speak of "The Submerged Tenth" of industrial England. And like
John Chrysostom, Booth added: "is not one in ten a proportion
scandalously high?"[45]

Yet such a proportion is subtly misleading. By speaking of the
poor as one-tenth only of the overall population of Antioch, John
wished to persuade his congregation that the problem of poverty in
Antioch could be solved. If only the Christian rich would be a little
more generous, the poor of Antioch would disappear. What John
deliberately forgot, of course, was that he preached to a congregation made up of persons of the "middling sort" who, although they
did not think of themselves as members of the "poor that have
nothing at all," lived under a permanent threat of impoverishment.

Impoverishment was what most ancient persons feared most for themselves. And with good reason. Impoverishment could come at any time, from any number of misfortunes: from ill-health, from the deaths of spouses, parents, and children, from economic and fiscal oppression, and from violence of every kind. To use a term favored by historians of early modern Europe, John's hearers lived in a society characterized by widespread "shallow" poverty. And for most of them, the "deep" poverty of actual destitution remained an ever-present possibility. "Deep" poverty was a state into which they might fall, and from which they might emerge again, scrambling back painfully into "shallow" poverty, on many occasions in the course of their lives.[46] Hence the tell-tale blurring of the category of "the poor" in late antique sources. *Penés, pauper,* even *ptôchos* (the usual classical Greek term for the "cringing" beggar) did service indiscriminately for the wide range of levels of poverty to which the average person might be exposed. In this sense, late Roman society resembled that of early modern France: "The *Ancien Régime* considered as 'poor' those who simply were liable to become poor. It is a confusion that says much about the instability of the conditions of life among the populace."[47]

John Chrysostom's hearers were less concerned than we are with a statistical estimate of the overall extent of "the poor." They were right not to seek to quantify the poor in this manner. For it leads to an unduly massive view of late Roman society. This was not a society marked by clear-cut cleavages, as if it were divided only between rich and poor, between solid citizens and a clearly defined class of the destitute. As we shall see in our next chapter, late Roman society was considerably more differentiated in its structures (and especially in the cities where the care of the poor was most hotly debated) than we have been led to expect by previous scholarship. But this did not in any way make it a comfortable society. In terms of the average person's expectations of success and failure, it was a society made up of countless *paupérisables* (to use the apposite term of Jean-Pierre Gutton when speaking of the poor of Lyons in the early modern period). It was a world of persons who considered themselves, and often with good reason, to be vulnerable to impoverishment. It was not only a world ringed by the silent specters of the destitute, which play so prominent a role in the Christian literature of the period.

Despite the rhetoric of conventional narratives of the "decline and fall of the Roman empire," there was, in fact, little that was new in this respect about the late antique period. An uneasy balance between "shallow" and "deep" poverty had been endemic in the ancient world. In its ecology, in its demographic patterns, in its epidemiology, and in its structures of political and economic power, the ancient Mediterranean had long been an unforgiving place. There was little to protect individuals, communities, and, indeed, entire regions, from periodic hunger, from phases of acute economic and political oppression, and from the constant necessity, for many, to wander in search of a better life.[48] Even at the height of the Roman empire, the prosperity and commercial enterprise that we associate with classical Rome floated precariously on the surface of an "ocean of scarcity."[49] By the year 300, things were certainly no better. But neither had they become dramatically worse. It would be an exaggeration to speak of the later Roman period as a whole as if it were characterized by massive and unprecedented impoverishment. I would not agree with Hendrik Bolkestein that, in looking after the poor in the later empire, the Christian church did nothing more than act as "a consoling presence at the deathbed of a declining world."[50] Instead, what is interesting about late antiquity is that we are looking at much the same poverty as had always been there. But we now look at it with the sharper eyes of Christians, for whom it was both a moral challenge and a spur to action; and, above all, we look at poverty with the eyes of Christian leaders (the bishops) for whom the existence of the poor offered, for the first time in the history of the Greco-Roman world, an opportunity to highlight their role in a new, post-classical society. But before we come to assess the public role of the bishops in the Roman empire of Constantine and his successors in the fourth century, we must look, inevitably briefly, at the evolution of the Christian church in the period between the mission of Saint Paul and the conversion of Constantine to Christianity in 312 C.E.

"It is more blessed to give than to receive": From Paul to Constantine

By the time of the conversion of Constantine, in 312 of the Common Era, Christianity was already a somewhat elderly religion. It was almost as old as the Roman empire itself. To contemporaries of Constantine, who reigned until 337, the days of Jesus of Nazareth were as distant as the last years of the reign of Louis XIV are to modern persons. Much had happened to the Christian communities since the days of Saint Paul. It is usually calculated that, in 312, between 5 percent and 10 percent of the inhabitants of the Roman empire were Christians. This figure is, of course, a guess. What may be more significant is that the Christian churches appear to have suddenly surged in membership in the course of the third century. They were still distributed unevenly throughout the conglomerate of widely different regions embraced by the empire. In crucial areas of the eastern provinces, such as Asia Minor and Syria, Christianity was already prominent. Christians had recognizable churches, socially visible leaders, and well-placed sympathizers. Elsewhere, Christianity remained confined to urban centers. In most regions it had not penetrated deeply into the countryside, and it was barely detectable as a presence in the northwestern provinces of the empire.[51]

By the year 300, Christians claimed to possess a firm canon of sacred Scriptures. On the subject of "love of the poor," these Scriptures gave conflicting messages, each of which was held to be equally valid, because equally an expression of the eternal will of God. In the Torah and the Prophets, which Christians received as the Old Testament, they were confronted with a message that stressed the obligation to show solidarity with distressed fellow Israelites. They heard prophetic utterances that denounced with the greatest vehemence, as abhorrent to God, the exploitation of their poor compatriots by the rich and the powerful. In the Gospels, they met the strangely unplaceable figure of Jesus of Nazareth. Here was a man who was often seen in the company of the rich and who received support from them. Yet he saw the life of his own disciples in terms of a stark call to poverty:

Blessed are you poor, for yours is the Kingdom of Heaven. (Luke 6:20)

If you would be perfect, go, sell all that you have and give to the poor and follow Me. (Matt. 19:21)

It is easier for a rich man to enter into the Kingdom of God than for a camel to pass through the eye of a needle. (Matt. 21:24)[52]

Last but not least, they read in the letters ascribed to Saint Paul the exhortations of a man who was notably untouched by the "social pathos" associated with the message of Jesus to his disciples, but who was deeply preoccupied by the problems and opportunities raised by the presence of wealth among the believers.[53] Paul's letters showed him to be an indefatigable builder of new religious communities, scattered throughout Asia Minor and the Aegean. He was acutely aware of the potentially divisive effects of wealth within the "churches." But rather than advocate absolute renunciation, he was convinced that the secret of the unity of believers lay in a steady circulation of goods among "the brethren." He wrote frequently in his letters about collections raised to support needy communities, and most especially to support "the poor among the saints" in Jerusalem.[54]

As a result, Paul came to express what would become the classic Christian notion of the "cheerful giver" (2 Cor. 9:7). The "cheerful giver" was a person prepared to make sacrifices for the sake of the community.[55] Paul's ideal was an *isotés*, a "leveling out," an equalizing, of resources between the brethren, achieved through collections of money made by the more affluent churches to relieve the needs of poorer churches:

So that your abundance at the present time might supply their want . . . As it is written [of the miraculous properties of the manna sent from heaven to the people of Israel]: He who gathered much had nothing over, and who gathered little had no lack. (2 Cor.8:14–15)

Thus, by 312, three separate messages—solidarity, renunciation, and the circulation of wealth among fellow believers—existed in somewhat discomforting proximity, one to the other, in the minds of all Christians. For the Christians of that time did not have at hand the works of modern scholars, who could have relieved them of the tensions generated by this awkwardly assorted tripartite conglomerate of demands. No one told them that they could separate these demands one from the other by placing each in a highly specific social and religious context. No historian of the Ancient Near East was present to point out that, in the Israel of the eighth and seventh centuries before the Common Era, the word "poor" had connotations entirely different from the poor of their own times. These "poor" were not the utterly destitute, images of whose misery would come to haunt the Christian imagination throughout late antiquity. The "poor" of the message of solidarity in Israel were self-reliant tribesmen, small farmers, even impoverished aristocrats, whose "cry" to God and to the powerful was not for alms but for justice and the cessation of violence.[56]

Nor was Professor Gerd Theissen present to make a crisp sociological distinction, which has been of great use to historians of the Early Church, between the world of Jesus of Nazareth, a world of stark alternatives, and the more comfortable world of Paul. The discomforting message of Jesus has been safely confined by modern scholarship to a single, vivid landscape—to the countryside of Jewish Palestine and Syria. Jesus' immediate circle of disciples in Galilee and their successors are held to have claimed his more radical utterances as authority for their own lifestyle. They were *Wandercharismatiker,* "wandering charismatics." As a result of the message of Jesus, they had taken to the roads of Galilee, Judaea, and later, eastward, to Syria, as rootless and, if needs be, penniless evangelists and popular healers. There they lived (so we are told) in an exciting world of their own, impinging little upon the Mediterranean urban communities founded by Paul.[57]

By contrast, the world revealed in the letters ascribed to Paul is that of *The First Urban Christians* (to use the title of the influential book of Wayne Meeks). These were relatively well-to-do, settled persons, who lived in large cities, such as Corinth, Ephesus, and Philippi. Paul's message to them can be summed up as a form of *Liebespatriarchalismus.* His ideal was that of a "loving" community made up of benevolent and generous householders. It was an ideal eminently suited to the distinctive social composition of an early Christian urban community. Social distinctions between rich and poor, between slaves and masters were accepted, but they were to be softened by generous giving and by gentle dealings.[58] Altogether, had Christians of later centuries known of these enviably clear-cut distinctions provided by modern scholars—between a very ancient Israel, a radical and predominantly rural "Jesus Movement," and the more staid views propounded by Saint Paul to urban Christians—their attitudes to wealth and poverty would have been less fraught with creative uncertainty.

What early Christians took for granted, as part of an inherited conglomerate of notions shared with Judaism, was that they were responsible for the care of the poor of their own community. Fellow Christians must be helped in their need, Christian widows and orphans must be protected by their fellow believers,

Christians must not be forced by economic necessity to lapse from the faith or to fall into the hands of unbelievers.

But if anyone has the world's goods and sees his brother in need, yet closes his heart against him, how does God's love abide in him? (1 John 3:17)

By the third century C.E., however, the Christian churches had developed a further category of persons who claimed support. The bishops and their clergy expected to be supported, either fully (in the case of the bishop) or in part (in the case of priests, deacons, and other servants of the church) by their fellow believers.[59] By adopting this system, Christianity brought to an extreme conclusion the implications of a silent revolution that had already accompanied the quickening of the tempo of religious life throughout the Mediterranean. Support for the clergy was the outcome, in Christian circles, of an unprecedented "democratization" of religious expertise and religious leadership that had affected many cults. Put briefly: persons of the lower and "middling" classes, who found it difficult enough to support themselves in normal conditions, now entered with gusto and in increasing numbers into the high enterprise of religion. Not being persons of independent means, they had to be supported by others. Hence a crisis that affected Judaism and many pagan cults quite as much as it affected the Christian church.

For we tend to forget how comfortably *de haut en bas* the traditional religious establishments of the ancient world had tended to be. Religious speculation was usually regarded as the preserve of philosophers and scribes, who came from the wealthy classes and so had the leisure to engage in such elevating and time-consuming matters. In this respect, the Jewish *Wisdom of Ben Sira/Ecclesiasticus* speaks for the intelligentsia of the Greco-Roman world as a whole: "The wisdom of a learned man cometh by opportunity of leisure: and he that hath little business shall become wise. How can he get wisdom that holdeth the plough . . . that driveth oxen, and is occupied in their labours?" (*Ecclesiasticus* 38:24–25).[60] The public religious establishment in most cities, the Temple-city of Jerusalem included, was usually in the hands of "an aristocratic oligarchy" whose members had sufficient wealth and leisure to maintain the cults alongside their other functions as leaders of society. Priests and public benefactors were often one and the same person.[61]

This is not the world that we meet in Early Christianity or, indeed, it appears, in Judaism after the destruction of the Temple. Already in the period of the Temple the religious and political establishment of Jerusalem had to deal with Pharisees. The Pharisees were a novel group, in that they were distinguished by a high level of commitment to religion and yet were drawn from an ambiguous "middling" class of persons. They were "neither leisured nor destitute."[62] It was from just such classes that the religious leaders of later centuries would come in large numbers—beginning, of course, with that most anomalous of all "Pharisees," Saint Paul.

The first Palestinian Christians were even less privileged. This is shown in a vivid account (preserved by Eusebius of Caesarea from the history of Hegesippus) of the meeting between the emperor Domitian and the surviving relatives of Jesus of Nazareth, which took place in around 90 C.E.:

> Domitian asked whether they were descended from David, and they admitted it. Then he asked them what property they owned and what funds they had at their disposal. They replied that they had only 9000 *denarii*, half belonging to each. This, they said, was not available in cash, but was the estimated value of 25 acres of land, from which they paid their taxes and supported themselves by their toil. [They were, therefore, small farmers, capable of supporting their own families and even a few servants: they were by no means members of the destitute poor.] Then . . . they showed him their hands, bringing forward as proof of their toil the hardness of their bodies and the calluses inflicted on their hands by incessant labor . . . Domitian . . . despising them as beneath his notice, let them free.[63]

What Domitian saw had reassured him. These were the rough hands of farmers. They bore the traces of *ponos*, of that need for unremitting labor which, since the time of Hesiod, had kept the peasantry of the Mediterranean firmly in its place, locked in a yearly struggle to wrest a living from the ungenerous earth.[64] Lacking leisure, persons caught up in the world of *ponos* were not free to engage in the time-consuming and dangerous pursuit of religious truth. Urban artisans were in the same position. When the brilliant writer Lucian dreamed of his future career, he faced the option of becoming a sculptor, like his uncle. But the choice of even such a prestigious skill was out of the question for a man with cultural ambitions. Lady Culture appeared to tell him so in no uncertain terms: "you will be nothing but a laborer, toiling with your body and putting in it your entire hope of a livelihood."[65] In the ancient world, toil and serious thought were held

to be incompatible. In presenting the craftsmen of Athens em-
barked on the incongruous venture of producing a play in *A Midsummer Night's Dream*, William Shakespeare expressed perfectly
the blunt social common sense of the ancient world. There was
little room in such a world for "Hard-handed men . . . / . Which
never labored in their minds till now."[66]

What the emperor Domitian could not have known was that, in
the religious sphere, the future lay with "hard-handed men" or
with those who were closer to them than they were to the elites.
Whether as "apostles" and later as bishops and clergy, or (in certain cases in the third and fourth centuries) as rabbis and their disciples, both Christianity and Judaism drew on the dedication of
persons who, without necessarily being poor farmers as were the
kinsfolk of Jesus, nevertheless had never enjoyed the guaranteed
leisure of the truly rich. Such persons found that they had to face
hard choices. They could renounce whatever livelihood they had
and live (like the poor) from the gifts of others. Or they could balance, as best they could, the demands of a modest employment
with the heavy demands of total dedication to the things of God.
In pursuing their dedication, they expected to receive encouragement, protection, even (eventually) regular financial support from
their fellow believers, on whose behalf they were engaged in time-
consuming religious activity.

As a result of this new situation, both Christian and Jewish
texts lingered anxiously on the issue of the relation between the
wealthier members of the community and a new class of "poor."
These "poor" were not the distressed fellow believers, whose right
to support nobody doubted. They were, rather, a new, notional
"poor." They were persons whose all-absorbing commitment to
religion left them with little or no time to support themselves. To
use an image current in both Jewish and Christian sources, such
persons were the succulent "grapes" whose prayer and study gave
savor and safety to the community. Their weight was to be borne
by the ordinary wood and trellis-work of wealth provided by the
less-expert rank and file of believers.[67]

This was by no means a smooth development. Paul would not
have written as he did, with such exquisite sensitivity toward the
problem of the use and abuse of wealth in the Christian community,
if his career as an apostle and collector of contributions for "the
poor" of Jerusalem and elsewhere had not taken place under the

shadow of a powerful negative stereotype—the stereotype of the religious entrepreneur for whom the launching of a new cult was, quite frankly, a source of money and prestige and an occasion to live at ease at the expense of his followers.[68]

Paul found himself forced on many occasions to make his own position clear. He assumed that "apostles" such as himself were fully entitled to the support of the Christian communities.[69] But he went out of his way to forego that right. Rather than be a burden to others, he was prepared to work "with toil and labor . . . night and day."[70] It was "these hands" that Paul showed to the elders of the Christian community of Ephesus. Those hands, which bore the same mark of toil as did the hands of the poor kinsmen of Jesus, were the proof of Paul's integrity:

I coveted no man's silver or gold or apparel . . . these hands ministered to my necessities, and to those who were with me. In all things I have shown you that by so toiling one must help the weak, remembering the words of the Lord Jesus, how He said: "It is more blessed to give than to receive." (Acts 20: 33–35)

This rare appeal on Paul's part to the direct words of Jesus (words that are not found ascribed to him in any Gospel) shows how acute the potential conflict between support of the normal poor and support of the "ministering" poor might become in many Christian churches.

The sharp pen of Lucian (whose own narrow escape from "toil" left him mercilessly aware of the devices of religious entrepreneurs in his own age) is one of the first glimpses that we have from an outsider into the inner workings of a Christian community. It is not a flattering glimpse. In the middle of the second century, if we are to believe Lucian, the eccentric Cynic philosopher Peregrinus set himself up for a time among Christians. He became "prophet, cult-leader, head of the community . . . He interpreted and explained some of their books and even composed many." As a result, the wiley Peregrinus lived in luxury, even when in prison: "For their first lawgiver [Jesus] persuaded them that they are all brothers one to another . . . So if any charlatan and trickster comes among them, he quickly acquires sudden wealth by imposing upon simple folk."[71]

Such suspicions lingered throughout late antiquity. In the middle of the fourth century, Basil, bishop of Caesarea (Kayseri, Turkey)

took it almost for granted that a rogue priest might set himself up
as leader in a new cult, "not from any notion of obedience or piety,
but because he preferred this source of livelihood, just as another
man would choose one or another occupation."[72]

A withering scorn for those who made money out of religious
enterprises was a characteristic reflex of those lucky few who did
not need to make money in the first place. But, in reality, religious
begging on behalf of a god and the profitable creation of new cults
were far from rare among the middling and lower classes. There
was no reason why gods should not show their power on earth by
attracting wealth as well as devotees.[73]

Thus, for a century before the conversion of Constantine, the
Christian communities were characterized by a sharply "bifur-
cated" notion of the duties of the rich to the poor. Not one group,
but two groups, claimed the support of the "cheerful givers" in
every congregation.

First, of course, there were impoverished fellow believers—orphans, widows, the sick, the imprisoned, refugees, and the destitute. As far as we can see, Christian almsgiving at this time was a
fiercely inward-looking activity. It did not include unbelievers.
Rather, it strengthened the boundaries of the community, like
solid rings of bark around a tree, by not allowing any fellow Christian to be forced by poverty to resort to help from nonbelievers.

Nor was it a random matter. The bishop and the clergy were
supported by a share of the offerings of the faithful. But they re-
ceieved these offerings, in part, in the name of the poor: they were
to redistribute what remained from their own upkeep to the widows, orphans, and destitute. The bishop was presented, above all,
as the *oikonomos*, as the "steward," of the wealth of the church.
This wealth was to be used by the clergy for the benefit of the
poor. In some circles, even private almsgiving was discouraged:
ideally, all gifts to the poor were to pass through the bishop and his
clergy, for only they knew who needed support.[74]

This last was an extreme opinion. But the centralization of
wealth in the hands of an energetic bishop could be decisive. The
letters of Cyprian, bishop of Carthage from 248 to 258, are impressive testimony to his use of wealth for the care of the poor in order
to reinforce his notion of the Catholic church as a closed, embattled community grouped around its bishop. Only those "poor" who
were known to have stood firm in times of persecution and to have

remained loyal to the bishop in the crisis that followed were to receive support.[75] Local heroes who had endured imprisonment in
times of persecution received allowances.[76] Cyprian provided for
refugees out of his own private funds, thereby saving well-to-do
Christians the shame of accepting alms as if they were members of
the indigent poor.[77] The boundaries of the Christian community
were protected. Christian traders were given bridging loans.[78] A
convert who had made his living by teaching acting (a profession
tainted by idolatry) was maintained by the poor fund of his local
church. Cyprian advised the bishop to send him to Carthage, where
the church, being wealthier, was better able to support him until
he learned a new trade.[79] A considerable sum—one hundred thousand sesterces, the equivalent of half the yearly salary of an Imperial secretary or of a month's wages for three thousand workmen—
was hurriedly collected in Carthage to ransom Christians captured
in a raid by Berber tribesmen.[80] Unfortunately, the list of donors
that was appended to this letter has not survived. Would that it
had. With it we might have had evidence of a Carthaginian Christian community of unexpected wealth and social complexity.[81] Altogether, in the words of Graeme Clarke, the translator of the *Letters* and the author of by far the best commentary upon them,
Cyprian's letters provide "practical evidence of the Church consti-
tuting a society within a society, a regular *tertium genus.*"[82]

Thus, a solid middle core of "cheerful givers" was called upon
to support two sharply different groups of dependent persons, each
of which was liable to considerable expansion—both the clergy
and the poor, with the clergy claiming to act as distributors of the
wealth of the church in the interests of the poor. Writing in 251, to
the bishop of Antioch, Cornelius, the bishop of Rome, emphasized
the extent of this double responsibility:

there can only be one bishop in a church in which are 46 priests, 7 deacons, 7 subdeacons, 42 acolytes and 52 exorcists, readers and doorkeepers
[154 in all: a group as large as most voluntary associations in Rome] and
more than 1500 widows and distressed persons [a considerable group, as
large as the largest association of artisans in the City].[83]

In 303, we learn that a police raid on the premises of the church
of Cirta (Constantine, in modern Algeria), a provincial capital,
found a storeroom with sixteen shirts for men, thirty-eight veils,
eighty-two dresses and forty-seven slippers for women, along with

eleven containers of oil and wine. Furthermore, we know that the church of Cirta had, besides its bishop, at least three priests, two deacons, two subdeacons, one grave-digger, and five readers. None of these were paupers. One reader was a schoolmaster and the other a tailor, a *sartor*—or, perhaps, even a skilled craftsmen in mosaic work, a *sarsor:* that is, he was exactly the same sort of skilled artisan as Lucian's uncle, the sculptor, had been and from whose trade Lucian had escaped to higher things.[84] But all the clergy—that is, the priests and deacons—and possibly lesser personnel as well, would have received from their bishop regular *sportulae*. These were gifts derived from a weekly division of the offerings of the faithful. The offering itself was a major ceremony, performed each Sunday. It involved a procession toward the altar and the solemn dividing up of the contributions of the faithful at a table loaded with offerings in cash and in garden produce.[85]

Thus, when Constantine decided to patronize the Christian church in 312 he found a body committed to a double charge: a duty to give to the poor and a duty to support the clergy. He also found among the Christian laity many well-to-do persons who had long been alerted to the need to scrutinize the clergy whom they themselves supported, to ensure that their money was spent to good effect. An ideology that linked the wealth of the church to the "care of the poor" and that made the clergy responsible for that care was firmly established in Christian circles before the conversion of Constantine. It would have been what a lay person (such as Lucian) would have known about the new sect.

After Constantine: Privilege and Poor Relief

In Constantine, the Christian churches were presented with a "cheerful giver" on a scale of which no previous generation of believers had dreamed. Throughout his reign, from the time of his conversion until his death in 337, Constantine placed gigantic Christian basilicas in many major cities. These building projects alone amounted to "a deluge of . . . publicity [that] exceeded any other program in precious stones realized by a ruler in antiquity."[86] The effect of such giving on provincial churches must have been stunning. The gifts of pious lay donors of previous years were dwarfed by imperial largesse. In 310, the rich widow Lucilla had secured the election of her candidate as bishop of Carthage through the judicious distribution, to the assembled bishops, of four hundred purses of coins. The gift was made to them to distribute to the poor. The poor saw nothing of that money. The bishops distributed it among themselves, and Lucilla's man became bishop of the second greatest see in the Latin West.[87] But, in 313, an imperial commissioner arrived at Carthage with some 3,000 purses of coins, as travel allowances for the supporters of the emperor's candidate, who was the opponent of Lucilla's nominee.[88] The "cheerful giver" of earlier times was now frankly outclassed by a Christian emperor.

Altogether, the conversion of Constantine brought a Christian church, previously characterized by well-organized but essentially inward-looking charitable endeavors, into a world in which the more outward-going "civic" ideal of public benefaction was still alive. The ideal had survived the crisis of the third century. In the Roman empire of Constantine and his successors, the Christian church did not face a *tabula rasa*, from which all features of ancient, classical society had been expunged.

The emperor remained a towering exemplar of old-fashioned euergetism. One of the most challenging discoveries of recent scholarship has been the extent to which, in the major cities of the empire (and even, on a lesser scale, in some provincial centers), a traditional, "civic" definition of the community was maintained throughout the fourth and fifth centuries.[89] The *annona* system had involved the mobilization of vast quantities of foodstuffs for distribution to the citizens of the cities, either free or at reduced prices. It continued to function. It was a system of distribution in which, as we have seen, the poor had no place. It was for citizens only. And it remained so. The *annona* system remained awesome in its scope and in the human effort involved in its success. In fourth-century Rome, some 150,000 citizens still received the *annona civica*. The supply of foodstuffs involved the herding, every year, from central and southern Italy, of sufficient pigs to yield five million pounds of pork, and the transport, mainly from Africa, of some twenty-five million *modii* (166,750,000 kilos or 18,300 tons) of grain.[90] In the sixth century, twenty-four million *modii* (160,080,000 kilos or 17,500 tons) were shipped from Egypt to Constantinople.[91] These, of course, are maximum figures. Not all of this cheap food for citizens was available at all times. Rather, the huge administrative effort devoted to the *annona* was maintained, whether it worked in practice or not, because it served to highlight the role of the emperors. The emperors had remained *euergetai*, public benefactors, in the old-fashioned manner. Their concern for the *annona* showed that they still "loved" their city and its citizen inhabitants.

Public benefactions by private citizens to their cities had diminished, in comparison with the *belle époque* of the second and early third centuries. But they were still practiced.[92] Local governors now tended to take the place of local *euergetai* in restoring and decorating the cities, but these men were mostly drawn from the civic elites. They shared with them a "collective memory" of classical urban life in which public benefactions were expected of prominent persons.[93] So firmly ensconced was the image of the *euergetés* as an ego-ideal of public life even among Christians, that the alert Louis Robert could use the sermons of John Chrysostom and Basil of Caesarea to illuminate the phraseology of second-century inscriptions in praise of civic benefactors. The few brilliant pages that Robert devoted to the subject are striking testimony to the survival, in late antiquity, of the classical language of euergetism.[94]

As members of the upper classes came to attach themselves in increasing numbers to the churches, they expected that their gifts to the poor and to the clergy should be surrounded with some of the sense of drama associated with acts of civic benefaction. They wished, in church also, to wear the ancient "halo" of a *euergetés*. Indeed, some succeeded in doing just that. On the mosaic floor of the late sixth-century church of Kissufim in the Negev, the lady Silthous is shown staring forward with an outstretched right hand, from which coins rain down in the gesture of the classical *megalopsychos*, the person of open-handed generosity. Her left hand clutches her robe in a gesture that makes the folded end of the robe seem like the *mappa*, the handkerchief by which the consuls would start the races when they presided over the games at Rome and Constantinople. In an otherwise remote provincial church, a pious Christian woman was able to show herself performing public benefactions to the Christian community in a manner that echoed ancient gestures associated with the greatest figures in the land.[95] As we shall see in our next chapter, such ambitious figures did not swamp the church of the fourth century.

Christian churches remained, in most places, doggedly low-profile, middling communities. But a new class of Christian *euergetai* had arrived, even if they were not yet widespread. Christian civic notables who could now be spoken of, in the same sentence, as both "first in the city council . . . and by reason of his piety, a lover of the poor," would expect a bishop to be a public figure like themselves, prompt and generous in looking after "his" city.[96]

The emperors thought the same. The disproportionate weight of imperial giving to individual churches was felt only on certain occasions and in the churches of a few regions: we should not exaggerate its immediate impact on Roman society. What mattered far more in the long run were the privileges that Constantine bestowed on the Christian church as a whole. These affected every church in the empire. They subjected the Christian clergy, as a body, to the extensive but demanding patronage of the Roman state. It would be the state, and not only the local congregation, that would now watch the Christian clergy carefully, to ensure that they made use of the support that had been offered to them with such generosity.

We must remember that the more the late Roman state of the post-Constantinian period is studied, the more it is revealed to have been a formidably ambitious institution.[97] Nowhere was this more apparent than in the wide range of privileges and exemptions that grew up in connection with a system of taxation and compulsory services that had been imposed with unprecedented determination on an empire-wide basis. The upshot of this development was a structuring of society in which the differential incidence of taxation proved crucial. If, in the words of the Supreme Court Justice John Marshall, "the power to tax is the power to destroy," then, in late Roman conditions, the right to avoid tax conveyed the right to prosper.

This was particularly true in the case of the Christian church. Under Constantine, Church property received substantial exemptions from the land tax.[98] More important still, the bishops and the clergy of all ranks were freed from personal taxes and from liability to the many forms of compulsory service that absorbed so much of the time and money of members both of the town council and of the humbler guilds of artisans.[99] In this context, it is important to bear in mind that, in the early fourth century, few bishops and even fewer clergymen were men of independent means. Most clergymen "doubled" as officials of the church and as traders, artisans, and small landowners.[100] Apart from the bishop (who was expected to be free from all other employments), the offerings of the faithful did no more than supplement the incomes of the other clergy. Constantine's tax exemptions were crucial to just such people. They did not only represent, for the average member of the clergy, an enviable exemption from expense and time-consuming duties. They were a clear mark of status. In every city of the empire, the bishop and his staff of priests and minor clergy now stood out as a miniature "aristocracy of the exempt."[101]

Yet Constantine's exemptions had been framed in a dangerously open-ended manner. It was unclear to what grades of the clergy they applied. Did they apply only to bishops and priests, or did they extend to the entire personnel of the Church, from deacons down to the humble gravediggers? It was also uncertain whether they were held by clergymen by virtue of their office alone or whether they could be passed on to their sons. Nor was it clear to what extent the private wealth of bishops might benefit from exemptions granted to the lands of the Church.[102] Above all, it was far from clear to which group of Christian clergy these privileges applied. All over Africa, as a result of the Donatist schism, every city had two bishops, each of whom claimed to represent the true, "Catholic" church. In the Eastern empire, the Arian controversies soon brought about a situation where each party victimized the other by means of imperial officials, who would be charged to review and to deny the privileges of the clergy of their rivals. In Alexandria, the privileges granted to the clergy and the poor relief attached to them changed hands between rival parties on at least three occasions within two decades, during the stormy tenure of bishop Athanasius. "Hostile audits" of the clergy of rival parties, and the return of clergymen to compulsory public duties in their home towns, were a regular feature of campaigns of intimidation, directed by Christian emperors against those who failed to follow the official line.[103] Altogether, the legislation of the reign of Constantius II (337–361) shows how the uncertain application of Constantine's generous policy of ecclesiastical privilege had, within two generations of his conversion, generated much pleading in the courts, much rhetoric, and a need for a clearer view of what, exactly, the Christian clergy claimed to have done so as to deserve their privileges.

The notion that priests should be "free" so as to worship God or the gods on behalf of the community was deeply rooted in the practice of the ancient Near East and of the Roman empire.[104] The "Catholic" clergy were treated as the successors to the pagan priesthoods. They were said to benefit the Empire by praying on its behalf to the one, true God: "since We are aware that Our State is sustained more by religion than by official duties and physical toil and sweat."[105] This was a claim that the Jewish *rabbis* also made on behalf of Israel: it was the devout study of Torah, and not the collection of taxes, that kept the world safe.[106] In fact, the Christian emperors took them at their word. Consistent monotheists, they granted the same privileges to heads of synagogues and their personnel as they had done to the Christian clergy.[107] Rabbis also claimed exemptions, if in a more *ad hoc* and contested manner.[108]

But such claims, though elevating, were somewhat vague. Officials tended to ask more mundane questions: What did the Church do for the community? The answer, of course, came from the former tradition of the accountability of the clergy for their use of the offerings of the faithful: the Church received offerings because it looked after the poor. As we have seen, this was already a commonplace in Christian circles. Hence, by a slight but significant shift of emphasis, traditional Christian charity to fellow believers within the Christian community came to be regarded as a public service, as a more general "care of the poor" performed in return for public privileges.

This refrain runs through the laws of the period. For instance, clergymen who continued to earn money as traders were exempted from the gold tax: for a clergyman's profits "should be administered for the use of the poor and the needy."[109]

The notion of "care of the poor" helped to define the place of the Christian church in Roman society. It acted as a discreet control on the clergy. They were to know their place—closer to the poor than to the top of society. Thus, in 326, a law of Constantine ruled that rich townsmen might not join the clergy. The emperors did not want the town councils to be drained by "lateral promotions" of their wealthy members into the new hierarchy of the Christian church, as bishops and clergymen. Rich town councilors were to continue to serve their city: "For the wealthy must be there to support the obligations of the secular world, while the poor are maintained by the wealth of the church."[110]

Constantine encouraged this tendency to define the Church as an organization charged with the care of the poor by allotting levies of food and clothing to the clergy, for the support of widows, orphans, and poor persons registered on the lists of the Church. Constantine's grant was acclaimed by Christians as the fulfillment of Isaiah's prophecy: "Kings will be your foster-fathers" (Isaiah 49:23).[111] These registered persons formed a *plebs* in miniature, to which an imperial gift of food had been granted. But, for the first time, they were defined, in strictly Christian terms, as "the poor." The amounts involved in these "*annonae* for the poor" were small compared with the prodigious quantities of grain shipped every year to the "civic" *plebs* of Rome and Constantinople. In 331, Constantine gave the clergy of Antioch a regular dole of corn to feed the poor. It was only 36,000 *modii* (214 tons: roughly the same amount, that is, as Julian the Apostate gave to the pagan priests of Galatia for much the same purpose). This was a risible sum compared with the 100,000 *modii* that even a small town such as Pozzuoli received each year as a "civic" *annona*, and with the 420,000 *modii* (some 3,000 tons) that Julian brought into Antioch to relieve a famine in 362/3.[112] But the purpose of such doles was to define an obligation. The clergy could be called to account by the state if they failed to make use of their privileges for the benefit of the poor. This happened, in no uncertain manner, to the troublesome Athanasius of Alexandria. He was accused of selling on the private market grain that Constantine had given to the church.[113]

Thus, far from signaling widespread acceptance of Christian values, the imperial laws and the attendant acts of imperial generosity reflected the exact opposite. They betray frequent challenges to the privileges of the clergy and the consequent need for greater clarity as to the exact purpose for which these privileges had been issued.

In this respect, it is easy to be blinded by the urgency and brilliance of fourth-century Christian preaching on "love of the poor." We tend to look always to the bishops as the organizers and facilitators of what were, at times, impressive ventures of poor relief. As a result, we have overlooked the constant, mute pressure exerted upon the Church itself by the expectations of lay persons— of lawyers, bureaucrats, and the advisers of the emperors—who needed to be reassured, in terms of the classical, "civic" model with which they were familiar, that the privileges of the clergy were being used for the public good. In the laws and in other, less-considered incidents in the history of Christian charity in the fourth century, we can hear a voice that we seldom hear in late antiquity: the voice of Christian lay persons. Many such Christians were now public servants. Their notions of giving to the poor did not necessarily coincide entirely with those of the clergy. Rather, they betrayed a strange mixture of the classical and the Christian. It is to this phenomenon that we must turn in order to conclude this chapter.

The best way to appreciate the new situation is to look briefly at the Christian institution that attracted the attention of the emperor Julian in 362 C.E.—the *xenodocheion*.[114] As Julian's letter to the pagan high priest Arsacius makes plain, Christian *xenodocheia* were already a prominent feature in many cities. Their exact size and purpose largely escapes us. Most would have been standard buildings, not easily distinguished by archaeologists. None were as large as the great *Misericórdias* and *Ospedali* of early modern Catholic Europe, or their Islamic equivalents, the splendid *imarets* of the Ottoman empire. To take one example: the hostel attached to the monastery of Saint Martyrius at Ma'ale Adummim, on the road from Jerusalem to Jericho, is a cramped building compared with the spacious monastery to which it is attached at one corner. It could have housed sixty to seventy persons squeezed together in two storeys. It would have housed mainly pilgrims on the main road to the Holy Places.[115]

We should not define the functions of the *xenodocheia* too rigidly. They received poor travelers, whether as pilgrims on their way to holy places or simply as wanderers in search of food and work. In Pontus, they had a name derived from local Christian usage—they were called *ptôchotropheia*, places for the "nourishing of the poor."[116] Such *xenodocheia/ptôchotropheia* also functioned as hospitals.[117] There was nothing strange in this. For ancient persons to travel to seek a god and to wait upon him (for long periods, if needs be) for a cure was a normal response to the onset of illness. In the fourth century, as in all later centuries, the rest and better diet provided at a *ptôchotropheion* was, in itself, a major agent of cure.[118] Furthermore, in the case of lepers, to offer a roof and a fixed residence for such poor wretches (often placed at a safe distance from the city) was a practical and altogether welcome way of controlling the disease and of allaying public fears of contagion. John Chrysostom was predictably unpopular when he placed his own leper house too close to a fashionable suburb in Constantinople.[119]

What needs to be stressed is that the Christian poorhouse-cum-hospital was a novel institution in the ancient world. Temples, of course, had always contained large sleeping quarters for those in search of healing, as at the incubatory shrine of Asclepius at Epidaurus. But the new *xenodocheia* were not necessarily connected with healing shrines. Only soldiers and slaves—that is, persons who had no family to look after them—had *valetudinaria*, hospital quarters in their camps and slave barracks.[120] To extend this facility to the poor in general and to associate it with any human settlement (with cities, with villages, or with the country estates of Christian landowners) was a new departure. By offering to shelter and to feed the wandering poor, the *xenodocheia* gave new prominence to a hitherto "invisible" class of migrants, to whose movements no one had paid much attention before.

It is also important to realize that, in Christianity itself, the appearance of the *xenodocheion* was a novelty. It was not there in the pre-Constantinian church, and, indeed, not, as far we can see, in the reign of Constantine. It is only in the 350s that *xenodocheia* clearly appear in Christian sources.[121] They appear first in the eastern provinces. So, when Julian referred to *xenodocheia* in 362, he was looking, not at an immemorial practice of the Christian church, but at a phenomenon associated with the reign of his hated Christian cousin, Constantius II.

In many cases, the new *ptôchotropheia* were added to the claims to tax exemption put forward by the clergy. The lands from which they drew their income and the rapidly expanding personnel required for their staffing posed, once again, the issue of ecclesiastical privileges enjoyed in the name of the "care of the poor." Bishops were not the only founders of such buildings. Many were set up by wealthy Christians. Some of these were government officials. When still a young man, Paulinus of Nola, as governor of Campania, had established (or expanded) a hostel for the poor by widening the portico in which they sheltered at the shrine of his favorite saint, Saint Felix at Cimitille.[122] Such persons could be approached by bishops, as fellow founders of poorhouses, to grant the *philanthropia*, the gracious gift of tax-exempt status, to the bishop's new hostels.[123]

A *xenodocheion* was a clearly defined building, of use to the community. To found one was a reassuringly old-fashioned way of showing public munificence. The builder of one such hostel for travelers was acclaimed by the *démos* of Neoclaudiopolis (Vezir Köprü, Turkey) in Pontus as a *euergetés*.[124] They were destined to have a surprisingly long life. In Western Europe, poorhouses first set in place by pious persons in the Roman cities in late antiquity continued up to modern times: an orphanage founded in sixth-century Trier, for instance, was still there to be reorganized by Napoleon![125] But most remarkable of all is the mosaic placed at the entrance of a hospital, now in the Museum of Ma'arat an-Numan in Syria. Laid down in 511 C.E. it shows Romulus and Remus being suckled by the wolf. It is an unexpected echo in a distant eastern province of the legend of the founding of Rome. The imperial associations of *Roma Invicta,* of Unconquered Rome, usually connected with the image have been lost. In a Christian hospital, the suckling wolf of Rome has been transmuted, rather touchingly, into an emblem of care for the helpless.[126]

Hence, the *xenodocheion* emerged in Asia Minor and elsewhere as a building for poor relief that still enjoyed a quasi-classical status. It was both a work of public, civic munificence and an act of charity. If the *xenodocheion* was associated with a bishop, it served to reinforce his claims to the tax exemptions allotted to the Christian church. It is against this background that I suggest we look carefully at one of the most spectacular, and certainly the most brilliantly publicized, venture in poor relief to occur in the fourth century. This was the relief of a major famine that threatened Cappadocia at some time between 368 and 370, as a result of the preaching and organizational energy displayed by a young priest of Caesarea (Kayseri, Turkey)—Basil. Basil would soon become famous as bishop of Caesarea. As Saint Basil of Caesarea, he is revered to this day as a pillar of Orthodoxy. Along with his younger brother, Gregory of Nyssa, and his friend from student days, Gregory Nazianzen (from Nazianze/Nenezi, Turkey), Basil was the central figure in a brilliant and ever-fascinating constellation of Orthodox talent later known as the Cappadocian Fathers. The campaign eventually led to the building of a *xenodocheion* that bore Basil's own name—the Basileias. It was a combined hostel, poorhouse, and hospital placed outside the ancient walls of Caesarea. It was still known by that name in the fifth century.[127]

l.t.
can
mislead

Basil's relief of the famine in Cappadocia and his subsequent building of the Basileias is a story so well known and so frequently narrated that we need to remind ourselves how many aspects of it remain unclear. The first issue is that of the inspiration on which Basil drew in undertaking this project. The tendency of modern scholarship has been to confine the sources of Basil's inspiration to within the Christian church. His project is presented as having emerged from an exceptionally radical current within the Church—from a monastic movement critical of society and deeply concerned with the fate of the poor. It is said that Basil's intention, in his years as a priest and bishop in Caesarea, was to harness the new monastic fervor to a socially useful aim. Monks were not to retreat into the wilderness as asocial hermits or as wandering charismatic groups. Rather, they were to take care of the poor and, by the example of their own poverty, to spur the rich to greater giving. No longer confined to the fringes of society, monasteries devoted to poor relief were to be set up in cities and in villages. In all this, Basil is said to have tamed the asceticism of an earlier, more turbulent generation, while retaining, in his sermons and in his views of monastic poverty, the radical critique of wealth and concern for the poor that had characterized its leaders. We are confronted, indeed, with a narrative of the activities of Basil between 368 and his death in 378 that is presented in terms of a highly edifying "synthesis": the genius and civic spirit of Basil achieved a lasting balance between the radicalism of previous ascetic leaders, on the one hand, and the social conservatism of the post-Constantinian church, on the other.[128]

This interpretation depends to a great extent on what we think of the career of a challenging and little-known figure—Eustathius of Sebasteia (Sivas, Turkey).[129] Eustathius is known to have been the mentor of Basil in the early stages of the young man's ascetic life. By 368, however, Eustathius was an old man, in his late sixties, with a long and embattled life behind him. Our current image of Eustathius portrays him as a monastic reformer and an upholder of radical measures to relieve the poor. But this image depends on two incidents, neither of which concerned Eustathius directly; they involved only persons held to be close to him.

The first occurred in 343, in what is now northern central Turkey. At a council of provincial bishops that met at Gangra (Çankırı, east of Ankara) in 343, unnamed "partisans of Eustathius" were condemned for upholding radical views on social issues.[130] They were accused of having preached that "the rich who do not alienate all their wealth can have no hope from God." They were said to have encouraged slaves to desert their masters by joining the monastic life. They were even said to have denied gender boundaries. They were accused of shaving the hair of women ascetics and of dressing them in the same outlandish monastic garb as men.[131]

It remains, however, an open question whether the radicalism associated with "partisans of Eustathius" really existed as an extensive movement in the regions of Pontus and Lesser (western) Armenia, to whose clergy the bishops of Gangra addressed their letter. Pontus was a region with which Basil had close contacts. His family was from Neocaesarea (Niksar), and his first experiment in the monastic life took place on a family estate between Amaseia and Neocaesarea (probably Kaleköy near the bridge over the Iris river, the Yeşil Irmak).[132] But it is far from certain that the "movement" of the followers of Eustathius existed as a serious threat outside the minds of the bishops of Gangra. When in a mood to purge their opponents, fourth-century bishops resorted all too easily to prefabricated "identikits" of unacceptable behavior. Some bishops were deposed for flamboyant abuses of power. The ascetic disciples of Eustathius were accused of holding unacceptably radical views. Though already prominent, Eustathius was not a bishop at that time. He was fair game for character assassination by association with imagined extremists.[133]

Altogether, it may well be that we moderns (unlike the stodgy bishops of Paphlagonia) rather wish that a genuine radical movement had once occurred in Asia Minor. The idea that Christian monasticism might have led to an exciting radical movement—a movement characterized by criticism of the rich, by the emancipation of slaves, and by the furthering of female agency through cross-dressing—appears, to many of us, to be too good not to be true.[134]

The second incident brings us closer to Eustathius, but, once again, only by association. When Eustathius finally became bishop of Sebasteia in 357, he consoled his rival, Aerius, by nominating him as head of the *ptôchotropheion* that already existed in Sebasteia. We learn of Aerius from the *Panarion* of Epiphanius of Salamis. It is our only account of the incident, written by a man notorious for the number of surreal "negative identikits" with which he approached any and every heresy. In Epiphanius' account,

Aerius is presented as having lived down to the worst suspicions of the bishops at Gangra. He broke with Eustathius on the issue of wealth and poverty. He accused Eustathius of being a money-grubber. He insisted that the Church should not accumulate money. The wealth of the Church should be dispersed immediately for the relief of the poor. Eventually, Aerius took a mixed group of male and female followers into the hills, wandering without shelter on the snow-covered mountain slopes that bordered the river Halys (the Kızıl Irmak), in northern central Turkey.[135]

Whether Aerius' actions can be seen as the logical extension of the social views of Eustathius himself remains an open question. The same doubt applies to Eustathius' activities in the period in which he had served as a priest in Constantinople, between 337 and 341. It has been suggested that Eustathius had brought to Constantinople a distinctive notion of poor relief. This was characterized by a redistribution of the wealth of the rich through a call to ascetic renunciation and through the insertion of monasteries into the life of the city as centers for the care of the poor. All this has been presented as part of the "package" of a distinctive social program associated with Eustathius.[136]

Constantinople was a booming new city. It was doubtless filled with destitute immigrants from Asia Minor. Famine victims from western Anatolia drained into the city in times of crisis, attracted by the foodstuffs that were constantly brought by sea to its busy quays. If there was a place where immigration was likely to bring about a "crisis of poverty" in the fourth century, it was in such a newly developed imperial center.[137] Constantinople would, indeed, have offered an exciting field of action for new, more radical forms of care of the poor. But there is no evidence that the Arian priest, Marathonius, who created for his church a lasting and popular infrastructure of poorhouses and monasteries, owed his ideas on poor relief to Eustathius.[138] Marathonius, in fact, was a former bureaucrat, a retired official of the Praetorian Prefect.[139] It is more likely that he looked to official quarters for his inspiration. He took up with unprecedented energy a system of poor relief, linked to the novel institutions of the *xenodocheion* and the hospital, that had already been set up, in Constantinople, by lay persons and that had been patronized by none other than the emperor Constantius II—that "stoney faced individual" who followed so loyally in the footsteps of his father, Constantine.[140]

Altogether, it would be wrong to see the activities of Basil of Caesarea between 368 and his election as bishop in 370 in terms of his relations with the radical monasticism ascribed to Eustathius. The campaign of preaching, the opening of the storehouses of the rich, the setting up of a soup kitchen, and the eventual creation of the Basileias should not be regarded as exclusively ecclesiastical and monastic affairs. Still less can they be presented as a modified version of the program of *la gauche évangélique,* "the Left-Wing party of the Gospel" (to use the ringing phrase of l'abbé Gribomont).[141] Such accounts leave out the towering background of the new Christian empire. They overlook the lively interest in the care of the poor evinced by Christian emperors and their officials. Basil's activities in relieving Caesarea at a time of famine are best seen as the actions of a man acting quickly and with maximum publicity in order to justify the privileges of his church. Beneath the gaze of an emperor and his highly placed officials, he created a publicly acclaimed system of poor relief that showed that the wealth and tax exemptions of the church of Caesarea were being used to good effect.

What Basil achieved, in this situation, was truly impressive. The crisis appears to have been caused by a winter drought such as often afflicts inner Anatolia. No snow or rain fell from an icy, empty sky.[142] The result was not the collapse of the entire ecology of the region. It was, rather, a food shortage, caused by the panic of the rich. Faced with the prospect of a famine of indefinite duration, they were unwilling to make available the grain already stored in their barns.[143] Furthermore, Caesarea was unusual in that it lay in the middle of an entirely agrarian region dominated by imperial horse ranches that were crucial for the cavalry of the armies of the eastern frontier. It was not supported by a network of minor towns, which could have served as intermediate points of distribution.[144] Caesarea stood alone. The threat of famine brought the destitute of an entire region to the gates of the city.

Basil did what he could. In a series of sermons, he showed that he had not been educated in Athens to no purpose. He knew how to "move the heart by the incantation of words."[145] The sermons he preached on this occasion were unusually "classical" in style. He challenged the rich to act as *euergetai* to the poor. He promised them the acclamation of the entire *démos* of the angels in heaven.[146] Basil's sermons, indeed, were intended to be the swan-

song of the ancient city. With an indignation rendered heavy with
classical resonances, he pointed to the urban façade of Caesarea.
Decaying walls and buildings towered all around, "great cliffs of
stone and marble," in which wealth that might have been spent
on the poor was frozen in useless stone by the mad drive for
"civic" fame.[147]

Eventually, the storehouses were opened. Basil used his own
wealth to found a soup kitchen, and could be seen in it, directing
his servants as they laid tables for the poor. He even embraced
lepers with the kiss of peace.[148] A little later, when a bishop, he
wrote to Elias, the governor of Cappadocia, to justify his recent
foundation of the Basileias. The extent of the new bishop's building activities and the amount of personnel attached to them had
stirred up opposition and had made the governor anxious: the
church was expanding the number of persons who might claim
tax exemption. Basil appealed to Elias as one classical *euergetés*
to another. How could a man such as the governor, "already com-
petent, single handed, to restore public works that have fallen
into ruin, to people uninhabited areas, and in general to trans-
form solitudes into cities," object to so useful a public work as
the Basileias?[149]

In this way, as early as 371, Basil laid the basis of the "civic"
myth of the Basileias. It was a myth that was taken up, a decade
later, after Basil's death. To his friend Gregory Nazianzen, the new
building (of whose scale, in fact, we know nothing) was Basil's
most solid achievement:

A noble thing is philanthropy [he told his hearers] . . . Go forth a little way
from the city, and behold the new city, the storehouse of piety, the common treasury of the wealthy, in which, . . . in consequence of his exhortations, the superfluities of wealth . . . escape the hostility of envy and the
ravages of time.[150]

Yet this can hardly have been the first time in the history of the
fourth century that a Christian bishop had to deal with a famine.
A decade or so earlier, Cyril, the bishop of Jerusalem, had sold the
votive silken hangings and the sacred vessels in his churches so as
to feed the poor.[151] Though singled out by later ages as classics of
Greek Christian rhetoric, even Basil's sermons were not, perhaps,
as original as they now appear to be. His sermon *Against the Rich*
was a performance "whose two-fisted radicality has made it justly

famous."[152] Yet we find that some of its most ringing phrases had already been used, a decade previously, by the great Syriac poet Ephraim of Nisibis when he wrote on the earthquake that destroyed Nicomedia (Izmit, Turkey) in 358. Both men spoke with dramatic vividness of the cupboards of the rich, crammed with wasting clothes and footwear that might have clothed and shod the poor.[153] The resemblances between Ephraim and Basil show that a discourse on the poor, marked by set phrases, was already widespread in Christian circles.

Much depends also on when, exactly, these events took place. The conventional date for the famine is 368. But an argument has recently been made for 370. The only major famine that is securely dated by an annual record of events is a famine that occurred in Phrygia in 370.[154] Phrygia and Cappadocia share the same climate. Both provinces could have been held, in late 369, in the grip of a winter drought whose terrible effects would slowly become apparent in the course of the spring and summer of 370.

It is hard to reach absolute certainty on such matters. But a date of 370 would place Basil's activities in an entirely different context from that which we would associate with 368. By 370 Basil was on the point of being elected as bishop of Caesarea. His activities fit into a pattern by which the heir-apparent of a dying bishop would establish his reputation as "lover of the poor" by acts of public generosity and, often, by the building of a church or *xenodocheion*.[155] Furthermore, in the spring of 370, the Christian empire in the person of the emperor himself was on Basil's doorstep. The emperor Valens was on his way to the East. Antioch would serve him as his headquarters. But Caesarea and the great ranches of Cappadocia were crucial to any strategy that involved the reassertion of East Roman power in Armenia. Basil had already been approached by members of Valens' court. One of these was referred to contemptuously by Gregory of Nyssa as head of the emperor's cooks. He was, in fact, the quartermaster general of the court. This was a court on the move. It intended, in the near future, to eat its way through Cappadocia.[156] Food shortages would be a matter of great interest to such a person. The emperor himself was concerned. At some time, Valens contributed imperial estates to endow Basil's schemes for the relief of the poor.[157]

By putting together these fragments of information we may have arrived at a stranger and truer view of Basil at this time. We see him from the perspective of the emperor and his entourage. His relief of the famine did not happen in isolation. It was not a purely ecclesiastical venture, inspired by a radical social vision of monastic origin. We are dealing, rather, with a strange alliance. A brilliant young priest, destined to be bishop and enabled by all the arts of classical rhetoric learned at Athens to present himself as the new-style *euergetés* of a Christian city in its hour of need, found himself collaborating closely with an emperor who was a notoriously morose and undereducated Latin speaker from the Balkans and whose theological views Basil did not share. But both men were committed to maintaining the social fabric of a crucial region. The incident is a striking outcome of the Constantinian settlement, by which the church was granted its privileges in return for a fully public commitment to the care of the poor.

It was not the only such incident. Let us end this chapter by looking eastward for a moment, to the Christian kingdom of Armenia. It comes as a surprise to realize that, in the 350s—that is, over a decade before the events that led up to the foundation of the Basileias in Cappadocia—a thoroughgoing system of poor relief had been put into place in Armenia. In the 350s, the patriarch Nersês had used extensive grants of royal land to create a network of hostels in which the poor were gathered.[158] His actions were presented quite frankly, in retrospect, as a measure of social control. The poor were gathered and supported by the local community, "so that these people should remain exclusively in their own lodgings and should not go out as miserable beggars . . . they should have no other concern but to rise from their bed every morning."[159]

We know of all this from Armenian sources written a century after the event. But even if we make due allowance for exaggeration, the idyll conjured up by P'awstos Buzand in the 470s takes us into a very different world from Basil's Caesarea.[160] The classical rhetoric of the *euergetés* and builder of a "new city" was absent. Nersês wanted something else from his project. Armenia was an intensely hierarchical society of Iranian structure. Vagrancy and any form of free movement among the peasantry was viewed with deep concern by the upper classes. In the same years as Nersês set up his ambitious network of poorhouses, thereby tying beggars

and lepers irrevocably to their own locality, the Armenian nobility
wiped out an entire city founded by King Arshak, because it had
attracted a population of runaway serfs.[161]
Nersês was no *euergetés*. He was a "protector of the poor" on
an Iranian model—a feudal lord charged with the good behavior of
a subordinate social class.[162] By instituting a poor relief based
upon Armenian equivalents of the *xenodocheion*, Nersês attempted to do nothing less than freeze the dangerous mobility of
the destitute in the upland valleys of what is now eastern Turkey,
Armenia, and the southern Caucasus. He did what he did so as to
ensure that "the order of the realm must not be destroyed."[163]

Yet although P'awstos presents him in an Armenian epic idiom,
Nersês was not an entirely exotic figure. He knew the eastern empire well. Movsês Khorenac'i (a later and frequently unreliable
source, who occasionally includes invaluable fragments of earlier
tradition) asserts that Nersês derived his program of poor relief
from Constantinople.[164] Given the faithfulness with which the
Christian kings of Armenia followed the policies of their overpowering East Roman neighbors, the Christian successors of Constantine, such borrowing direct from the capital is not as strange as we
might think.[165] Once again, it is the "stoney-faced" Constantius II
and his circle of Christian public servants, and not, as has been
suggested for Armenia also, the maverick Eustathius of Sebasteia,
who emerges as the pace-maker in a new venture in the care of the
poor.[166] The *xenodocheion*, in particular, was a peculiarly flexible
institution. It could stand in the middle of a Greco-Roman city;
but its solid walls could also protect—and confine—the poor on
the edge of a mountain village or in the shadow of an Armenian
noble's residence.

Seen in this perspective, Basil and Nersês had one thing in common. For both men, "care of the poor" involved more than spontaneous initiatives on the part of the Christian clergy. A widely publicized scheme of poor relief attached to conspicuous new buildings
was, in both cases, a *quid pro quo* for the heavy privileges offered
to the Church by a Christian state.[167]

And so it was that, in the course of the half century between
the reign of Constantine and the activities of Basil of Caesarea, an
ancient concern that those who enjoyed privileges should make
their presence felt in the community by tangible actions edged

Christian charity into ever greater prominence in Roman society. In our next chapter, we will continue the story, by seeing how the bishops of the Roman empire made use of their new prominence, so as to act as "governors of the poor" in the late fourth and fifth centuries.

① the control of the poor became an 'ideology' of power — the soul of the empire.

2 "Governor of the Poor"

The Bishops and Their Cities

In a Coptic Egyptian collection of *Questions and Answers* from the sixth century of the Common Era, the patriarch Cyril of Alexandria was asked to lay down the qualifications of a good bishop: "The gift of prophetic visions [he was imagined to have said] is of no use to a bishop, compared with giving to those in need."[1] Even the Devil had no doubts on that matter. Speaking through a possessed person in sixth-century Gaul, he reminded a bishop of his basic duties. He was not to waste his time supporting a saintly, persecuted colleague: "All that is required of you is to look after the property of your church with diligence, lest any resource for the support of the poor be diminished."[2] The art of the good bishop, indeed, was the art of "governing the poor."[3]

Given the general consensus in all regions of the Roman and post-Roman world of the fourth, fifth, and sixth centuries, that the primary duty of the bishop was the care of the poor, it is particularly important to define with some care what contemporaries meant by the term "poor." The historian of this period cannot be sufficiently alert to what the framers of the English *Poor Law Report* of 1834 referred to as "the mischievous ambiguity of the word *poor*."[4]

Christian sources of this period help us very little to resolve such ambiguities. As we have already seen, Christian literature, and especially Christian preaching, tended to tilt perceptions of the poor toward the most extreme forms of poverty. From the fourth to the seventh centuries, the imaginative horizon of late antique Christianity was ringed by wraithlike figures of the utterly destitute, assembled in crowds on the margins of society, at the church door and at the gates of the city. Such figures seemed to need no further definition. When the Psalmist spoke of the believer

who could *understand [who was] the poor and needy* (Ps. 40:2),
Christian preachers assumed that this must refer to some more
mysterious, hidden form of poverty. It could not refer to the bla-
tant misery around them. The condition of the destitute spoke for
itself: "shivering in their nakedness, lean with hunger, parched
with thirst, trembling with exhaustion and discolored by under-
nourishment."[5] When Christian preachers in the Latin West used
the word *pauper*, it usually carried with it overtones of ultimate
destitution and humiliation that made each poor person an image
of the suffering Christ.[6]

Although such persons existed in all regions of the late antique
world—and, at times, congregated in the cities in heartrending
numbers—they by no means exhausted the definition of what it
was to be "poor." As a result, Christian emphasis on compassion
for the visibly destitute has led to a distortion of our evidence similar to that which characterized nineteenth-century accounts of
the "poor" of London. Like those Victorian sketches of the life of
the "lower classes," Christian rhetoric "had the conceptual effect
of pauperizing the poor by first creating the most distinctive, dramatic image of the lowest class, and then imposing that image
upon the lower classes as a whole."[7]

It is important to be clear on this issue. As a result of the "pauperizing" of the image of the poor prevalent in late antique Christian sources, we have been led into a circular argument. It has long
been assumed by social historians of the later Roman empire that
the society of the fourth and fifth centuries was marked by an
acute degree of polarization between the "rich" and the "poor"
and by a massive increase in impoverishment, both among the
peasantry and among the middle and lower classes of the cities.[8]

Yet we must remember that much of the evidence for this dramatic view comes from Christian preaching on the "care of the
poor." When, for instance, we read the sermons of Basil of Caesarea, his evocation of the avarice and luxurious lifestyle of the
rich leads us to conclude the obvious—that "excessive poverty co-
existed with excessive wealth in Cappadocia."[9] We have tended to
take for granted that Christian preaching on the poor registered
faithfully the onset of an acute crisis in late Roman society, associated with widespread impoverishment and with the development of a "chasm" between the rich and the poor. Christian
sources have been taken to have provided, as it were, a faithful

wrongly

"photograph" of that crisis. As a result, the charitable activities of
the Christian church have often been interpreted as a heroic attempt to ameliorate a grim and largely novel state of affairs, associated with the general decline and fall of the Roman empire.

Paradoxically, a poignant Christian rhetoric, tilted toward the
evocation of extreme forms of the human condition, has combined with the most sternly unsentimental, "hard-nosed" assess-
ment by modern scholars of the structural weaknesses of late
Roman society, in such a way as to present a world marked by
glaring contrasts between the impoverishment of the many and
the oppressive wealth of the few. Our sense that similar developments have happened in our own times, in many Third World
countries, adds moral sharpness to our judgement on late Roman
society. In the words of Andrew Wallace-Hadrill, speaking of an
earlier period of Roman history: "The vast riches squandered by
the elite . . . and the contrast with the undoubted squalor experi-
enced by the poor, tempt us into polarizing the culture of the elite
and the culture of the masses. It is easy (and perhaps it is morally
satisfying) to dramatize this contrast."[10] But he rightly warns us
not to do so.

A highly polarized image of the later empire has come to be
taken for granted as the "reality" of late Roman social relations.
The result of this has been a notable lack of sensitivity to the
more subtle, intermediate gradations of late Roman society, especially as these existed in the Roman and post-Roman cities of the
Mediterranean and its hinterland. It is only in the last decades
that further research, led by archaeologists, has come to alter this
conventional image of the social structure of the later empire.
The archaeologists have challenged social historians to realize
the extent to which our previous insistence on a brutal "bi-polar
divide" in Roman society, between the rich and the poor, between
town and country, has oversimplified our image of the later
Roman world.[11] As Peter Garnsey and Caroline Humfress have
put it, in their remarkably fresh-minded synthesis of recent
scholarship, "Polarities are blunt tools of analysis . . . the meta-
phor of a vertical spectrum or continuum may enable us to probe
more deeply."[12]

Regional archaeological surveys of the later empire—especially,
but not exclusively, of the eastern provinces—reveal a very different world from the desolate impression conveyed by Christian

lots in the middle

archaeology (vs) lit. sources

sources. Far from being a world from which all wealth and prosperity had drained into the hands of the few, leaving the mass of the population in a state of undifferentiated misery, archaeologists have revealed landscapes filled with thriving villages, dotted with comfortable and unpretentious farmhouses, in which the cities had changed their structures, but had by no means lost their vitality.[13] It is a far more differentiated society than we had once thought. The time has come to pay attention to the intermediate classes who, in the present state of scholarship, exist in a "grey zone" between the well-documented splendor and luxury of the rich and the dramatically depicted destitution of the poor.

Nowhere is it more important to avoid a distorted image of late Roman society than in the study of the Christian church. For, despite its official privileges and its occasional ability to recruit members of the upper classes as bishops and clergymen, the Christian Church stood squarely in the middle of Roman society. It occupied the extensive middle ground between the very rich and the very poor. "Middling" persons formed its principal constituency. The church tended to recruit its clergy from among the more prosperous artisans and from the fringes of the class of town councilors. True aristocrats and men of high culture were *rarae aves*, rare birds indeed, in what was, overwhelmingly, a more subdued, more "middling" world. It is, of course, the writings and sermons of the brilliant exceptions who fill the columns of Migne's *Patrologia Latina* and *Patrologia Graeca*. We should not underestimate their influence. The presence of only a few such persons might set the tone of clerical society as a whole in their province. But the slow labor of the *Prosopographie chrétienne* and detailed study of the wealth and personnel of the clergy in various regions has made us realize how few of them filled the ranks of the church in most places and at most times.[14] Few clergymen and even, in many regions, few bishops rose above the *mediocritas*, the fragile sufficiency, of the humble schoolteachers whose social world has been conjured up with such vividness by Robert Kaster in his study of the late antique *grammaticus*. As a teacher of Greek or Latin grammar, the *grammaticus* played an essential role in an educational system that was regarded as the foundation of Greco-Roman civilization. Chosen *grammatici* enjoyed tax exemptions for the same reason as did civic doctors: "for [in the words of a later Syriac summary of Roman law], like doctors, they cure the soul."[15] A few *grammatici* made brilliant careers. For all that, the average *grammaticus* remained very much a "middling" person:

> The combination of high and low standing marked the profession . . . In contrast to the overwhelming mass of the population, his birth, means, and culture placed him in the small circle of those free from ignoble employment. Yet for all that he was a social pauper in the world of the elite. Compared with the imperial aristocracy of birth or service, he was no more than a "mere *grammaticus.*"[16]

The same could be said of most "mere" bishops and clergymen in the church of the fourth and fifth centuries.

What needs to be stressed, in assessing the social texture of the later empire, was that such persons were in an uncomfortable position. We have found that late Roman society was not as drastically "polarized" between the rich and the poor as we had been led to suppose. The class of "middling" persons was more extensive and more differentiated than we had thought. But such persons did not enjoy the autonomy and the protection that we associate with a modern "middle class." The powerful and the truly rich remained overbearing presences in a society where so many self-respecting persons lived uncomfortably close to the widespread "shallow poverty" that had always characterized an ancient society. It was a tense situation. As Keith Hopkins has put it succinctly, by reason of the "steepness of the social pyramid . . . Roman society demanded an uncomfortable mixture of pervasive deference to superiors and openly aggressive brutishness to inferiors."[17] In a world where so many persons thought themselves to be "social paupers," Christian talk of "care of the poor," and the all-embracing ideology that went with it, could come to mean far more than mere charity to the destitute.

Let us, therefore, look out for a moment at this world of vulnerable "middling" persons, that pressed in around the Christian bishop and his clergy. For all their new, official privileges, the clergy had much in common with such persons. Bishops might come to be drawn increasingly from the relatively secure class of town councilors, and would have counted as belonging to the top of local society. But their clergy were by no means so privileged: they usually came from humbler backgrounds. And it was through their clergy that the bishops made contact, on a day-to-day basis, with the poor. Clergy and laity both stood on the same treacherous slope that tilted downward toward poverty. They shared the constant, often bitter, struggle to achieve a measure of sufficiency above the utterly destitute poor to whom the bishop's care was officially directed. "Middling" persons had always needed protectors. They had always shown impressive ingenuity in their search for some form of social "safety-net" against impoverishment. Now, through the bishops and clergy, they sought the protection of the church—an institution made up largely of persons like themselves. In the fourth and fifth centuries, they came to seek shelter within the ever-widening penumbra of the bishop's "care of the poor."

In the first place, we must be clear as to the nature of the social groups who were most directly involved in the safety-net offered by the Christian church. We are dealing with a largely urban world. Up to the seventh century, the great cities of the eastern Mediterranean—Constantinople, Antioch, and Alexandria—along with Rome and Carthage in the West (up to at least the middle of the fifth century) remained the focus of attention. Their churches were by far the most wealthy and their ecclesiastical establishments the most extensive.[18] The smaller towns of Gaul, Spain, Italy, Asia Minor, and Syria changed greatly between the fourth and the seventh centuries. But they remained central to the care of the poor.[19] In some regions of the West, many towns became no longer recognizable as "Roman" cities. Yet the continuing residence of the bishop and his clergy in the towns, combined with the town-based structures of the bishop's "care of the poor," provided an element of real continuity. In Gaul, by the year 600, the Christian basilicas around which the care of the poor was organized were already many centuries old. The cities themselves and the roads leading into them were dotted with *xenodocheia* and similar poorhouses founded by bishops and by pious lay persons.[20]

Despite many changes in urban life, the inhabitants of the cities remained different from the rest. Those in danger of impoverishment were close to a "safety net" of protection, carefully built up over time in the cities. By contrast, real poverty, silent and untended, existed in the countryside. Passing through northern Gaul in the late fourth century, Saint Martin of Tours pointed out to his disciples the archetypal figure of enduring human misery: "He saw a swineherd, shivering with cold and almost naked in his garment of skins. 'Look at Adam' he said, 'in his garment of skins,

thrown out of Paradise and herding swine.'"[21] In East and West
alike, even the most prosperous countryside was filled with such
sad figures. When we read of the "care of the poor" in Christian
sources, we must always remember that we are not invariably
reading about those who suffered most in late antiquity. We are
often reading only about those whose proximity to urban bishops
enabled them to make their claims heard.

It is not that the Christian church did not encourage charity in
the countryside. As we saw in our first lecture, the Christian
model saw the world as universally divided between "rich" and
"poor," and expected the rich in any setting to look after the poor
of their locality. Such charity certainly occurred around rural
monasteries, around the figures of hermits, and in the out-
buildings of the villas of pious Christian landowners.[22] Basil of
Caesarea, for instance, went out of his way to develop in Cappadocia a system of country bishops—of *chorepiscopi*—whose *raison
d'être* was to look after the needs of the rural poor.[23] These services, however, were unevenly distributed and erratically maintained. In the course of the sixth century, there was a perceptible
shift to the countryside in many regions, such as Gaul, Asia
Minor, and Syria. As a result, the care of the poor became more
available, through favored rural churches and, above all, through
the foundation of rural monasteries.[24] But the structures of Christian poor relief were slow to follow this shift. Many areas were left
unattended to. Even in a region covered by as fine a grid of ecclesiastical organization as was Egypt, the care of the poor remained
in the hands of the bishop. The country clergy appear not to have
had many resources of their own with which to deal with local
poverty.[25]

We should have no illusions as to the quality of the "middling"
persons who lived in these towns. From the fourth century onward, we are not dealing with the robust *cives* and *démos* imagined by a "civic" model of society. Such people may have existed
in classical times: although, as we have seen, there is good reason
to doubt whether the boundaries between solid, resident "citizens"—the ideal core of the city—and the more fluid categories of
the "poor" and the "stranger" were ever as rigid, in reality, as they
were made to appear in the "civic" model of classical times.[26] But
by 400, there was no doubt that the inhabitants of the average town
were a distinctly shabby lot. Analysis of the extensive Christian

cemetery of Tarragona "suggests a high infant mortality, that most of the 'modest' inhabitants were involved in strenuous physical labor, and that few reached old age."[27]

The rich residents of the city towered above such persons. To take a local example from Israel. The seafront of Caesarea Maritima has been shown to have been occupied, in late antiquity, by three extensive villas. Each took up an entire city block. Their spacious courtyards and reception halls were covered with mosaic floors and lined with columns of choice marble. Private warehouses clustered around them, with "outlet" shops attached, which sold their owners' products on the public street. Dominating the view of the city as one approached from the sea, these private mansions formed an unbroken line that merged, at their northern end, with the palace of the imperial governor of Palestine and with his extensive office buildings.[28] It was a truly daunting display of private wealth closely allied to public power. These were the houses of the *ktétores*, the *possessores*, the great landowners of the district. Such persons tended to replace the more diffuse governing class of the city, which had been associated since classical times with membership of the local town council. Unabashedly rich and powerful, they became the privileged secular intermediaries between the emperor's representatives and the cities.[29] Throughout the empire, similar persons resided in or near the cities. At Apamea (Abamiya, Syria) the houses of the resident aristocracy tell the same story: "They were grand mansions, evidently of a rich and sophisticated aristocracy . . . They lived in their spacious domains, almost entirely closed to the outside . . . By the time of Justinian, these people were living as they had for three or four hundred years."[30]

It was considerably more difficult to define the status of those who lived beneath such solid wealth and power. Late Roman lawyers viewed these intermediate classes with a disabused eye and with a distinct lack of enthusiasm. As we have seen, a surprisingly wide body of the inhabitants of many towns continued, in the late antique period, to be treated as *cives*. It was as "citizens," and not as members of the poor, that the "people" of Rome and Constantinople received the cheap foodstuffs provided by the "civic" *annona*.[31] But, in the eyes of the lawyers, there were citizens and citizens. They saw society as headed by a readily identifiable class of *honestiores*, of "more honest persons"—to use the terminology adopted in the second and third centuries—that was clearly distinguished from the *humiliores*, the "more humble." The *honestiores* were defined less by wealth (because their wealth could usually be assumed) than by their public status. This derived from the holding of office, either in the imperial service or as members of the ruling class of the cities—as members of the town council or, later, as we have seen, as "landowners." In small cities, of course, town councilors could be relatively humble persons. Consequently, they were extremely anxious to maintain their status as members of the "more honest" classes. It was crucial for them, for instance, that they should not be liable to flogging.[32]

Beneath the *honestiores* there stretched the colorless and ill-defined mass of *humiliores*, of "more humble persons." The lawyers of the fourth and fifth centuries remained, significantly, indifferent to the Christian categorization of society into "rich" and "poor." Late Roman secular idiom preferred to speak of categories that carried overtones of relative social vulnerability: the *potentiores*, the "more powerful," were contrasted with the *tenuiores*, the "weaker." The *tenuiores*, the "weaker" persons, were spoken of as *viles*, as "cheap," as *abjectae personae*, as "persons of low profile." They were persons characterized by a *plebeia vilitas*, by "a low quality of life, as befits members of the *plebs*."[33]

If late Roman urban society had its *classes dangereuses* among the lower classes, then they were these, the *tenuiores* of the cities. For they provided the manpower for dangerous urban riots. They were not easy to control. They were men without honor. Without honor, they were difficult to coerce. They had no status to lose and no wealth that might be threatened by fines. They could only be beaten, not blackmailed, into submission. Their daily behavior showed this only too clearly. Not for them the ceremonious decorum, associated with *paideia*, by which the "more honest" classes were expected to patrol themselves. They were free to be loud-mouthed and rowdy. Basil wrote to warn his monks that the fact that they now wore the clothes of the poor did not mean that they could behave badly like the poor. It was not for them to play around, to shout like any *démotés*, like any "man of the people," "accustomed to hitting and to being hit."[34]

Yet, on closer investigation, this view from the top gives way to a picture of the population of late Roman cities as built up, like a fragile honeycomb, by layer upon layer of humble persons. These groups stretched downward, from the direct dependents of the great and the clerks in the city offices, through minor town councilors, petty landowners, and members of the teaching professions to the *corpora*. The *corpora* were carefully organized associations of artisans. Much of the policing of the city and its safety from fire hazards depended on such groups. They were held responsible for the good behavior of each neighborhood. Last of all, there were always a considerable number of free laborers.[35] All of these were well aware that they stood above the destitute "poor." But none of them could be certain to avoid impoverishment without going out of their way to seek protection from above.

We are looking at a world where, in late antiquity quite as much as in the classical period, good behavior and its *quid pro quo*, entitlement, were guaranteed by membership of distinct bodies. The late antique graffiti on the seats of the theater and the hippodrome in a provincial capital, such as Aphrodisias, make this plain. They show benches reserved for the members of every professional group in the city, as well as seats for the Jews and for supporters of the circus factions.[36] Long after the *civis* had ceased to be a vivid figure in the social imagination, a mute notion of citizenship survived, almost by default. The cities of late antiquity had by no means forgotten that membership of a distinctive group (whether it was formal membership of a trade association or the general identification of a *démotés* with the affairs of his city) conferred entitlement, and that absence of such membership spelled vulnerability to dire poverty.

All over the Roman world, it was on just such persons that the Christian church depended for its day to day finances and for the recruitment of its clergy. Both before and long after 312, the Christian churches continued to draw on the sheer will to give of each local community. In the fourth and fifth centuries, quite as much as in the third century, we should not imagine that the "wealth of the church" consisted in secure endowments of land. The landed wealth of the churches accumulated only gradually, in a piecemeal manner. Not until the sixth century did the estates of major churches (such as the churches of Rome and Alexandria) come to rival those of secular great landowners. These churches were exceptional. Smaller churches were never so fortunate.[37] All over the Roman world, from the burgeoning churches of major cities to the small church in a midget town such as Durobrivae (Water Newton) in northern Britain, the "wealth of the church" was the creation of its "cheerful givers." It was lay persons of the "middling" class who made the regular, weekly offerings for the poor and the clergy. It was they who provided the silver vessels and the silken hangings for the altar. It was they who would cover the floor with mosaics, each contributing the relatively small sums needed for so many square feet of mosaic work, proudly marking the patches with their names and even, on occasions, with their portraits—of which the image of the Lady Silthous scattering coins in the church at Kissufim (Negev) was an unusually ambitious example.[38] In this, Christians followed the same practice as did the Jews in the building and decoration of their synagogues. The donor inscriptions of both groups show very clearly the horizons of the possible for a religious institution made up of self-respecting but by no means overwhelmingly wealthy persons.[39]

A dramatic incident illustrates the modest nature of the finances of most provincial churches in the early fifth century. In 411, the ascetic couple Melania the Younger and her husband, Pinianus, came to reside in Africa as refugees from the sack of Rome. They were representatives of a truly wealthy senatorial family. They had already begun to distribute their fortune to the poor. They settled in Thagaste (Souk Ahras, Algeria), on a family estate that was larger and better appointed than the city itself. Melania's Latin biographer (possibly a monk from Rome) spoke with admiration of its private bath house, of its independent artisan workshop, and of its dependent villages that supported both a Donatist and a Catholic bishop. This was real wealth. By contrast,

The town of the very blessed bishop Alypius, named Thagaste, was small and exceedingly poor . . . [Wherewith Melania] adorned the church of this holy man with revenues as well as offerings of both gold and silver treasures and valuable silken veils, so that this church which formerly had been so very poor now stirred up the envy of . . . all the other bishops in that province.[40]

Not to be outdone by the sudden good fortune of Thagaste, Augustine's congregation at the seaport town of Hippo (Bône/Annaba, Algeria) made their own bid for funding. They attempted to attach Melania's husband, Pinianus, to their church by forcibly ordaining him as a priest. Anxious to distance himself from the rapacity of his flock, Augustine was quick to point out to the mother of the Roman couple that it was, of course, the "poor" in the congregation who had been the most enthusiastic supporters of the scheme. Their life would have been considerably more comfortable if a "cheerful giver" of senatorial dimensions, such as Pinianus, were permanently resident among them.[41] The attempt failed miserably. The wealthy couple soon departed for the Holy Land. Their spectacular passing through provincial Africa only served to illustrate how rare such truly wealthy patrons were. Most churches in most areas of the Roman world were left to their own resources. Altogether, the dull creak of financial stress (real or imagined) in a religious community made up of "middling" persons committed to supporting both the poor and their own clergy formed a constant background noise to the Christian notion of "care of the poor."

Yet we should not underestimate the financial "muscle" that could be built up, through constant giving over the years, by just such persons. In sharp contrast to the secular traditions of urban beneficence, the strain of giving within the church was supposed to rest not only on the rich, but on every believer. As in Judaism, the obligation to give alms applied to all Christians. To give little but often was what was expected of the "cheerful giver" of modest means. In the words of rabbi Eliezer: the "breastplate of righteousness" acquired by almsgiving was made up, like the small round scales of the scale-mail armor of third-century cavalry, of innumerable small coins.[42] In the Early Church, coins were expected to "gather sweat in the palms of the hands" of the believer, for whom giving was a real sacrifice (often made possible only through fasting, so as to offer money usually spent on food), before the coins were given, after due consideration, to support the deserving poor or to feed and lodge a traveling evangelist.[43] Things had not changed greatly by the year 400. Preaching in Carthage, Augustine still cited the passage, taken from an Early Christian manual, *The Didache*, as if it were a passage from Scripture itself.[44]

This was a world characterized by the slow but steady piling up of wealth for religious purposes that was very different from the "explosive rhythm" of the civic occasions on which urban benefactors of the *belle époque* had dispersed their surplus wealth as *euergetai*.[45] By contrast, the pattern of giving that supported Christian care of the poor was mediocre but predictable. It had a flexibility and a tenacity that enabled the bishop's activity to touch every level of the poor and of the potentially poor in every city in which there was a Christian community.

Given these resources, gathered doggedly from relatively humble persons, the natural reaction of the bishops and clergy was to look after their own. For the distress of fellow-believers of the "middling" classes directly affected the workings of the church. A newly discovered letter of Augustine makes this plain. In Africa, in 420, economic distress among the town councils and the city guilds had resulted in an immediate shortage of clergy. For no guild was willing any longer to release any of its members to serve the church, as they would have done in more prosperous times. The crisis, in Augustine's opinion, could only be resolved by administrative measures to halt the impoverishment of these respectable but vulnerable pillars of the community. He advocated the setting up in Africa of the institution of *defensor civitatis,* "defender of the city." This involved the appointment of a legal representative with powers to protect the community from unjust tax demands. It was a purely secular device that had been applied, sporadically, in other provinces.[46] Interventions such as this, by bishops, were intended to relieve the "poverty" of the intermediate classes of the cities as a whole. They bear little relation to the "pauperized" image of the poor, as consisting only of a mass of destitute persons.

Basil of Caesarea had faced analogous problems in Cappadocia. In 372 he petitioned the Praetorian Prefect, Modestus, to lighten the tax burden on the inhabitants of the mining villages of the Taurus mountains. Modestus was asked "to bestow salvation upon a pitiful rustic people."[47] In fact, these remote mining communities were directly linked to Basil's own city. They supplied the ore needed by the imperial arms factories of Caesarea. By protecting them, Basil strengthened an alliance between the clergy and members of the artisan guilds, an alliance that occurred in many Greek cities in the fourth century.[48] When Basil was summoned, on one occasion, before a hostile governor, the arms workers turned out in force on behalf of their bishop:

For men at work in these trades are especially hot- tempered and daring, because of the liberty allowed to them . . . Torch in hand, amid showers of stones, with cudgels ready, all ran together in their united zeal . . . What then was the conduct of this haughty and daring judge? He begged for mercy.[49]

Furthermore, the willingness of the clergy to use church funds to give financial support to fellow believers, which is so evident in the correspondence of Cyprian of Carthage in the third century, continued to be called upon in the fourth century. In around 330–340, Heriêous wrote to the priest Paiêous in Egypt on behalf of "our brother" Pamonthios:

> To those who have fallen into . . . misfortune the word of the Lord exhorts us to give succor; to all, and most to our brethren. Since therefore our brother Pamonthios, having fallen into no common vicissitudes, has suffered most shamefully at the hands of pitiless and godless men so that he is compelled, one might almost say, to lose our *blessed hope* (Titus 2:13), for which reason he sought us to make application by these present letters to your brotherliness . . . that you too . . . may help him, remembering the command of the blessed Apostle not to forget those who are weak, not only in the faith but even in the affairs of the world.[50]

Pamonthios was a wine dealer who had borrowed money to pay his taxes. Now his creditors were about to foreclose on him. He was by no means "poor," but, without the help of his fellow Christians, he soon would be. The day-to-day work of the church was to firm up the position of vulnerable "middling" persons such as Pamonthios quite as much as it was to take care of the destitute.

We can see this most clearly in the case of the role of the bishop as the protector of the "widows and orphans." We should not underestimate the implications of what appears, at first sight, to be a banal obligation, inherited from the early church.[51] For what we know of the demography of the Roman world and of similar societies suggests that the destruction of the family unit by the death or desertion of male protectors and wage earners was the single greatest cause of poverty.[52] In the later Roman empire, as in late medieval Florence, widows and orphans were by no means an "archaic," "Biblical" category, whose protection and alleviation were peripheral to the effort to halt the dire processes that made for urban poverty. Far from it. In the later empire, as in late medieval Florence, the widows represented a category of the poor on which Christian charity could set to work with a reasonable hope of thereby alleviating a major source of poverty.[53]

We must remember, however, that the category of the widows and orphans frequently represented a group of self-respecting persons, who felt entitled, not to relief from a pre-existing state of

destitution, but, rather, to protection from the danger of impoverishment. Many already had claims on the church. They were not
necessarily strangers to the community. They had been the wives
and children of male members "in good standing" among the
faithful. They were a privileged example of a category of respectable, but vulnerable, persons who avoided impoverishment by
clinging to the church.

One is struck by a continuous tendency toward a "social up-
grading" of the "widows of the church." This occurred especially
(but by no means exclusively) in the case of those widows who
were enrolled in the privileged "order of widows." Of all the
groups who depended directly on the bishop for their sustenance,
the widows—both those formally enrolled in the "order of widows" and the many others supported by church funds—remained
by far the most vocal and the most difficult to control.[54] One suspects, in such widows, the fierce sense of entitlement of those
who had come down in the world. Reforming bishops, such as John
Chrysostom, were shocked to find that so much money devoted to
the care of the poor was absorbed by the support of persons who
were by no means poor. Rather, as widows, they belonged to the
category that we would call "Distressed Gentlefolk."[55] The large
role that widows and orphans play in the correspondence of bishops, in their relations with officials and lawyers,[56] shows one
thing: a society that had only very recently become "sensitized to
poverty"[57] remained acutely sensitive to an ancient anxiety about
the dangers of impoverishment among the relatively well-to-do.

The fate of the widow, reduced by the loss of her husband to the
status of a purely "private" person, without social support of any
kind and totally dependent on her own resources, stood as an
omen for the potential vulnerability of an entire section of late
Roman society.[58] Men and women alike, they all could come
down in the world. It was for such people that the bishop offered
protection. The emperor Justinian once deprived the widow of a
wealthy town councilor of Ascalon of her inheritance through a
legal verdict. Then, having robbed her in this manner, "in order
that this woman might not thereafter be assigned to the ranks of
the beggars," he granted her a pension of one gold piece a day.
Three hundred and sixty five *solidi* a year was no pittance: it was
the equivalent of the income of a governor or of a bishop. With a
hypocrisy that enraged Procopius, but of which the pious emperor

was probably entirely unaware, Justinian had played the bishop to her. Like a bishop, he had kept her from impoverishment: "For it is my custom to do whatever is pious and righteous."[59]

At the end of our period, the correspondence of Gregory the Great illustrates the latitude with which the bishop of a wealthy see could interpret his duty to take "care of the poor." At the bottom of the scale, a blind man, Filimud, received an annual food allowance that amounted to half a *solidus* a year.[60] But Gregory's maternal aunt and the widows of two eminent persons received, respectively, 40 and 20 *solidi* a year, and grain allowances of 400 and 300 *modii*. This would have enabled them to maintain a large household.[61] Three thousand refugee nuns settled in Rome received each a pension of 2 *solidi*.[62] This was as much as a member of the classical *plebs* of Rome had received in foodstuffs each year from the *annona*.

A late biographer of Gregory emphasized the extent of the paperwork that went into his care of the poor. The "great parchment volume" in which he kept his poor lists could still be read in ninth-century Rome. Would that they had survived![63] He also stressed the courteous discretion with which Gregory supported what later centuries would call the "shame-faced poor"—impoverished members of the upper classes.[64] It is a sensitivity echoed by the rabbis in the *Talmud*. They toyed with surreal cases of déclassé persons being maintained in the state to which they were accustomed, and emphasized the need to spare such persons the shame of appearing to beg for alms.[65] Yet there is more to it than that. Gregory wrote at a time when the urban structures of Italy were reeling under the impact of continued, largely rural warfare. His predecessor, Pelagius I, had reacted to the crisis in the same way. In 557, he wrote urgently to the bishop of Arles, to send him supplies of cheap clothing that had been earmarked for the poor—hoods, tunics, and short cloaks: "for there is such shortage and lack of clothing in this city that I cannot without grief and heaviness of heart look at our men, whom we knew once as well-born and well-to-do."[66] In Italy, as in many similarly embattled cities of Gaul and Spain, to gather a privileged, settled, and clearly registered section of the population around the bishop, as "the poor of the church," was to maintain the last relics of the ancient *plebs romana*, holding its own, now through Christian charity, in a dangerous world.

There is one corollary to the development by which the bishop became the protector of the *plebs* of the late Roman cities as a whole, as well as a provider for the poor. I wish to touch upon it in passing, although it raises a topic that deserves extensive treatment. That is: in the bishop's "care of the poor" one class of persons is strikingly absent—there are no slaves.[67] Christian practice and preaching on the "care of the poor" was produced by and for free persons only. Christian charity acted so as to console the free in their destitution and to protect the free from impoverishment. Slaves had no part in this process of consolation or protection, because it was a process that involved the destinies of free persons, who were not "owned" exclusively by any one protector.

Slavery remained a very real presence in many regions of the late Roman and post-Roman world. In many cities, domestic slavery was prominent.[68] Slave labor could still be found in the countryside. The barbarian invasions brought on a period of prolonged insecurity, characterized by a *guerre guerroyante,* in which relatively small armies terrorized the countryside in order to break the will of the towns. Such conditions led to spectacular local revivals of the slave trade.[69] Furthermore, the long established practice of exposing children at birth, to be collected by slave traders, or the custom of selling one's children in times of need, ensured that one feature of poverty, so tragically visible in early modern Europe—the appearance of large numbers of child beggars—was discreetly avoided in late Roman conditions.[70] Persons whom other societies would have recognized instantly as "poor" passed rapidly, at birth or in childhood, into the silent ranks of the slaves.[71]

But, although slaves were seen as objects of compassion by Christians, they were not considered to have destinies, as free persons did, for which the bishop and clergy might consider themselves to be responsible. The destiny of slaves was held to rest in the hands of their masters and mistresses. It was for the owners of slaves, and for no one else, to ensure that slaves were fed, clothed, and protected. Slave owners were urged by Christian preachers, as they had been urged in pagan times by philosophers, to control themselves and to abstain from cruelty and from sexual abuse of their slaves. With his characteristic blend of realism and insistence on the primacy of the heart, Augustine accepted the slave owner's right to speak harshly to his slaves. "For if he did not . . .

perhaps he would be failing to keep control of his household." It was better to do it that way:

> by harsh and frightening words rather than by savage beatings . . . [But] do not let him say these proud words in his own heart, not in the eyes and ears of God . . . let him reflect on the frailty of his flesh, once he has put off his rich man's clothes . . . Let him turn his thoughts to what he was like in his mother's womb, naked and helpless, just like that poor slave of his.[72]

Christian slave owners were encouraged to use the church as a *locus* for the freeing of their slaves.[73] They could be rebuked (and even shunned) for excessive mistreatment of them. In return, the church negotiated, with considerable care, the occasions on which slaves might seek sanctuary in the churches and might be received into monasteries or as members of the clergy.[74]

It is, perhaps, revealing that one use of the church for which slave owners later became notorious seems not to have been resorted to in late antiquity: old slaves were not freed by their masters, so as to save the cost of their support, in the expectation that they would be looked after as the "poor of the church." This happened in eighteenth-century Brazil and was denounced as a constant burden on the resources of the great Baroque *Misericórdia* of Bahía/Salvador.[75] It is an indication that the late antique Christian church, despite its rapid development of a novel system of *xenodocheia* and of hospitals, was slow to develop institutions of such a scale that they could be used as "dumping grounds" for elderly dependents. Old people's homes were mainly associated with monasteries, where elderly monks had to be cared for. Yet the old would have made up a sizable proportion of the population liable to destitution. The Christian church, though it urged kind treatment for elderly servants, was not in a position to absorb such poverty. There was only so much that it could do.[76]

By contrast, Christians defended with the greatest tenacity the distinction between the free and the unfree. They attempted to ensure that free persons never crossed that dread boundary. The fact that the children of the unfortunate Pamonthios were in danger of being sold off as slaves by his creditors was a principal reason for the appeal on his behalf.[77] Jews reacted likewise. In 291, the synagogue of Oxyrhynchus paid a large sum to redeem and manumit a middle-aged woman and her two sons.[78]

The ransoming of captives taken in barbarian raids (that is, of

free persons perceived to be in imminent danger of enslavement)
counted as one of the most heroic deeds that a bishop could perform. It certainly involved the greatest immediate outlay of cash,
and occasionally led to the dramatic, and long-remembered, melt-
ing down of church treasures.[79] As an old man, Augustine was
forced to intervene to bring to a halt a vigorous "internal slave
trade" run by Roman merchants who preyed on the peasantry outside Hippo. He drafted passionate petitions to the emperor.[80] He
went out of his way to consult a professional Roman lawyer on
the rights and wrongs of the situation. Could a landowner sell his
own peasants as slaves? Could free parents sell their children into
slavery?[81]

In the matter of slavery, as in so much else in late antiquity, ancient boundaries held firm. The core of free persons expected to
receive a high degree of protection from their bishop. Slaves, by
contrast, were left to the protection of their owners. Thus there
was nothing inconsistent with Gregory the Great's actions when
he wrote to the military governor of Africa to send him prisoners
of war, taken from barbarian tribes. As slaves, these would work
the estates of the church, which, in turn, would support the
"poor" of Rome.[82] Free persons supported by the labor of slaves,
the "poor of the church" were, in Gregory's Rome, recognizable
echoes, somewhat the worse for wear, of the once-triumphant
populus romanus.

If we turn to the sermons and letters of Saint Augustine (some
of which have only recently come to light) we find a fully documented case of a Christian leader who, for all his notorious brilliance as a theologian, acted and spoke, on a day-to-day basis, very
much as the average bishop of the Western empire in its last days
was expected to act and speak. From this abundant evidence we
can gain a sense of the wide spectrum of persons who, at different
times and for different reasons, came to Augustine's attention as
members of the "poor."

The destitute poor are a constant presence in Augustine's
preaching in Hippo and Carthage. He knows that the winter and
the empty months of summer, before the harvest, are hard times
for them.[83] He says once that they mobbed him on his way to
church, begging him to preach on their behalf, and to urge his
congregation to be more generous in giving alms.[84] His sermons
often reached the level of *pathos* shown by John Chrysostom, the

master-preacher of charity, in Antioch and Constantinople. They show the homogeneity and resilience of what had become a Mediterranean-wide discourse on the poor.

> For now, by God's will, it is winter. Think of the poor. Think of how the naked Christ can be clothed. Pay attention to Him [to Christ, in the person of the poor] as he lies in the portico, as He suffers hunger, as He endures the cold.[85]

He also traced, with clear eyes, the ups and downs of the vulnerable members of the "more humble" classes, as they moved, in a perpetual "random oscillation of . . . households,"[86] up to and away from the edge of destitution.

> But perhaps you have been made utterly poor and needy. You had some little family property that had supported you, which was taken away from you by the tricky dealing of a rival. You groan, you grumble against the times you live in . . . Yesterday such a man was groaning that he had lost his property. Today, backed by a greater patron, he is grabbing the property of others.[87]

But it is, above all, in the ranks of the clergy that we see most clearly the struggles of the potentially impoverished to maintain a foothold through the church. The fact that Hippo was the major seaport of Numidia encouraged the drift of the unfortunate, the enterprising, and the resentful from the smaller towns and villages of the hinterland. Donatianus of Suppa lived for a time in Hippo off the alms of the church. He proved to be useless as a member of the lesser clergy. Finally, Augustine made him door keeper to the shrine of Saint Theogenes, "so that he should have something to live off."[88] Donatianus had lived down to the expectations of a contemporary astrologer, Firmicus Maternus, whose lore reached back, over centuries of poverty, to Hellenistic Egypt. He was one of those whose stars "had made to work as door keepers, forced by beggary to do this service."[89] But this was by no means how Donatianus saw himself. He expected to return to Suppa (where he may still have had connections) as a full clergyman, having made his fortune—so he said—as a pillar of the church of Hippo!

Young Antoninus, future disastrous bishop of Fussala, had come to Hippo with his mother and his mother's lover. The family lived for a time on the alms of the church. Then Augustine intervened to regulate the situation. Antoninus and his "step-father" were given places in the monastery. His mother was put on the *matricula*, the formal list of the "poor of the church."[90] Once again, what we see in this family are not beggars but *déclassés*. Antoninus' subsequent career shows this clearly. He made up with a vengeance for his period of poverty. Created bishop of Fussala, a hilltop village of the hinterland, on the strength of his knowledge of Punic, Antoninus set about victimizing his congregation in Fussala and the neighboring villages. In 420, Augustine was taken to see (among other things) the gaping holes in the houses from which Antoninus had plundered stone ornaments with which to build his new bishop's palace.[91] Antoninus, the bully bishop, was a member of the "poor" for whom the church had done only too well. More welcome, by contrast, was Leporius, a penniless refugee of high status from the fallen Roman frontier on the Rhine. Made priest by Augustine, he was able, on the strength of his prestige alone, to raise enough money to build the first *xenodochium* of the church of Hippo.[92]

It is useful to linger on these specific and well-documented cases. They give a human face to those who, at one time or another, counted as members of the "poor of the church" without necessarily joining the ranks of the destitute. The overwhelming impression left by this evidence is of the extreme diversity of this care, and of the many mechanisms that were used to carry it out. The poor of late antiquity (as in later Christian societies) were implicated in a "mixed economy of care."[93] Some were relieved from fiscal burdens by the interventions of the bishop. Some were given employment in the church. A large number were formally enrolled on various "poor lists": 3,000 were on the list of widows and orphans in fourth-century Antioch, 7,500 were on the poor rolls of the church of Alexandria in the early seventh century. A provincial church, such as Gaza, may have supported about 200 persons a year, each receiving the equivalent of half a year's wages of a skilled artisan.[94] But, although the organization of poor relief by the bishop and clergy was prominent, it never stood alone. Beggars were actively commended to the charity of believers. John Chrysostom, for instance, was firmly of the opinion that the growth of poor relief through the church had caused the average Christian to become slack in giving alms in person to the poor and in offering hospitality to strangers. If individual Christians were more generous, he argued, the clergy would not be burdened with the time-consuming business of poor relief.[95] Some poor persons received from their bishop licenses to beg. In the sixth century, Nicetius of Lyon gave such a license to one poor man:

he had obtained from him letters bearing his signature, with which he went to beg for alms at the houses of pious people. After the saint's death, he continued to use his letters, persuading charitable people to give him quite large sums in memory of the saint.[96]

A collection of ostraca from Upper Egypt—that is, of broken pots on which messages were written in Coptic, the native language—give us an unexpected glimpse of a bishop and his priests in action around the year 600. In one such ostracon, bishop Abraham of Hermonthis brought the full weight of his authority to bear on a local strong man, Psalis:

Since I have been informed that Psalis ill-uses the poor and they have told us saying: "He is ill-using us and making us poor and wretched." He that ill-uses his neighbor is excluded from the feast. [That is, from the fellowship of believers at the Eucharist and at festivals.]

Psalis, wrote Abraham, was like Judas, like those who struck Jesus, like Gehazi, like Cain, like the accusers of Daniel and Susanna. Clearly written, the tile was meant to be declaimed in public.[97] A beggar was sent to an other person:

May the Lord bless thee and all that thou hast, men and beasts. Be kind and have pity on this poor man.[98]

Abraham's priest was to read a message to Patermoute:

beg him to show mercy on this widow, that the Lord may bless him.[99]

A landowner was taken up on his promise:

Since I spoke to thee . . . regarding the poor, and thou didst say whoso thou findest, send him to me: so now have pity on these two persons whom I send thee. God knows, they cry aloud to the pity of everyone daily.[100]

His clergy had to know how to approach a grandee in the right way:

Be so kind—I worship the footstool of your feet—to settle this affair. For it is written, *Therefore strong peoples will glorify thee.* (Isaiah 25:3)[101]

Altogether, these scattered fragments give us some idea of what it was like, in late antiquity, to "come under the shadow" of a conscientious bishop.[102]

Such activity depended to a great extent on the energy of individual bishops and on the wealth of their churches. In the fourth century, however, an institution was created that did much to fuse the bishop's official "care of the poor" with more wide-ranging powers to act as protector of the potentially impoverished members of his flock in every city. This was the bishop's court—the *episcopalis audientia*.[103]

At the very beginning of his reign, Constantine had ratified the right of the bishop to act as the supreme arbiter of civil suits brought before him by the faithful. This was a traditional practice, long current in the pre-Constantinian church and in Judaism. The right to arbitrate created, in effect, a new court, a new venue of arbitration, known as the *episcopalis audientia*. Constantine's legislation was not intended to set up a novel form of jurisdiction. As in Roman law, the bishop was treated as an arbiter. He had to be chosen by the mutual consent of both parties. What Constantine did insist upon was that, once the case had been brought before the bishop, it should be terminated by him alone: no party was allowed to appeal to a further arbitrator.[104]

The validation of the *episcopalis audientia* was a characteristically Constantinian device. It was both grandiose and opportunistic. It enabled the emperor to demonstrate his respect for Christian bishops. At the same time, it recruited an intermediate institution, more in touch with the humbler classes of society than was his own bureaucracy, in an attempt to "put a cap" on litigation. Quick and cheap arbitration in the *episcopalis audientia* ensured that the governors' courts would not be clogged by protracted lawsuits.[105]

We know very little about the cases dealt with in the *episcopalis audientia*. The fact that, in 362, the emperor Julian the Apostate accused the clergy of Bostra of "tyrannizing" their city, through the manner in which they adjudicated suits concerning wills and the division of property, shows that the *episcopalis audientia* was far from being a court open only to the poor.[106] It seems to have offered its most successful services to the relatively well-to-do, who could not afford to be bankrupted by prolonged litigation in the imperial courts. Non-Christians were prepared to convert so as to make use of its services.[107] Yet Augustine's activities as a judge also show him reaching far down the social scale. He dealt with disputes over rents between landlords and peasants.[108]

As we have seen, he sought legal advice on the rights of impoverished parents to sell their children.[109]

One would wish to know so much more about the *episcopalis audientia*. It is one of the great regrets of late Roman history that, compared with the vivid sermons on the "love of the poor" that fill so many volumes of the works of the Fathers of the Church, we should know so little about the activities of the bishop's court. A crucial aspect of the presence of the church in late Roman society remains as silent and unseen as the dark side of the moon.

What we do know, from the complaints of Augustine, is that the business of the *episcopalis audientia* could be immensely taxing. When he wrote *On the Work of Monks* he told his readers that at no time did he regret the loss of the ordered leisure associated with the monastic life as sharply as when he sat in his court "suffering the burdens of the unpredictable onrush of complex lawsuits brought by outsiders on matters of secular law, having to decide them by pronouncing judgment or to intervene to bring about a settlement."[110] The bishop's court usually met in a *secretarium*, an audience hall, adjacent to the bishop's basilica.[111] On that occasion, the bishop was expected to sit, like a judge, on a high throne.[112] The bishop could delegate aspects of the work of arbitration to members of his clergy and even to skilled laymen.[113] But, in whatever way the business was conducted, the practice of the court made him, for good or ill, a prominent figure. One bishop (Basil of Ancyra) could even be accused by his enemies of sitting in judgement like any governor, imprisoning litigants and torturing witnesses.[114] Whether used for good or ill, the continued presence of the bishop's court and the ethos of "judgment" that surrounded it gradually came to influence the inhabitants of every city.

Hence a significant development that is associated with the regular practice of the bishop's court. The business of the court was conducted according to the rules of Roman law. There can be no doubt about that. Yet the process of arbitration—from the first appeal to the bishop to his final verdict—took place in an atmosphere charged with expectations of judgment that did not belong exclusively to the Roman world. Augustine, for instance, was in the habit of justifying his verdicts by appeal to the Scriptures.[115] This meant that the daily practice of justice, in Christian circles, was imperceptibly colored by an ideal of the just judge associated with the Old and New Testaments—that is, with books that brought into the late classical present echoes of a model of society that was rooted in the ancient Near East and oblivious to the values of the classical city.

In the Near Eastern model of society, the "poor" were a judicial, not an economic, category. They were plaintiffs, not beggars. To give "justice" to the "poor" was a sign of royal energy—whether this was the energy of a king or of a god.[116] It was an attribute of royalty that was displayed most fully on the accession of the ruler.[117] For in giving such justice, the new king showed the reach of his power. He deliberately brushed aside intermediate authorities—local oligarchies, local patrons, heads of families—so as to deal directly with those who had been deprived of all protectors but himself. Hence the importance, in representations of royal justice, of the appeals of widows and orphans.[118] They were a class of the "weak" who, in normal circumstances, would have depended on the protection of their immediate kin and locality. Now the king stepped in to take up their case. The laws of Urukagina of Lagish (2400 B.C.E.) make plain that it was a sign of royal power to ensure that "the orphans did not fall prey to the wealthy . . . the man of one *shekel* to the man of a *mina*.[119] Hammurabi (1729–1680 B.C.E.) declared that the purpose of his laws was to protect the "poor," "so that the strong may not oppress the weak." He did so, appropriately enough, after he had successfully oppressed everybody else. Hammurabi's laws were "laws of righteousness, which Hammurabi the strong king established."[120] They were issued after Hammurabi had created a kingdom in which the "provincial administration had systematically by-passed local authorities, and was geared to the enrichment of [his] distant capital in Babylon."[121] For a god not to reach out to the poor was to court replacement. As the son of the Canaanite god, Krt, informed his father:

Thou hast let thy hands fall . . .
Thou didst not judge the case of the widow
nor uphold the suit of the oppressed.
Descend from thy rule that I may reign.[122]

In order to obtain such justice from above, the petitioner had to adopt the position of the "poor"—that is, of a person with no other protector but the king. This did not mean that he or she was economically destitute. Rather, the "poor" person was the person of any status who waited, humbly but insistently, for the answer of the great.[123] To be poor was to have a claim. The monumental clarity and poetic elegance of the juxtaposition of the term *ze'aqah*, "the cry," that elicited its remedy, *z'daqah*, "justice," was not lost on the great Hebraist Saint Jerome as he commented on Isaiah 5:7.[124] It conveyed an ethos of justice—firm, paternal, and mercifully swift—that appealed to many humble late Roman persons who found themselves living, in many ways, in a post-classical world in which Old Testament conditions reigned.

I would suggest that an almost subliminal reception of the Hebrew Bible, through the chanting of the Psalms and through the solemn injunctions of the bishop in connection with the *episcopalis audientia*, came to offer a meaning to the word *pauper* very different from the "pauperized" image of the merely "economic" poor. The pauper was a person with a claim upon the great. As with the poor of Israel, those who used the court of the bishop and attended his church also expected to call upon him, in time of need, for justice and protection.

These expectations were built up over time on the ground around the bishop, through the daily practice of his court. But they also received stunning confirmation in the realm of high politics. The late fourth century saw a series of spectacular interventions by Christian bishops on behalf of entire communities. Uncertain of his control of the cities of the empire, Theodosius I had encouraged appeals by bishops. They highlighted his sovereign prerogative of mercy.[125] In 387, bishop Flavian of Antioch was allowed to gain amnesty for the city of Antioch after a major tax revolt. In 391, the citizens of Thessalonica were not so fortunate. The punishment planned by Theodosius for a riot escalated into a horrendous massacre. But it was Ambrose of Milan who made the emperor do penance for the act. Ambrose did so in a manner that deliberately cast himself in the role of an Old Testament prophet, and Theodosius as king of ancient Israel, who had failed to listen to the "cry of the poor."[126]

These were not isolated incidents. A newly discovered letter of Augustine shows the bishop of Hippo, in 419, waiting anxiously for news of a similar amnesty, obtained by the bishops of Africa after a tax riot in Carthage. Before this letter was discovered, we knew nothing whatsoever of the riot nor of the campaign for amnesty that followed it.[127] This campaign took a party of senior African bishops all the way through Rome and Ravenna to the edge of the Pyrenees, on a journey of over 1,500 miles, in search of the authorities.[128] In another letter, we learn that the ever enterprising Antoninus of Fussala had gained letters from the senior bishop of Numidia, so as to sail to Italy to negotiate the release of captives—probably fiscal debtors under arrest.[129] Augustine's home town, Thagaste, had already created a legend suitable to the times. In the days of persecuting emperors, bishop Firmus of Thagaste was said to have defended with such steadfastness the rights of a suppliant who had fled to the church for protection that the emperor, duly impressed, had "granted amnesty without difficulty."[130] A local legend such as this, which circulated in humble Thagaste, already looks forward to the actions of the great aristocratic bishops of the early medieval West.

Incidents such as these are reminders that the history of the rise of the Christian church in Roman society can not be reduced to a few dramatic "turning points," associated with vivid and carefully publicized confrontations between bishops and emperors, as was the case of the relations of Theodosius I with bishop Flavian of Antioch and with Ambrose of Milan. There may have been many such maneuvers, constantly repeated on a small scale, of which we know nothing. The old tradition of embassies sent by cities to the emperors—dramatic affairs, whose heroes had braved the dangers of travel and the wrath of the rulers—was taken up by Christian bishops who appealed, now in terms reminiscent of the ancient Near East, on behalf of the "poor."

The infiltration of an ancient Near Eastern model of justice may explain a certain "upward slippage" of the notion of the "poor" in Christian texts of this time. In 419, Honoratus was elected bishop of Mauretanian Caesarea. It was an irregular election, of which Augustine and his colleagues disapproved deeply. Not so Honoratus' own congregation. When the letter of the senior bishops was read out, declaring the election of Honoratus to be invalid, there was a riot. All concerned, and "most of all the poor"—*maxime pauperes*—opposed Augustine. These *pauperes* were not the destitute. They were the average inhabitants of Caesarea, glad to have an effective bishop to represent their interests. Honoratus had already been at the imperial court.[131] The majority of Honoratus' congregation was "poor" only in that they had put themselves in his hands, as a judge and intercessor. Like the townsmen of Palaebisca, in Cyrenaica (modern eastern Libya), they knew what they wanted in a bishop: "a champion of men's affairs . . . able to injure his enemies and do good to his friends."[132]

The Coptic collection of *Questions and Answers* with which we began this chapter hints at a similar "slippage." When Cyril discussed a disputed election, he envisioned a case when the town authorities—the *prytaneia*—might be opposed by the *leptodémos*—the body of lesser citizens. This was a traditional, "civic" definition of the city that made use of Greek loan words. A little further on, however, the classical term *leptodémos* is abandoned. Cyril was content to speak bluntly, in Coptic, of *ñhéke*, "the poor."[133] Shorn of its "civic" structure—in which the citizen body was traditionally divided between the ruling authority, the *prytaneia*, and the rest, the *leptodémos* or *démos*—the late Roman city had settled down as a city in which the powerful ruled "the poor." But, in return, the "poor" expected to enjoy the protection to which they were entitled on the basis of an Old Testament model of society.

By contrast, in towns of Asia Minor where the classical tradition remained strong, the opposite occurred. The poor did not replace the *démos*. Instead, in a combination that would have puzzled classical persons, they became the *démos*. In Stratonikeia (Eskihısar, near Milas, Turkey), a city with a long tradition of public benefactions, the pious Maximus received an honorary inscription near the church. His gifts had shown "how good it was not be anxious for earthly possessions." The inscription was set up by the town council, the ancient *boulé*, and by the *akteanoi poliétai*, the "destitute citizens." It was the poor of the city who now granted public honors in collaboration with the *boulé*, as the *démos* had done in classical times.[134]

The laudatory epitaphs that were placed on the tombs of bishops in late fifth- and sixth-century Gaul show the completion of this process. They balance, in classical terms, the two aspects of the bishop's role as protector. The bishop was praised, equally, for having given sustenance to the needy, to the *egeni* and the *inopes*, and for having given *peace* and *justice* to the *cives*.[135] Altogether, the bishops had come to see themselves as so many avatars of the great dispensers of justice in the Hebrew Bible. Maurilio, the saintly and effective bishop of Cahors, was praised by Gregory of Tours as a man who had brought into the present an ancient, preclassical style of government:

He was just in his judgments, always ready to defend the poor of his church from the hand of unjust judges, according to the words of Job [Job 29:12–16]: *I delivered the poor who cried out, and the fatherless who had no one to help him. The mouth of the widow blessed me. For I was an eye to the blind, a foot to the lame and as a father to the weak.*[136]

With such figures, and with the wide section of urban society who had come to look to them for protection, we have traveled a long way from the image of utterly destitute beggars with which we began this chapter. In the next chapter, let us carry forward this development, which we have followed principally in the fourth and early fifth centuries, into the fifth and sixth centuries. For at that time, the language of "poverty" and the image of the poor as the bearers of claims on the great, which had been so present in ancient Israel, came to seep out of the churches. It added a novel tincture to the language of public relations. It became a language that was increasingly found to be apposite to describe the quality of the relation of the emperor to his subjects, and of the weak to the powerful.

We will also see how Christian thought and preaching had concentrated on the mysterious and enduring presence of Christ among men—and most especially on the poignant notion that, somehow, Christ was still hidden in the ranks of the poor. This mystique of the poor provided the members of a rapidly changing and abrasive society with a new language with which to express its hopes and its fears. It enabled early Byzantines to think about the maintenance, under strain, of a minimum of social cohesion, and to express a high-pitched yearning for solidarity in what had, by the sixth century, become the first post-classical Christian society.

3   "Condescension"

Poverty and Solidarity in the Eastern Empire

We have seen so far that the rise to prominence of the notion of the "care of the poor" in late Roman society was by no means a simple process. It can not be treated as if it were the inevitable effect of the diffusion, throughout the Roman world, of *Das Evangelium der Liebe und Hilfleistung*, of "The Gospel of Love and Charity,"[1] that had been preached by the Christian church from its very beginnings. Rather, in our first chapter we saw that the rise to privilege of the Christian church after the conversion of Constantine in 312 dramatically altered the scale of Christian charity, the nature of its institutions, and the meaning that such charity took on for a still partially Christianized world. It was no longer a fiercely inward-looking matter, directed to the needs of the faithful alone. "Love of the poor" became a public virtue, which bishops and clergymen were expected to demonstrate, in return for public privileges. But neither was the emergence of a new society, in which "love of the poor" held a prominent place, a function only of increasing pauperization and of the increasing polarization of late Roman society between the "rich" and the "poor." We are dealing, rather, with a change in the social imagination. Late antiquity witnessed the transition from one model of society, in which the poor were largely invisible, to another, in which they came to play a vivid imaginative role.

It has proved easier to characterize this change than to explain it. It did not occur only because the classical vision of society simply collapsed, as the destitute poor pressed in upon the city, forcing themselves on the attention of the authorities by their unprecedented numbers. What we may be dealing with, rather, was the ability of the Christian church to find a place within the city for outsiders of all classes. A perpetual "Brownian motion" of persons from place to place had characterized the ancient Mediterranean in all centuries. In the cities, there were always people who were strangers, most of whom were considered *de trop*, immigrants with no place in the community. In late antiquity, however, the Christian church, with its empire-wide networks (which claimed to treat fellow believers from whatever region as potential "fellow citizens") and its new institutions—an expanding clergy and new systems of poor relief—was able to attach to itself, in every city, a number of persons who, previously, had had nowhere to go. The experience of Augustine as bishop of the coastal city of Hippo (Bône/Annaba, Algeria), which we discussed in the last chapter, shows how this might happen. Destitute and *déclassé* immigrants from the hinterland found a place on the poor rolls of the church of Hippo or in the church's monasteries and convents. "Middling" persons, even distinguished refugees from as far away as the Rhineland, were welcomed into the clergy. The bishop was charged with the integration of strangers. When a young man, Augustine himself had come as a stranger to Milan, in 385, in order to teach rhetoric in the city. It was Ambrose who welcomed the young African, as part of his duty—*satis episcopaliter* (Augustine wrote), "very much as befitted a bishop."[2] Such activity betrayed a new flexibility in making good use of immigrants. It does not mean that late antique cities were passing through an unprecedented demographic crisis, brought about by overpopulation and by excessive immigration of the destitute from the countryside.

A major demographic crisis did, indeed, occur a millennium later. In many areas of western Europe in the early modern period, the upholders of the more manageable medieval image of a hierarchical and paternalistic society (in which the poor, in theory at least, had an allotted and largely unproblematic role) found themselves faced by novel social developments with which they were unable to cope—an uncontrolled rise in prices, unprecedented numbers of the vagrant poor, and an ominous rise in "shallow" poverty among the working classes as a whole.[3] Tempting though it might be to see a parallel between the conditions of the later empire and those of early modern Europe, the analogy is misleading. We are dealing with profoundly different societies, both in the mentality of their governing classes and in the texture of poverty itself in each of them. The late antique and early medieval world was closer, in many significant ways, to a society as exotic to us as nineteenth-century Ethiopia than it was to the states of early modern western Europe.[4]

No demographic changes on the scale associated with the population pressure of early modern Europe seem to have occurred in late antiquity. Nor, for all the initiatives taken by Christians in the late antique period, did late Roman society ever pass through anything as drastic as the spasm of organization that set in place the work houses, the great hospitals and orphanages, the systems of poor relief, and the general, close surveillance of the poor that we associate with the social policy of governments and local authorities in the sixteenth and seventeenth centuries.[5] These were on a different order of magnitude from anything that occurred in the Christian church in the late antique period. Early Christian writings on the care of the poor were extensively reprinted and translated, in the sixteenth and seventeenth centuries, in support of new, Humanist ideals of social order. The classic sermon *On the Love of the Poor* of Gregory of Nazianze, the Cappadocian friend and admirer of Basil of Caesarea, played this role in early sixteenth-century Lyons, as did similar Patristic sermons in late seventeenth-century Russia.[6] But these were distinguished ghosts from an unimaginably distant past. The early modern cities to which their message was applied bore no relation whatsoever to the world of late antiquity.

The later empire showed few inhibitions in attempting to organize its subjects and to collect and redistribute their wealth for its own purposes. But, when it came to the issue of the care of the poor, it did very little compared with the states of early modern Europe. For instance, it was only in Constantinople, his new capital, that Constantine and his successors maintained a system of cheap burial for the poor that embraced the entire lower-class population of the city. At the start, Constantine's burial scheme was a characteristically "hybrid" venture. It combined Christian charity—in which the provision of decent burial for the poor and for strangers had always played an important role—with an emperor's grant of "civic" privileges to the citizens of "his" new city. The scheme was extended to some other towns.[7] But Constantine's initiative stood alone. No late antique organizational venture can be compared to the massive civic institutions for the care of the poor created in the early modern period. Rather, what changed in late antiquity was the definition of the bonds of society. Traditional

patterns of giving and traditional links of patronage and protection
were redirected. New social networks were created that reached
out, past the traditional core of "citizens," to embrace an ill-
defined, but symbolically charged, group of "the poor."

Wealth was encouraged to flow further down the social scale.
Acts of giving that could still be represented in terms of the traditional generosity of a *euergetés*, of a public benefactor of his city,
were now performed, in the Christian church, for the benefit of
"the poor." Such acts were extensively publicized in Christian
texts. We are dealing with a society that still knew how to praise
the generosity of the rich in old-fashioned terms, even when this
generosity took place on a considerably more moderate scale than
had been the case in the glory days of the high empire, and even
when the givers were new figures—imperial governors rather than
local notables, bishops, and pious men and women rather than
civic leaders.[8]

Such acts of Christian generosity showed that a process of
"Christianization of euergetism" was well under way in the post-
Constantinian church.[9] Their resonance was enhanced by the
echoes they evoked of the classical *belle époque*. It was satisfying
to write about them in old-fashioned terms, and especially if it
was possible, thereby, to make invidious comparisons between
such actions and the wasteful spending of traditional civic benefactors. They held a vivid place in contemporary sources. As a result, they have caused modern scholars to direct if anything too
much attention to them.

For what is less vividly documented in Christian sources may
have proved equally decisive in the long run—that is, the spread to
the late antique population as a whole of the Christian and Jewish
practice of almsgiving. Unfortunately, apart from innumerable
sermons that urged the faithful of all classes to give alms to the
poor, the actual practice and impact of Christian almsgiving in
late Roman society remain unknown. We must remember that
almsgiving was not a totally novel departure. To be a beggar had
always been one form, among others, of earning money in the ancient Mediterranean. It was considered dishonorable by respectable persons and slightly uncanny. But it was a device used with
little shame by the lower classes. To give to such beggars was a
routine matter. It was a gesture largely untinged with the social
pathos associated with Christian and Jewish notions of "love of

the poor."[10] The destitute (along with malcontents and enterprising scroungers) had long gathered around the great temples in the cities and in the countryside.[11] Jerome, and many other Christians, took for granted that pagans also could enjoy a reputation for piety through their almsgiving.[12]

Yet, despite a measure of continuity with pre-Christian practice, there is every reason to assume that almsgiving became more frequent in late antiquity. This meant one thing. In Jewish and Christian circles, a steady drizzle of small sums, given irregularly to the poor by individual believers, was taken for granted. Constant small sums changed hands.[13] As a result, local almsgiving, by believers of every class, may have considerably reduced the impact of the occasional large sums provided by the great—by the rich and the emperors. In a world where almsgiving was widely practiced by everyone, "Christianized euergetism," though memorable, was not the only way in which wealth now reached the poor.

What we do know about is the amount of money that came to be dispensed, on a yearly basis, by bishops in many areas of the late antique world. As we saw in the last chapter, the bishops of major cities had "poor rolls" that included thousands. In the late fifth century, the bishop of Ravenna had at his disposal some 3,000 *solidi* per year for the care of the poor. Such a sum was the equivalent, every year, of the outlay of a contemporary civic notable for the repair of the public baths of his city. It was an impressive sum, one that could have supported some one thousand poor persons.[14] Even in a small provincial town, Anastasioupolis (Dikmen Hüyük/Beypazarı, Western Turkey) on the main Roman road to the East, a conscientious bishop could devote some 325 *solidi* of his living allowance to the poor.[15]

These statistics are precious just because they are so few. But even if there were more of them, they would not tell the whole story. In an ancient society such as the later Roman empire, the novel availability of wealth to spend on the poor was less important than was the downward extension of the networks of patronage and protection associated with the bishop's "care of the poor." In the last chapter, we saw how this extension took place. The bishop and his clergy came to be intimately involved with the protection of the *tenuiores,* of the "weaker" classes of the late Roman cities as a whole, as well as with the destitute poor to which their care was officially directed. The care of those who were vulnerable to impoverishment on all levels of urban society, and not only the care of the destitute, was crucial to the consolidation of the power of the bishop as a local leader.

Hence a paradoxical development, characteristic of late antiquity. A long "civic" past ensured that the average inhabitant of a late Roman city felt that he or she had an even stronger claim than had the poor to the attentions of the bishop. The expectations of such persons silently but firmly reimposed ancient boundaries on the social vision of the clergy. Slaves, for instance, were notably absent from the care provided by the Christian church. For they were not free persons, entitled to seek protection on the same footing as the *leptodémos*, the "little people" of the city. As a result of this pressure, the classical model of society—which saw the city as a gathering of privileged fellow citizens—did not give way, brusquely and irrevocably, to a more austere and universal Christian model that saw the world as divided only between the "rich" and the "poor." In practice, Christian poor relief, although officially directed to the destitute, never focused on that class alone. It never neglected the "middling," "weaker" classes who had once made up the mass of fellow citizens in ancient towns. In many late antique cities, the new "care of the poor" tended to merge, in a hybrid manner characteristic of so much of late antiquity, with the maintenance, in a new form, of ancient safeguards that protected the city's inhabitants, both individually and as a whole, against oppression and impoverishment.

Hence the title of this book, *Poverty and Leadership in the Later Roman Empire*. With the establishment of the Christian bishop as the "governor of the poor," a new form of leadership emerged in the cities of the late Roman and post-Roman world. Not only did this leadership claim to have put down roots to the very bottom of society through the bishop's care of the poor; but through the extension of this care of the poor to include so many members of the "middling" classes, new conduits were opened up for the exercise of protection and for the conveying of appeals to those at the very top of society—especially to the emperors and his officials. As we have seen, these new forms of protection and appeal were exercised vigorously all over the Roman world, not only by well-known bishops on famous occasions but also by innumerable, lesser-known bishops and clergymen on a more routine basis.

I also pointed out, in the last chapter, that this development was accompanied by the emergence of a new language, taken mainly from the Hebrew Scriptures, with which to express claims on the rich and the powerful. It was a decisive change. Slowly, over the course of the fourth and fifth centuries, the relation between the emperor and his subjects, and between the different classes of society became tinged with a new *pathos* generated within the Christian church. The relations between the believer and God, between subject and emperor, and between the weak and the powerful came to be swallowed up by a single, elemental image—the image of the relation between the poor and the rich and powerful to whom the poor "cried out" not only for alms but for justice and protection.

We should not underestimate the rhetorical force in late Roman society of what was, in effect, a novel "master image." It was an image originally formed in the highly stratified, monarchical societies of the ancient Near East. It accepted towering asymmetries of power and wealth between "the poor" and those to whom they looked for help. But it also functioned in the Near East, as it would function in the later empire, as a language of claims that was calculated to bridge just such daunting social distances. It was the duty of the powerful (and, indeed, it was regarded as a special ornament of their power) to listen to "the cry" of the poor.

As officially recognized spokesmen of "the poor," in the wide sense of spokesmen to the emperor and to the local authorities of the needs of the various vulnerable classes within their cities, the bishops of the fourth and early fifth centuries played a decisive role in introducing this "master image" into public discourse. All over the empire, Christian bishops, clergymen and monks fostered a nonclassical image of society by the simple process of speaking as if society were, indeed, divided primarily between the rich and the poor, the weak and the powerful, according to a Biblical, Near Eastern model. But we must always remember that the bishops did not act alone. They came to deploy a particular "language of claims" that laid great emphasis on the plight of the poor.[16] But they did so within a wider situation. It is to this state of affairs that we should first turn.

We are faced, in the later Roman empire, with a situation analogous to that which has been described by present-day commentators on human rights—that is, with what these commentators have called "an advocacy revolution." The imperial government did not become any more humane or any less oppressive in these centuries as a result of such an advocacy revolution. But ways of appealing to its representatives did change considerably, both in complexity and in tone, in the course of the fourth, fifth, and sixth centuries.

From around 300 onward, the later Roman empire was characterized by an unprecedented degree of closeness of the state to the lives of its subjects. For the first time in its long history, the Roman empire had become a presence that could not be ignored by the majority of its inhabitants.[17] Modern scholars are agreed that the expanded presence of the Roman state did not necessarily bring as much misery upon its subjects as we had once thought. It was not the overweight, totalitarian monster that it appeared to be to those who studied it (with marked repugnance) in the 1920s and 1930s. It may not have exercised a significantly greater degree of control over its subjects than previously. But its representatives were now everywhere.[18] As a result, the growth of the late Roman state appears to have brought about a heightening of the intensity of interaction between the state and its subjects. Large segments of the population that had not previously come within its purview now found themselves engaged on a regular basis with Roman officials.

Let us take a few, small but revealing examples from one exceptionally well-documented province, Roman Egypt. We owe our knowledge of many crucial late Roman tax edicts to the fact that they were preserved in the archives of relatively humble Egyptian farmers. One farmer who kept such laws, Aurelius Isidore of Karanis in the Fayum, could not even sign his own name in Greek. But he needed to have copies of these documents in order to defend his property.[19] In Egypt, it has been plausibly suggested that the spread of functional literacy in Greek, and then in Coptic, may have had much to do with the need of ordinary taxpayers to protect themselves against a highly literate and active bureaucracy.[20] The bureaucracy both increased its own demands on the "weaker" classes and, at the same time, drew them closer to the state by eliciting from them an endless stream of petitions. Aurelius Isidore belonged to a large class of men "unafraid to use the system." He appealed frequently to local officials. In 299, he was on to the prefect himself: "I betake myself to Your Magnificence in order to make this complaint."[21]

At the same time, we can see that the nature of petitions brought before officials in Egypt changed markedly. They took on a notably more melodramatic tone. In the words of the Russian scholar, Arkady Kovelman, "Roman petitions [of the classical period] mostly resemble treatises, while Byzantine petitions [from the later Empire] are like novels."[22]

We should not underestimate the prevalence in late Roman society of the rhetorical skills generated by the drafting of innumerable official petitions. Reticence in the expression of grievances was not a characteristic of the age. The late Roman state worked on the principle summed up in the American adage: "It is the squeaky wheel that gets the grease." In order to attract the attention of the representatives of a gigantic and highly centralized bureaucracy, every wheel that needed grease had to emit long and piercing squeaks. Understatement was not encouraged. When called upon to explain the meaning of the last words of Jesus of Nazareth on the Cross, *My God, my God, why have you forsaken me?*, Nilus of Ancyra (Ankara, Turkey), a Christian writer of the fifth century, pointed out that these words, of course, could not mean that God had deserted Jesus. Far from it. Rather, Jesus Christ (as the sacrificial representative of the entire human race) was simply following late Roman practice in bringing before God, in the most dramatic language possible, the prayers of a fallen humanity:

It is like a legal representative pleading before a provincial governor on behalf of a group that has suffered oppression. "Most just of rulers [he would say] we have been afflicted, we have been ground down, we have been drained of all resources."[23]

It has proved only too easy to take the language of late Roman petitions at their face value. Historians have conjured up a horrendous image of the later empire by putting together the many dramatic complaints that fill the sources of the late antique period. They have, as it were, glued together innumerable "snapshots"— culled largely from petitions and from the denunciation of abuses in the imperial laws—in order to create a composite picture of terminal corruption, inertia, fiscal oppression, widespread impoverishment, depopulation, and the recession of cultivation.[24] We should be careful not to do this. Many of the abuses denounced in the late Roman period were common to the ancient world in general: they can not be treated as symptoms of unprecedented crisis. There is much evidence (textual and now archaeological) to show that many complaints were grossly exaggerated: for instance, the claims made in many texts that high taxation led to drastic depopulation and to a recession of cultivation cannot be substantiated.[25] As with the former view of the later empire that saw it as a brutally polarized society (mentioned in the last chapter), scholarship has changed in recent years. There is little room for so melodramatic an image of the period.

Furthermore, by taking the dramatic litany of grievances contained in late Roman petitions too literally, we have tended to overlook a remarkable aspect of the functioning of late Roman society. We know so much about the abuses of this period precisely because the late Roman state had created mechanisms for their expression. The emperors themselves, by inviting denunciations and petitions from their subjects, had created around themselves a quite unusual "culture of criticism."[26] This is not to say that the "culture of criticism" automatically led to reform, still less to any form of popular participation in government. Rather, the expression of grievances was encouraged as a device of imperial surveillance. It was only by eliciting appeals from every side, and often from competing groups, that a distant and majestic emperor could keep in touch with what was happening along the edges of his immense and cumbersome governmental machine. It was part of a policy of "divide and rule." Different sections of the government were encouraged to denounce the abuses of the others, while, at the very top of society, the emperor and his court struggled to remain the focus of attention for their distant subjects by offering the hope of an ultimate redress of grievances.[27] The "advocacy revolution" of which the bishops took advantage was brought about by the peculiar tensions created by the presence of an extended and highly centralized administration, in which top and bottom struggled to maintain communication with each other.

It has usually been believed that the later Roman Empire saw a diminution of direct appeals to the emperor from members of the lower classes, such as had characterized the "classical" Roman empire.[28] But this impression is misleading. What we have, rather, is a greater penetration of late Roman society by the representatives of the emperor. It was these representatives, rather than the

emperor himself, who found themselves tenaciously besieged by
appeals from all classes. In 245, a group of villagers from the Eu-
phrates was content to wait for eight months in Antioch, so as to
obtain a final judgment from the Praetorian Prefect.[29] In the reign
of Justinian, in the 530s, the peasants who caused disruption by
streaming into Constantinople were by no means all of them land-
less immigrants. They were disturbing because they were registered taxpayers who had abandoned their villages for the time
being. They were not destitute. Rather, they were groups of farmers, often entire villages, who would come up to town to seek redress against their landlords. They were quite prepared to remain
there until they had worn down the patience of the central
courts.[30]

Not only did humble petitioners continue to address the courts.
The social and cultural range of those encouraged to act as bearers
of such appeals widened dramatically. Bishops, clergy, and holy
men joined with zest in the "advocacy revolution" associated
with the expansion of the late Roman state. They competed with
the lay elites as the spokesmen of their localities. They did so because they could claim to represent the lower classes of the cities.
But they were also positively encouraged to come to court as part
of the policy of "divide and rule" practiced by the emperors. As we
have seen, they tended to speak of those whose needs they represented, in generic terms, as "the poor." They used religious language, based on the prayers of the Psalms, that looked insistently
upward in the expectation of mercy from the great. The constant
upward pressure of appeals, linked to a new language of claims,
both betrayed and furthered the fragmentation of the traditional
upper classes. This fragmentation was the most fully documented
and significant development in the public life of the later Empire.

As I have dealt at length with this theme, in 1992, in my book
*Power and Persuasion in Late Antiquity: Towards a Christian
Empire*, I shall be brief here. The "classical" model of the relation
between city and empire had assumed that the leading classes of
every city were the sole "natural" protectors of their fellow citizens. Their monopoly of the patronage of their city and its region
acted as a control on the mechanisms of appeal to the emperor and
his representatives. In this way, the local elites had succeeded, in
the early centuries of the Roman empire, in shielding what was, at
that time, a remarkably under-bureaucratized central government

from the pressure of appeals. Furthermore, the outright dominance of local oligarchies in their cities, a dominance expressed
and reinforced by acts of public beneficence toward the *démos*,
saved the imperial government the considerable cost of policing
the cities.[31]

It was a system that had worked, ideally, on a "symbiotic"
model of power. The elites established what has been called "a
cozy" relationship with the imperial government.[32] In the Greek
East, in particular, the upper classes had always stressed the bonds
of a shared culture, created by a traditional education, a *paideia*
based upon study of the ancient classics. Great weight was placed
on the shared observance of codes of deportment associated with
the poise and humane good nature associated with the golden age
of classical Greece.[33] The emperor and his representatives were
treated as members of the same, intimate circle: they were approached as "fellow initiates" in *paideia*. It was assumed that, by
virtue of their shared *paideia*, the rulers of the Roman world
would be sensitive to the demands of their upper-class subjects.
For instance, they hoped that the emperors would be moved by a
shared sense of pity for their calamities. When the city of Smyrna
was flattened by an earthquake in 177 or 178, the cultivated emperor Marcus Aurelius was believed to have shed tears on the
pages of the appeal addressed to him by the rhetor Aelius Aristides. It showed that the emperor was a "lover of cities" like themselves.[34] They also hoped that Roman governors would be re-
strained by a shared sense of shame from breaches of the common
code of upper-class decorum—most notably, that Roman officials
would abstain from high-handedness and violence in their dealings with the well-to-do.[35]

It hardly needs to be emphasized that this "symbiotic" model of
power had always been somewhat tenuous. It had become seri-
ously eroded by the fourth and fifth centuries. Yet it is important to
remember that it was never entirely abandoned in the late antique
period. Government remained "the art of the possible." And, in
that "art of the possible," the classically educated local elites continued to play an important role. Imperial government always depended for its smooth running on the collaboration of the local
aristocracies. The emperor's bureaucracy continued to be recruited
from among them. But, at the same time, the "cozy" model, associated with the classical empire, gave way appreciably to the more

frankly "vertical" image of society that had been fostered in Christian circles. A citation from Saint Paul's *Letter to the Romans* has recently been discovered on a mosaic in the office of the imperial tax authorities at Caesarea Maritima: *If you would not fear the authority, do good.*[36] In the fifth century, for Christians and non-Christians alike, it was an altogether apposite citation. "Fear," felt by all for a distant emperor—and not the urbane collusion of an educated upper class with its rulers—was what brought in the taxes. The Christian "master image," which registered a dramatic tension between dependence and the hope of mercy, made greater sense to more people in a world where an autocratic imperial system had appreciably sharpened the vertical "tilt" of society. By the sixth century, a civic notable of Gaza, for all the culture of his city and his high local status, was expected to consider himself as humble as "any member of the poor"—*hena penéta*—on reaching the presence of the emperor at Constantinople.[37] It is against the background of this situation that we must set the emergence of the Christian master image of social relations, especially as it appeared in its sharpest form—that of the image of the relations of the rich man to the beggar. It was a master image that both assumed and strove to overcome perilously wide social distances.

The relationship with the poor had always been charged, in Jewish and Christian circles, with a sense of overwhelming asymmetry. It expressed a "vertical" relationship between God and the believer. Every believer was to God what the beggar was to the giver of alms—a being utterly dependent on the mercy of another. Seldom in the history of religion (and never before in the history of the Greco-Roman world) had the essence of the human relationship to the divine been concretized in such starkly social terms, and in social terms characterized by such stark asymmetry. The parallel between the state of the beggar before the rich and of the believer before God was a theme that John Chrysostom, the greatest Christian preacher of almsgiving to the poor, stressed insistently as he preached in Antioch and Constantinople between 386 and 404:

When you are weary of praying and do not receive an answer to your prayers to God, consider how often you have heard a poor man calling and have not listened to him.

It is not for reaching out your hands to God [in the Early Christian *orans* gesture, of prayer with outstretched arms] that you will be heard. Stretch forth your hands, not to God, but to the poor.[38]

It was an analogy of brutal simplicity. God was to the believer as the rich man was to the poor. For the poor looked up to the rich man as to a minor "god" on earth. This frank acknowledgment of social asymmetry was further confirmed, for medieval Byzantines, when, through contact with the Slavonic world, they learned that *bogat*, the Bulgarian word for wealthy, came from the same root as *Bog*, the word for God.[39]

"Care of the poor," therefore, concretized the central tenet of an austerely transcendent monotheism—the dependence of all creatures on the generosity of an all-powerful giver. Expressed most frequently and most urgently in the language of the Psalms, the Christian church fostered a religious language that seeped into every level of its activity. Citations of the Psalms appear, carved on inscriptions or set in mosaic, in churches from all over the Empire: "Bow down Thy ear, O Lord, for I am poor and needy" (Psalm 86:1 AV) appears on a mosaic from Gerasa (Jerash in Jordan);[40] "He raises up the poor from the dust and lifts the needy from the dungheap" (Psalm 113:7) appears on a carved inscription from Bregovina in southern Serbia.[41] Faced by such citations of the Psalms, which express the upward cry of believers to God, it is often impossible to tell whether they were originally placed there to celebrate some downward gesture of almsgiving to the real poor by a pious Christian connected with the church where the mosaic was placed.[42] It is often more likely, given the religious tone of the age, that the "poor" in question included all human beings, as they stood before God. For instance, it was by imploring God to listen to the "prayers of the poor"—that is, in effect, of the entire population of the land—that the Monophysite liturgy of Egypt prayed for the annual rising of the Nile.[43]

Given this religious climate, Christian petitioners found no difficulty in applying the language of the Psalms and of other parts of the Hebrew Scriptures to entirely practical situations. The language of prayer gave moral weight and poignancy to their petitions. By the sixth century, it is as a *philoptôchos*, a "lover of the poor," that a magistrate or a great landowner might be approached, not for alms but for justice and favors. A letter of request written in both Latin and Greek (perhaps as an exercise in writing such appeals) reminded the recipient (in Latin) that "good and bad, senators, emperors and the poor" were all equal: "the envy of death has made all one" (Wisdom 2:23–24). The person addressed is then advised (in Greek) in the form of a catena of Biblical quotations: "Let not thy mind of its own will turn aside, neither neglect the supplication of the poor, of those that cry out in distress."[44] Relations on a great estate might be tinged by similar language. Piioutios, a defaulting tenant returning to his landlord after a three-year absence, asked for the return of the farm he had leased. Piioutios was no pauper. But he went out of his way to speak of himself as the "slave" of his "benefactor and lord."

Your all-glorious lordship's love of the poor and of Christ, going out all over the land, has caused many of its people to have recourse to your lordship, as they come forward and receive justice and pity.[45]

Thus, a language of petition evolved, between the fourth and the sixth century, that sought protection and relief in terms of the Biblical claims of the poor on the rich. Yet, despite the undoubted rhetorical weight of this language, we should not think of it as engulfing late Roman society as a whole. In many areas of society and for many purposes, the profane processes of justice and taxation remained sternly untouched by Christian *pathos*. Centuries-old formulae continued to be used in Egypt and elsewhere. Like stiff sheets of ancient canvass, they bent very little to the new, more plangent mode of Christian petition-writing. At the end of the sixth century, we see in the papyri of Dioscoros of Aphrodito a full range of appeals. Some officials are, indeed, appealed to now as "lovers of the poor." But others are not. One governor is approached by an appeal to his "inborn and habitual sense of justice, that runs in the blood of Your Magnificence . . . as befits a descendent of Olympian Zeus."[46] Olympian Zeus as the guardian of justice was a concept taken from Hesiod and frequently repeated in the praise of governors in the later Empire.[47] It is not a sentiment that we might expect to hear in the age of the most Christian emperor Justin II. The phrase shows the tenacity of other, confidently non-Christian ways of viewing the working of society in late antiquity.

Nor were such governors encouraged to look as if they were particularly loving to the poor. The statues set up for officials in the cities of Asia Minor in the fourth, fifth, and sixth centuries show men with stern faces and piercing, hard eyes. They were not men given to sentiment. Rather, they had been sent from Constantinople to maintain law and order. To the notables who erected such statues, a governor was to be "a vigilant hero who cuts down the rude strength of the lawless."[48] It was only when such persons became bishops that they were expected to show great "love of the poor." Gregory of Langres, the ancestor of Gregory of Tours, had spent forty years as count of Autun. In that capacity, "[h]e was so rigorous and severe in his pursuit of criminals that scarcely one guilty person was able to escape." Only later did he become a bishop; and, after his death, he achieved a reputation for having opened, by a miracle, the doors of the state prison.[49]

Indeed, if anything, the reputation for being a true "lover of the poor" was projected away from the harsh realities of governmental control on the local level to the distant figure of the emperor. As is often the case in highly centralized and extended autocracies (one thinks of Tsarist Russia), the emperor was viewed as the person most likely to yield to Christian appeals. Such a belief preserved the hope in Christian circles that, despite the abrasive methods of the emperor's representatives, a mysterious reservoir of mercy existed, at the distant center, which might soften the workings of a hard-driving imperial system.

Hence it is important to identify clearly the precise areas of late Roman society where the Christian master image of the relation between rich and poor was developed, and the purposes for which it was deployed. It was the favored language of a specific group, of bishops and holy men called upon to act as protectors of the weak. It provided such persons with privileged access to the great. But we must remember that, for all the success of the Christian church in establishing itself at certain levels of late Roman society, its representatives still had to fight an uphill battle to maintain their own position as spokesmen of "the poor" in a world where powerful groups (local notables and imperial servants) were little affected by such language.

If we turn, once again, to late Roman Egypt we can trace the manner in which a specifically Christian language of petitions crystalized, vividly, around local Christian leaders.[50] In the middle of the fourth century, the priest Miôs wrote to Flavius Abinnaeus, the military commander at the post of Dionysias (Qasr Qarun) in the Thebaid. He asked him to release from military service his brother-in-law, the only son of a widow:

But if he must serve, please safeguard him from going abroad with the draft of the field army . . . [for one who gives] *a drink of water to one of these little ones shall not lose his reward.* (Mark 9:41–42) . . . May God [give] a return to you for your charity.[51]

Similar requests were made to a well-known holy man, the visionary John of Lycopolis. John's gift of prophecy had led him to be consulted by the emperor Theodosius I himself. He had foretold Theodosius' victory in a civil war. But John could also be approached by less exalted persons, for more humble needs. A papyrus shows him receiving a request from Psois, who claimed exemption from the draft on the grounds of an injured finger. John had already helped Psois to pass on a bribe to the appropriate official. The papyrus is in a flustered Greek; but John also received requests written in Coptic. As a holy man who shared the language of the local population, John acted as a channel through whom the requests of native Egyptians could be passed on to the imperial authorities.[52]

By the middle of the fifth century, the scattered writings of Shenoute of Atripe enable us to see a Christian discourse of the poor developing in a highly competitive situation. Shenoute found himself confronted by an old-world civic benefactor, Gesios, a leading notable of Panopolis (Akhmim). Gesios was a pagan. He celebrated public banquets in honor of the gods according to a long Egyptian and Greek tradition. The great White Monastery of Shenoute stood right across the river Nile from Panopolis, at Sohag. What was at stake in the clash between Shenoute and Gesios was nothing less than the religious leadership of the region. And with this leadership went the economic solvency of the White Monastery. For surplus wealth extracted from the peasantry by Gesios, through rents and levies for feasts, might flow in the form of free-will offerings to support the monks of Shenoute if Gesios were defeated. Faced by such an opponent, Shenoute "assumed a discourse of economic inequity."[53] He regularly denounced Gesios and similar pagan notables as oppressors of the poor.

It was as a protector of the poor that Shenoute was able both to denounce and to mingle with the great. His biographer, Besa, made much of Shenoute's eventual visit to the imperial court. He went to Constantinople, Besa insisted, only as a defender of the poor: "He went to the royal court, to the pious kings, because of the oppression which local governors were inflicting upon the poor."[54] There were, in fact, many reasons why bishops and monks might make the journey to the court. In 342, the bishops at the council of Serdica had complained that African bishops went often to visit the emperors, so as to canvass for official appointments for their lay friends. Henceforth, the council ruled, bishops should go to court only if they were bringing appeals on behalf of widows, orphans and the distressed.[55]

Thus the interventions of bishops and monks were authorized and at the same time discreetly delimited, by the insistence that they should act as spokesmen of the poor. For a monk such as Shenoute, it was *de rigueur* to appear in Constantinople looking as poor as any beggar. Apa Victor, representative of the great Pachomian monastery of Pbow, huddled with the poor at the gate of palace, as the proud patriarch Nestorius was ushered with pomp into the imperial presence.[56] When Saint Sabas, head of the Great Laura in the Judaean desert, came to the court of the emperor Anastasius in 511,

the *silentiarii* [the ushers to the throne room] at the doors, while admitting all the rest, repelled this great luminary . . . they did not admit him since he looked like a beggar and viler than all, when they saw him wearing dirty and much-patched rags.[57]

The stolid poverty of such men identified them at once with the plight of those on whose behalf they claimed to speak.

For what was truly distinctive about the Biblical language of petition was the manner in which the most urgent claim of all upon the great was presented as if it came from the very edge of society. We should not underestimate the rhetorical power of a view which insisted that the highest God was most present at the lowest reach of the human community. From the imaginative point of view, this is not altogether surprising. The poor already lived in a silent, other world, closer to the forgotten dead than to the living. They were barely visible creatures, whose very existence was forgotten by the rich. In that sense, they mirrored only too faithfully the insistent silence of God. Discussing the traditional doctrine of the poverty of Christ, the modern Protestant theologian Karl Barth catches with great sensitivity, in the summary of his own views, a late antique sense of the forgotten poor as symbols of the exclusion of God. As a "poor" man, writes Barth, Christ "shares as such the strange destiny which falls on God in His people and the world—to be the One who is ignored and forgotten and despised and discounted by men."[58]

By the same token, to turn to the poor, and to be mindful of them, was to turn directly to God Himself. In the words of the Jewish *Midrash:*

Rabbi Abin observed: the poor man stands at your door, and the Holy One, blessed be He, stands beside him, on his right hand; as it is written *Because He standeth at the right of the needy.* (Psalm 109:31)[59]

To give alms to the poor was to find oneself, instantly, standing in the Presence of God.[60] By bringing God Himself into human society in the form of a human being, Jesus of Nazareth, the Christian doctrine of the Incarnation added yet greater density and dramatic power to that notion.

Here we must be particularly careful to avoid the sentimental accretions of more recent forms of Christianity, in order to catch the precise, sharp flavor of late Roman Christian attitudes to the person of Jesus of Nazareth as a member of the poor. Jesus was observed to be a humble man of the lower classes, as were His disciples. To pagan critics of Christianity, this obvious fact was enough to explain His career in the most unflattering manner. The illegitimate child of a disowned mother, and so driven to desperate expedients, Jesus had naturally (like many of his equally enterprising lower class contemporaries) turned to religion to make a living. He had acquired in Egypt the knowledge of sorcery, which had enabled him to perform miracles and to gather followers.[61] There was nothing at all strange in this. Such behavior was only to be expected of a *vilis persona,* "a person of low quality" on the make.

Suspicions of this kind accompanied the person of Christ and of his apostles throughout these centuries. According to the emperor Julian the Apostate, Jesus and his apostles had recruited "the lowest elements" around him, "content if they could delude maidservants and slaves."[62] We should note that Christians did not answer such criticisms by romanticizing the image of the poor. Rather, the theme of the poverty of Christ (and of his disciples, the Apostles) was put forward so as to rebut the claims of the rich, of the powerful, and of the educated to enjoy a special relationship with God. They insisted that Christ's lowly social status had been deliberately chosen by Him, so that no human being should have any doubt as to the direct source of His power. It was an utterly supernatural authority. It owed nothing whatsoever to human structures of power, prestige, or culture. To be born among those who had no such advantages, and to choose his first disciples from among such persons, ensured that the success of His message would be recognized to be utterly miraculous, as patently coming from God alone. Rather than be born in Great Rome, as the son of an emperor or of some great legislator, Christ had been born

in an inconspicuous country, in an unimportant village, to a poor virgin, so that He should draw all humanity to him noiselessly and without display . . . All his deeds were poor and insignificant, humble and unnoticed by many, so that His Godhead alone should be recognized in them.[63]

Not only did the authority of Christ and his Apostles require the support of no human power. Their poverty showed that His grace was not bestowed upon any human being on the strength of pre-existing human status or of pre-existing human accomplishments. As Augustine put it, with characteristic trenchancy, in a newly discovered sermon addressed to a partly pagan audience in a small African town:

we have to remind ourselves that our Lord Jesus Christ came not only for the salvation of the poor but also of the rich, not only of commoners but also of kings. He refused all the same to choose kings as disciples, refused rich people, refused the nobly born, refused the learned; but instead he chose poor, uneducated fishermen, in whom his grace would shine through all the more clearly . . . And if he had first called a king, the king would have said it was his rank that was chosen; if he had first called a learned man, he would have said it was his learning that was chosen. Those who were being called to lowliness and humility would have to be called by lowly and humble persons.[64]

Altogether, the observed poverty of the historical Jesus was a minor theme in Christian belief at this time. What fascinated contemporaries, rather, was the high-pitched image of the universe—and of society—implied in the paradox of the Incarnation. By becoming a human being, Christ, the emperor of heaven, had joined himself to the destitute "poverty" of human flesh. The Incarnation was an act of *sunkatabasis*, an awesome act of condescension, by which God Himself had stooped to earth, to make Himself directly available, as a human being, to the "cry of the poor."[65] The words of Gregory of Nyssa were frequently cited in subsequent centuries:

What could be a greater show of self-abasement on the part of God, the emperor of all, than to come, of His own free will, into a sharing of our destitute nature. The pure and undefiled takes on the stain of being human, and, passing through every stage of the deep poverty of human life, comes so far as to have experience of death. Look and see the measure of His voluntary poverty—that Life should taste death.[66]

The contrast was not between a lower-class Jesus and the upper classes of this world. It was the contrast between two worlds that mattered for Gregory of Nyssa: the majesty of God and the destitution of the human condition had been joined in the person of Christ. In the words of Saint Paul in his Second Letter to the Corinthians (8:9):

though He was rich, yet for your sake He became poor [the verb is formed from *ptôchos*, a beggar: "He beggared Himself"] that through his poverty [*ptôcheia*] you may become rich.

Exegesis of this passage inevitably tilted the notion of the poverty of Christ toward the most "pauperized" image of the poor. Having enjoyed the high state of being God, Christ, by the mere fact of becoming human, had fallen into utter destitution: He was the *ptôchos*, the *pauper par excellence*.[67]

Yet, at the same time, Christ had retained the hidden fullness of his divinity. For late Roman Christians, if Christ was a beggar, he was a beggar of a very special kind. As God "hidden" in human flesh, his figure was charged with the disquieting aura of archaic folk-tale. He was a king wandering the world in beggar's rags, an Odysseus returned, unknown, to Ithaca.[68] It was a belief that, we may suspect, drew considerable weight from ancient sediments of beggars' lore. The Greco-Roman world had long been accustomed to beggars who wielded the curse of exotic and threatening gods. In the first chapter, we saw how one such *agurtés*, one such beggar for a god, had raised enough money to set up a statue to Syrian Atargatis.[69] Even the cries of the humble beggars outside the church in Antioch were charged with numinous associations. The beggars besought passing Christian women, invoking all that was most precious and most vulnerable in their lives—their beautiful, clear eyes, ever in danger of glaucoma, the health of their infant children, the safety of husbands traveling in distant lands.[70] If it was wise to listen to the abjurations of such beggars, then the claims of a beggar who might turn out to be God incarnate in disguise must certainly be met.

In this way, the aura of the incarnate Christ passed to the poor.

Late Roman Christians lingered on the great scene of the Last Judgment in Matthew 25:

When the Son of man comes in his glory, and all the angels with him, then he will sit on his glorious throne . . . Then the king will say to those at his right hand, "Come, o blessed of my Father, inherit the kingdom . . . for I was hungry and you gave me food, I was thirsty and you gave me drink, I was a stranger and you welcomed me, I was naked and you clothed me, I was sick and you visited me, I was in prison and you came to me . . . Truly I say to you, as you did it to the least of these my brethren, you did it to me." (Matthew 25:31, 34–36, and 40)

Gifts to the poor were gifts to Christ. They would gain, for the believer, entry into heaven.

For a late Roman preacher, such as John Chrysostom, this passage amounted to a statement of "continued redemption" offered by Christ, first, as the historical Jesus, on the Cross, and now, in the present, through the poor.[71] To approach the poor with mercy was to receive mercy from Christ, who lingered among them. John repeatedly urged this theme on his hearers:

For He was not satisfied even with death and the Cross only, but He embraced being poor also, and [nowadays] being a stranger, a beggar, and naked, and being thrown into prison, and undergoing illness, so that He might, by that means, call you back . . . saying: "If you are not mindful of me for having hung on the Cross for you, at least show mercy on Me for My poverty [in the present poor]. And if My poverty does not move you [in the poor], at least be moved by My sickness, be softened while I am in prison . . . I was athirst when hanging on the Cross, I am athirst [today] also in the poor, that both by what I have been and by what I am now, I may draw you to Myself, and make you charitable, so that you may save yourself."[72]

We should note that the language of the continuous, mysterious indwelling of Christ in human beings was more than a language of compassion, directed downward, as it were "vertically, only toward the poor, as an extreme pole of the human condition. It was a language that was also applied "horizontally," as it were, by John and by contemporary preachers to act as a language of group solidarity. In John's sermons, its objects were most usually the *ptôchoi,* the beggars. But the indwelling of Christ could also serve to emphasize the solidarity of the Christian community as a whole. All baptized Christians, irrespective of their wealth and poverty, were "members of Christ." They all bore the "image of

Christ" in themselves.[73] Ideally, they were all bound together in a tight, organic unity through shared participation in the flesh and blood of Christ, distributed at the Eucharist.

It is significant that Chrysostom's sermons on the poor took place under the shadow of the Eucharist. His most impassioned passages came at the end of each sermon, immediately preceding the "Kiss of Peace"—in which the faithful were expected to forgive each other their enmities (by such a kiss) before sharing in the consecrated bread and wine.[74] Through the Eucharist, Christ gave his unique flesh and blood to every Christian. Chrysostom and many Eastern fathers believed that a shared divinity, quite literally, ran in the veins of all who shared in the orthodox Eucharist.

As the majority of the population came to be baptized Christians, shared participation in the Eucharist was appealed to so as to erect an ultimate, mystical barrier, to protect the body of each believer against violence and neglect. Bishop Rabbula of Edessa, from 412 to 437, preached with horror against the wild-beast shows that continued to be maintained throughout the major cities of the Eastern empire. Such shows provided a sense of *apolausis*, of "civic" good cheer. They were given by governors and by the leaders of the cities to their fellow citizens. But for Rabbula, the flesh of Christian *venatores*—the late Roman equivalents of *matadors*, pitted with long pikes against the onslaught of lions and savage bears—was nothing less than flesh joined to God in the Eucharist. It appalled him to think that such flesh would be mauled by beasts.[75] The following monastic anecdote circulated at the same time:

An important person took great pleasure in watching wild beast shows, and hoped for one thing only, to see the fighters wounded by the animals. One day he fell into danger and cried to God: "Lord, come to my help in this misfortune!" The Lord came to him, His body covered with wounds, and said: "This is how you wished to see Me; how then have I the strength to save you?"[76]

It was in these ways that the leaders of the Christian church had come, by the middle of the fifth century, to create a new language of solidarity. It was a language appropriate to a relatively new social and political situation within the Eastern Roman empire. We should not underestimate the extraordinary degree of homogeneity achieved, in the fifth and sixth centuries, by the centralized structures of the Eastern Roman empire. All roads now led to Constantinople, as New Rome, in a manner that they had never led to Rome at an earlier period. Coinciding with this development, the penetration of late Roman society by the religious language of Christianity, especially by the language of the Psalms, tinged the relationship between rulers and subjects, just as it had tinged the relations between the rich and the poor, with a sense of the need to bridge great distances, distances that somehow echoed the gulf that existed between God and man. From the emperor, now wrapped in majesty and believed to reign by "the grace of God" alone, downward, the spread of monotheism in late Roman society had the effect of bringing a sharper, more melodramatic note to the problems associated with the symbolic expression of cohesion in a Christian society.

But this high-pitched monotheism had also helped to create an ambitious language of solidarity. This was based on the paradox that a high God, precisely because he was all-powerful, must be both immeasurably distant and, at the same time, ever-present. An acute sense of distance was balanced by a sense of the closeness of God. With the rise of Christianity, this paradox came to be expressed in its most extreme form through continued debate on the doctrine of the Incarnation. Here, in the person of Christ, was a human being in whom the very top of the universe, "the emperor," was linked to the very bottom, to the "beggar" of human flesh. The joining of human and divine in Christ was a charged statement of the ultimate cohesion of the universe, secured by a mighty act of *sunkatabasis,* of "condescension" on the part of God. It could also act as a symbol of the ideal cohesion of society. Widely separated segments of society—emperor and subjects, rich and poor—were bound together by mysterious ties of common flesh and common belief. Those at the top should learn to respect these ties and "condescend" to listen to those at the bottom.

It is perhaps more than a coincidence that the same generations in which an imperial court became permanently resident at Constantinople, under the son and grandson of Theodosius I, Arcadius, from 395 to 408, and Theodosius II, from 408 to 450, witnessed the detonation of the Christological controversies associated with the Council of Ephesus (in 431) and the Council of Chalcedon (in 451). These controversies focused obsessively on the extent and the nature of the joining of God and humanity in the person of Jesus of Nazareth.[77] For, in Constantinople, the emperors, now the undisputed focus of the entire Eastern empire, had to deal with a problem that had beset the monarchical system of the Roman empire from its beginnings (as, indeed, it had previously beset the Hellenistic kingdoms of the Greek East). The emperors had always had to elaborate ways of combining a sense of remoteness from their subjects with a human touch, with a sense of closeness to the hopes and fears of the average person. They had adopted alternating styles of majesty and accessibility. Christian ritual and Christian piety now provided new symbolic forms with which to express the uncanny combination of the godlike and the human in the person of the emperor. What was debated at the court at this time was a problem analogous to that debated by the theologians in the Christological controversies—the relation between the godlike, official *persona* of an emperor and his human nature.

The ceremonial exaltation of the emperor was central to the running of the late Roman state. The army took its oaths on the majesty of the emperor: for the emperor "second only to God is to be loved and worshipped by the human race."[78] Bishop Ambrose of Milan was not a man easily unnerved by emperors. Yet even he observed that, when the emperor appeared in procession from his palace in Milan, the "blaze of the purple" led onlookers to see "something godlike" in his face.[79] In the court of Theodosius I, the "adoration of the purple" became the central ceremony of contact between the emperor and his servants: fortunate officials were called forward to kneel and kiss the hem of the emperor's robe.[80] In the carvings around the base of the obelisk set up by Theodosius I in the Hippodrome of Constantinople, the emperor is shown hovering serenely, on a different plane from other humans, above his courtiers and the people of the city.[81]

Yet, at the same time, Theodosius I, like his predecessors from the time of Augustus, had been careful to maintain the human touch. Christian institutions helped him to do this. His wife, Flacilla, visited the poor houses and hospitals of Constantinople without retinue and without imperial robes. The insistent physicality of her care of the poor asserted that the imperial couple did not feel themselves above the common lot of humanity: "she brought the pot, fed them soup, gave them their medicine, broke them bread and served them morsels . . . performing with her own hands all the tasks usually given to servants."[82] In interceding on behalf of condemned persons, Flacilla was said to have reminded Theodosius that he, also, was mortal. The emperor's "godlike" right to grant life, through amnesty and the commutation of capital punishments, was held to be based on a carefully nurtured capacity on the part of Theodosius to recognize the fact that—despite appearances to the contrary—the ruler of the Roman world was also human.[83] The *"exalted tapeinophrosyne,"* the exalted self-abasement of Flacilla, "humanized the monarchy."[84]

It was Theodosius I's grandson, Theodosius II, who made the fullest use of Christian ceremonials and of Christian sentiment so as to practice an art of imperial deportment that emphasized the constant pendulum swing between the "godlike" and the "human" in the person of an emperor. Theodosius II had been brought up in the purple. He knew what to do on state occasions, "how to gather up his robes, how to take his seat, and how to walk . . . how to restrain all laughter; how to assume a mild or formidable aspect as the occasion might acquire."[85] But he also knew how to join in with the people of Constantinople, as a fellow Christian and a fellow human being. Unlike the restless military emperors of the fourth century, Theodosius II had grown up in Constantinople and seldom moved from it. It was "his" city in a way that it never was for Constantine. A shared Christian piety made him accessible to "his" people. At the news of a victory, he led the entire crowd in the Hippodrome (assembled, according to tradition, to receive the official declaration of triumph in the presence of the emperor, in the imperial box that led from the palace) into the Great Church. In this way, Theodosius II came to incorporate the great basilica (the future Hagia Sophia of Justinian) that stood only a few hundred yards from the Hippodrome and the imperial palace into the pendulum swing of Christian and profane, personal and official.[86] On another occasion, as a winter blizzard swept down on the city from the Black Sea, "the emperor himself in unofficial dress went into the midst of the multitude," gathered in prayer on the field of the Hippodrome, and joined with them in singing hymns.[87] When Theodosius II attended the Eucharist at the Great Church on the high festivals of the year, he did so without his armed bodyguard and without his imperial diadem. For a "godlike" emperor, this was a novel and stunning gesture of humility.

For we, whom always rightly the weapons of military authority surround, and [for] whom it is not proper to be without bodyguards, when entering God's temple, abandon our weapons outside, taking off our diadem, and by the appearance of the lessening of our majesty, there is reaped by us all the more awe for the majesty of empire.[88]

Monks who visited Constantinople from the provinces reported that the emperor wore a hair-shirt beneath his purple robe: beneath the unearthly shimmer of the imperial regalia, Theodosius II bore normal, human flesh, as much in need of penitential discipline as that of any monk.[89]

It was such an emperor who, in 428, selected Nestorius, an Antiochene priest with a reputation as a brilliant preacher, to be patriarch of Constantinople. Nestorius was a product of what has been called the "Antiochene School." It was axiomatic to him that God, in his very nature, was utterly transcendent. He was eternally removed from human suffering. God might come close to human beings; but their natures remained utterly separate from each other. Yet this God was not entirely remote. What amazed Nestorius was that the *will* of God should, in a manner so profound as to resist logical analysis, choose to abase itself so as to join itself entirely with the will of a chosen human being. The will of God had joined the will of Jesus so completely that the human will of that unique person, the Christ, did not achieve only a rough approximation to the will of God—as was the case for even the most holy of human beings. Rather, the will of Jesus Christ became a perfect "mirror image" of God's will. No greater closeness between God and humanity was possible. It was enough, for Nestorius, to stand in awe at the downward reach of God, in engulfing in his grace a human being who was enabled by that grace to achieve what all human wills had striven to achieve—total harmony with the will of God.[90]

Nestorius came to Constantinople very much as the emperor's man. He forwarded Theodosius II's own agendas. He urged the emperor to cleanse the empire of heresy. He imposed new controls on the monks of Constantinople. He preached against the more lewd aspects of the games in the Hippodrome, thereby attempting to make the Hippodrome, the joining point between the emperor and "his" people, more worthy of a pious monarch. Above all, he exalted the position of Theodosius II as emperor. Only Theodosius was allowed by him to enter the consecrated space around the altar, when gifts were brought at the time of the Eucharist. His elder sister, Pulcheria, was excluded. She had been in the habit of entering the sanctuary with her brother. A splendid altar-cover, dedicated by the princess, marked her out as a benefactor of the church on a par with Theodosius. Nestorius would have none of this. The emperor must stand alone, unique among the laity of the East Roman world, in the sacred space allotted to the clergy.[91]

Through his alliance with the emperor, Nestorius entered a world where the ceremonial life of the imperial court gave regular imaginative support to his central notions of the nature of the relations between God and humanity. In the rituals of the court, the essential separateness between the emperor and his subjects was emphasized so that it could be bridged by acts of studious good will. The emperor, for instance, was expected to fraternize with his soldiers. He would appear without his great purple robe, dressed only in a military uniform tied by the heavy, jewelled belt of a senior officer. But, Nestorius pointed out, during this encounter the emperor remained throughout the emperor. He did not "become" a soldier. In the same manner, God never lost his essential separateness from humanity, even when, with supreme good will, he condescended to unite his will with that of the man Jesus.[92]

A sense of unbridgeable separateness between God and man, similar to that between an emperor and his subjects, hovered over the thought of Nestorius. It influenced his choice of images and affected the manner in which his thought was perceived by others. Nestorius hesitated to admit the pious formula, by which the Virgin Mary was spoken of as *Theotokos*, as "she who bore and gave birth to God." This reluctance on his part made it seem as if Nestorius thought of Christ as owing His "godlike" dignity simply to an "external," "official honor" bestowed on Him by the "grace and favor" of God.[93] His enemies made cruel use of his cautious language. It was only too easy to imply that Nestorius thought that Jesus had begun His life as an ordinary human being, who had been "promoted" to equality with God, much as the son of an emperor could be declared an *Augustus* by his father. Such a promotion had happened at the age of nine months to Theodosius II, immediately after his baptism. On that occasion, courtly bishops had likened the event to the baptism of Christ in the river Jordan. Arcadius' elevation of his son, Theodosius, was likened to the declaration of God made above the head of Jesus: "This is my Beloved

Son in whom I am well pleased" (Matthew 3:17).[94] In such an atmosphere, it was easy for caricatures to develop, which made it
seem as if Nestorius treated the closeness of God to Christ as no
more than a "promotion" analogous to those effected according to
court protocol in the imperial palace.

One does not know whether, had he remained at Antioch, Nestorius would have developed his Christology with the same brit-
tle clarity, by the choice of images taken from the corridors of
power. Extreme views were foisted upon him by his enemies.
Nestorius' own intellectual fussiness and ironic manner exposed
him to caricature. But the fact remains that it was in this manner
that his preaching was remembered by those who heard him and
who circulated his opinions. They were particularly alert to such
issues because they lived in an atmosphere dominated by the
presence of an imperial court, in which the emperor Theodosius II
himself had come to express in Christian form the ancient tension between "godlike" majesty and humanity in the person of
the emperor.[95]

If Nestorius made one, crucial mistake, it was the mistake of
any religious system that appeared to replicate a little too faithfully the styles of social and political relationships current in the
world around it. What the patriarch's views gained in terms of in-
stant intelligibility, by appeal to well-known court ceremonials,
they lost by overlooking the dark heart of the matter. They overlooked what was yearned for in an emperor, and in an entire society. A sense of the essential separateness of the emperor, relaxed
by carefully chosen moments of accessibility, was the daily norm
in Constantinople. But the emperor's subjects wanted more. They
wanted something more imponderable. They wanted a sense of
closeness to the emperor and to the powerful that was based on a
mystique of cohesion and on a sense of solidarity. Such solidarity
did not arise (as Nestorius hinted in his preaching on the relation
between God and the human person of Jesus of Nazareth) through
anything as crisp as the clear joining of two intrinsically separate
wills. It grew, rather, from a more murky but tenacious sense of
kinship, grounded on shared human flesh and on an ability to treat
the sufferings of others as if they were one's own. If the emperor
was truly as distant from the sufferings of his subjects as the God
of Nestorius seemed distant from the suffering humanity of
Christ, then the mounting *pathos* of Christian appeals to the em-

peror and to the great might have an empty ring. The chill truth
might be that the "godlike" emperor Theodosius and those around
him did not, after all, share in the hopes and fears of those they
ruled.

Only two weeks away by ship from Constantinople, across the
eastern Mediterranean, Cyril, patriarch of Alexandria, was pleas-
antly disappointed by what he heard of the preaching of Nestorius.
He would break the man (as his uncle Theophilus had broken John
Chrysostom in 404). And, in breaking Nestorius, he would break
the prestige that had come to accrue to the patriarchs of Constantinople, as a result of the presence of the imperial court.[96] Historians do not need to love Cyril. He has been described as "one of
the most unattractive figures of the annals of the Church."[97] He
knew what he wanted and how to get it done. Eventually, Cyril
ensured that his views would be upheld by paying out in bribes to
members of the imperial court one thousand and eighty pounds of
gold, 77,760 gold coins, the equivalent of the salaries of thirty-
eight minor bishops, of a year's food and clothing for nineteen
thousand poor persons—and twenty-five times as much as the
largest sums dispensed for the ransoming of captives by any Western bishop.[98]

Yet Cyril was not merely a bully. He was a master politician.
He chose his ground with an uncanny instinct for the mood of his
times. He was also a formidable and utterly sincere wielder of a
specific religious language that was deeply rooted in the theological traditions of the see of Alexandria and in the Christian piety of
his age.[99] He pursued the views of Nestorius with single-minded
ferocity and with genuine horror. He held them to be contrary to
the deepest wishes of a fallen humanity to regain its lost intimacy
with God. In his opinion, Nestorius had made God as remote
from humanity as was a "Persian monarch."[100] We should not
underestimate the deadly appositeness of such an accusation.
Many leading members of East Roman society were deeply concerned that the imperial autocracy might go the same way as the
court of the Persian King of Kings as Greeks had always imagined
it. Theodosius II might become a ruler totally withdrawn from his
subjects, secluded in the veiled depths of his palace. Before he became bishop of Ptolemais in Cyrene, Synesius had warned the father of Theodosius in no uncertain terms of the dangers of just
this development:

This majesty and this fear of being brought down to the level of men by becoming an accustomed sight causes you to be cloistered . . . doing very little, hearing of little . . . so that you live the life of a sea-anemone in the depths of the ocean.[101]

Synesius wrote for those around the court on behalf of his own region. Cyrene (eastern Libya) was a distant province, perched at the furthest southeastern tip of the East Roman empire. Its inhabitants needed to be reassured that, if they had grievances that brought them to Constantinople, they would not be confronted with the closed palace of a "Persian" ruler.

What Cyril proposed against Nestorius was a joining of God and man that rested on a quasi-physical, "natural" solidarity between God and human nature, achieved in the unique person of Jesus Christ.[102] It was a daring solution. The "condescension" of God to humanity was based on a joining deeper by far than the mere "juncture" proposed by Nestorius. It was a "natural" unity that was as strong as it was amazing and impenetrable to reason.

But, for Cyril, the very impenetrability and uniqueness of the bonding of God and humanity in the person of Christ guaranteed a level of solidarity between God and humankind that was no abstract doctrine. Just because it was veiled in mystery, Cyril's language spilled out into every level of the Christian imagination. It became a master image of solidarity, in the first place between God and humanity, but also, by refraction, between the emperor and his subjects, the rich and the poor, the weak and the powerful. Christians of all classes, who sought to "imitate" God in their actions, must now imitate a God who had committed Himself (through the incarnation) to intimate and enduring solidarity with every aspect of the wretchedness of the human condition. If the rich and the powerful were "like God" to the poor, then they must learn to be like a God who had opened himself up entirely to human suffering and who was "naturally" capable of compassion for fellow human beings. They must show the same degree of condescension and of fellow feeling for the poor.

For Cyril and for those who supported him, God and humanity were not joined by anything as basically external and as *de haut en bas* as the decision of a sovereign God to join His *will* with that of human beings. He wrote to Nestorius in no uncertain terms that God and humanity had been brought together as a single unity "from the very womb" of Mary.[103] God was held to humanity, as it

were, through the virgin Mary. He was bound by ties of kinship incurred through sharing with all other humans the human flesh of
a human mother. His insistence on this theme was the secret of
Cyril's success. A language of high-density solidarity, magnified
because veiled in mystery, was his *leitmotif*. It was with this
theme in the forefront of his message that he subjected the emperor Theodosius II, the imperial princesses, and the clergy and
people of Constantinople to a deluge of long letters and doctrinal
statements in what amounted to the theological equivalent of saturation bombing.

To modern persons, it is the Christology of the "School of Antioch" that appears to be the more attractive. The distancing of God
from the human sphere allowed theologians of that school to concentrate on the human person of Jesus of Nazareth. They presented a figure that has often been acclaimed as closer to the "historical" Jesus of modern times than was the awesome Jesus of
Cyril, a human being whose very flesh was saturated with the divine in a such a way that the mere touch of His hand was sufficient to heal the sick.[104] Yet the Jesus of Nestorius was by no
means the mild "historical Jesus" of modern sentiment. Supporters of Nestorius, such as Theodoret of Cyrrhus, saw Jesus, rather,
as a human being whose union to the will of God had led him to
transcend the body as no other human person had ever done. As a
result of His example, human beings were challenged to strain
their wills to the utmost, so as to ally them with the will of God.
By so doing they would rise far above the sluggish flesh. The Jesus
of Nestorius was an appropriate model for the awesome holy men
of Syria. A "fleshless" pillar-saint such as Symeon Stylites and
similar extreme ascetics admired by the Christians of the region
showed what even ordinary human wills could do in overcoming
the body, when following out the will of God.[105]

For early Byzantines, a "historical" Jesus was not at all the sort
of figure they most desired. They wanted to sense, in the bonds of
the flesh that linked Jesus to his mother, and so to themselves, a
guarantee of solidarity between man and God that went deeper
than mere will. Hence the crucial role, in the fifth and sixth centuries, of the rise of the cult of Mary as *Theotokos*, as "she who bore
and gave birth to God." In taking human flesh from Mary, God had
become not only human, but humane. The raw majesty of His divinity was, as it were, "mellowed" by drinking in the human milk

of Mary. Breast-feeding, we should remember, was a weighty matter for fifth-century persons. The baby was normally suckled for a long period—up to three years.[106] The milk that the child received was not thought of as mere milk. It was liquified flesh, identical with human blood (it was, indeed, blood turned white lest its gory color terrify the infant).[107] The mother's milk was the direct source of the physical identity (and, in a more mysterious manner, of the character) of the child. By suckling Jesus, Mary had made God human. She had instilled in him, through the process of taking in human milk, the capacity for fellow feeling for fellow bearers of human flesh that was regarded as the foundation of all human sentiments of compassion, of mercy and of fellowship. Even the most miserable human being had once been suckled at the breasts of a human mother. Every person could appeal to the powerful for mercy because, despite their vast social distance, they also had hung upon a mother's breast.[108]

In icons of the sixth century, Mary is not yet shown suckling the infant Jesus. But she is shown with the infant Jesus seated in majesty on her lap, in such a way as to appear still bound to her womb. He receives the touch of Mary's right hand on His knee.[109] This was a gentle reminder of His kinship with the human race. In the icon connected with the converted Pantheon of Rome in the early seventh century, the hand of Mary is gilded. For it was the touch of that right hand that linked Mary to Jesus, and, through Mary, it linked all human worshippers, through shared human flesh, to God. Such representations of Mary's physical closeness to Christ answered an enduring streak in Christian popular piety: in the wise words of Henry Chadwick, the "fundamental factor [in such piety] is . . . [the need] for a figure in complete solidarity with us."[110]

These controversies happened in an empire in which, as we have seen, the tension between distance and solidarity had generated an entire new language of claims upon the great. The issues were debated in Christian congregations long schooled by preaching such as that of John Chrysostom to value the mystical solidarity of the Christian community, and to see the figure of Christ lingering still among the poor. It is not surprising, therefore, that the Christological controversies broke over the Eastern empire like a thunderstorm. By and large, the views of Cyril carried the day. The intervention of the patriarch of Alexandria was able to ensure that, in future centuries, any apparent return in the direction of Nestorius raised the chill possibility of the unraveling, once again, of the bonds of solidarity between God and man.

It was sincere fear of that possibility that caused what later became known as the "Monophysite" dissidents to oppose the compromise creed proposed at the council of Chalcedon in 451. They did so out of loyalty to the views of Cyril. The judicious balancing of human and divine in the person of Christ set forward at the council of Chalcedon (in a formula commonly associated with the *Tome* of Pope Leo) became anathema to such persons. If humanity and God were, in any way, allotted separate and autonomous spheres, then the danger was that God might withdraw into His own sphere, and leave humanity to fend for itself.[111] For the Monophysites, only an uncompromising emphasis on the "single" nature of Christ, a being in which God and human were forever combined with unique intimacy, would avoid that chill possibility. Hence, eventually, a division of the churches of the East that has lasted up to our times.

Let me be clear on this issue. It is not my intention to propose a purely "social" explanation of the Christological controversies that racked the Eastern empire in the course of the fifth and sixth centuries. This has been attempted and has failed. The religious issue of the closeness of God to humanity was serious enough, in and of itself. The passions this issue aroused do not need to be explained, as if they were fueled by deeper forces, by social grievances or by nationalist aspirations[112] To privilege such factors, as if only they were "real" and as if the theological speculations of the fifth century were airy nothings, is to overlook the nature of late antique religion. The full weight of an entire religious culture, in which the issue of the joining of heaven and earth haunted pagans, Jews, and Christian alike, weighed in on the Christological statements of all parties. How God could be at once so distant and yet so present to humanity was a living theme. It joined pagan metaphysical speculation in the neo-Platonic schools with the preoccupations of Christian theologians.[113]

Yet, the historian can not but be impressed by the constant recurrence, in this debate, of images drawn directly from the political and social life of the Eastern empire. A particular vision of society and its discontents was part of the air that all parties breathed. It would be wrong to suggest that the division between

Monophysite and Chalcedonian can, in any way, be reduced to a "lining up" of divergent social visions. It was, rather, the opposite. Each side, in its different ways, appealed to much the same basic image of a good and of an "ugly" society. But each was convinced that the views of its opponents ran counter to that vision. The Christian inhabitants of the Eastern empire had developed a sharp sensibility as to what constituted an "ugly" society. It was one in which the "cry of the poor" was not heard, where bishops and monks were not listened to, where appeals to common bonds of shared flesh and of shared belief were not acknowledged, and where a gap as vast and empty as the sky separated the humble from the powerful. A theology that threatened to separate God from humanity in one way or the other was held to resonate with sinister appositeness the much-feared drifting apart of East Roman society. Monophysites saw this clearly in Nestorius and thought that they saw it in the followers of the council of Chalcedon. Chalcedonians reciprocated in kind. They claimed that the manner in which the Monophysites had merged the human and divine in the person of Christ presented the world with a Jesus whose flesh could not be thought of as the same as that of normal human beings—a "Manichaean," ethereal creature, who could not truly share the human feelings of his worshippers. For either side, it was the same model of solidarity that appeared to be placed at risk by the views of their opponents.

If we turn to late fifth-century Antioch, we can see most clearly the imaginative consequences of the notions of solidarity that had been mobilized in the course of half a century of Christological debates. At that time, Monophysite opinion had made a victorious incursion into Antioch, the former homeland of the views of Nestorius. The conflict-laden atmosphere of the city enables us to glimpse the images and the fears that rallied popular opinion in favor of the views of Cyril. Congregations watched carefully for hints as to what their bishops really thought about the extent of the gulf between God and themselves. In the 440s, Bishop Domnus of Antioch was seen, by horrified catechumens whom he was instructing for baptism, to have raised his right hand high above his head and to have pointed his left hand downward.[114] The extravagant gesture of separation showed what the bishop really believed about the solidarity of God and humanity in Christ: not much. For Domnus' widely separated hands implied that he

thought that the best humanity could hope for was a "mere joining" of two separate entities across a vast gulf. So distant a joining
would soon unravel.

It was important to bridge the gulf. Some time in the 470s,
Peter the Fuller, a hotly contested Monophysite patriarch of Antioch, deliberately added a phrase to the traditional litany of praise
which addressed Christ as God. To the phrase, "Holy God, Holy
and Mighty, Holy and Immortal One," he added "Who was crucified for us." To upholders of Chalcedonian orthodoxy, this addition betrayed a blasphemous confusion of thought. No one could
say that God Himself had died on the Cross. Yet, for the Anti-
ochenes, there were times when God needed to be reminded, in no
uncertain terms, that he had shared human suffering with those
who now turned to him in prayer in times of catastrophe—of
which the most dreaded, of course, were the earthquakes that occasionally shattered the towns of northern Syria. Crowds in the
great courtyard outside the principal church of Antioch were held
spellbound when a specially trained parrot, his wings outstretched
in the gesture of the Crucified, and undaunted by the Chalcedonian Establishment, squawked the anthem with its provocative
addition. Isaac of Antioch wrote an entire poem in Syriac on the
incident. Would that every Christian thought like that learned
and intrepid bird![115] The addition "Who was crucified for us" guaranteed that the Monophysite God was a God intimately connected to the afflicted world. As Isaac wrote, in a further poem on
the incarnation: "Look on the cause of His mercy, the body that
He borrows from us . . . Learn the reason for His graciousness, His
own human hunger and thirst."[116]

It was such a Christ that still lingered in the poor. When the
great Monophysite theologian Severus preached as patriarch of
Antioch, between 512 and 518, he preached very much as the heir
of John Chrysostom. John had spoken eloquently on the care of the
poor when he was a priest at Antioch. His insistence on the intimate blending of the divine and human in Christ and, by extension,
in the figure of Christ among the poor, came close in sheer intensity to later, Monophysite views.[117] A century and a quarter later, in
the days of Severus, little had changed at Antioch. The poor remained ever present. They clustered around the bishop, following
his movements every day.[118] Poor strangers were buried by the
Church in communal graves, known as *Pandektai*, as "Grab-Alls."

Their anonymous deaths were celebrated in a collective memorial service once a year. Severus pointed out that the well-to-do lavished money on the care of the souls of their own deceased kin; but they never bothered to turn up to remember the souls of the anonymous poor.[119] Women in their full finery still brushed past the beggars on their way into the church: "and you do not even turn your face towards them."[120] The poor of sixth-century Antioch remained as they had been in the days of John Chrysostom and, indeed, as they had been since the days of ancient Sumeria. They were still "the silent ones of the land."[121]

But this was not how Severus saw them. Severus' language took on an even heavier tone than that of Chrysostom when he preached on the continued presence of Christ among the poor. For Severus, the Monophysite, the Incarnation had bound God irrevocably to humanity. In the well-chosen words of Roberta Chesnut's study of *Three Monophysite Christologies,*

all suffering has come to be that of Christ . . . all human beings, no matter how lowly, take on the significance of having belonged and continuing to belong to God.[122] Let us approach to touch the bodies of our brothers, the poor [Severus insisted], as we would touch Christ's holy and untainted side.[123]

Egypt was destined to become staunchly Monophysite, out of loyalty to the patriarchs of Alexandria, who maintained, in their most intransigent form, the teachings of Cyril.[124] In the 430s, a great abbot such as Shenoute of Atripe had no doubt as to the local meaning of the victory of Cyril at Ephesus. As we have seen, Shenoute was an indefatigable author of petitions and of denunciations of the great. He made plain, in a Christmas sermon, the immediate social lesson of the victory of Cyril's views on the nature of the Incarnation:

And the inhumane governor who is heartless in his dealings with the poor, and especially he who is heartless to servants should turn his thoughts to the One Who was the truly Rich One, and Who, while He was Lord of all things, made Himself poor and made Himself a servant for the sake of humankind.[125]

And so it is appropriate to end this stormy period in the imaginative history of the transition from a "classical" to a Christian model of society with a popular work, written in Coptic in the sixth century. The anonymous author of this Coptic collection of

Questions and Answers allowed the patriarch Cyril to have the last word in this great debate. Why, the author asked the patriarch, did God become a human being? Cyril's answer was unambiguous. The Incarnation was necessary for the fair conduct of the Last Judgment. For if God had not identified himself with human flesh, the Devil would be able, at the Last Judgment, to challenge God's right to condemn the heartless who had failed to show pity on the poor. For as God had never been incarnated, so the Devil would claim, he had never himself felt the hunger and thirst of human beings. Why should human beings be condemned by him for having failed to understand the misery of their fellows, if he had not done so? The rich and powerful were entitled to have lived the way they did, as serenely unruffled by human misery as was God himself. Only a God who, in becoming Christ, had taken into his very being the thirst and hunger of humankind, could with perfect sincerity condemn the rich for lack of fellow feeling for the poor.[126]

What we have followed, in the course of these three chapters, is the shift from a classical, "civic" model of society to the medieval and Byzantine model of a Christian society, characterized by the division between "rich" and "poor," in which the rich were constantly challenged to bridge that division by "acts of mercy" to the poor. This model emerged slowly in the centuries that followed the conversion of Constantine in 312. A variety of practical devices and adjustments, directed principally to the public "care of the poor," but tending to work more diffusely through all levels of society, led local communities to turn, increasingly, to the Christian bishops for leadership and for the representation of their needs to distant authorities. This development did not happen in isolation. It was accompanied by the rise of a new religious language, based on an ancient Near Eastern model of society that proved increasingly apposite to the growth of a more powerful state and of sharper distinctions between the classes.

But this language did not only convey a sense of social distance. It was also used to convey a sense of solidarity. It was a language of claims, based upon appeals to the common bond of human flesh. It challenged the rich and powerful to be aware of the sufferings of their fellow humans, as God himself had shared in human suffering. In the early Byzantine period, it came to be deployed with ever-greater frequency and with considerable urgency. For, in the "vertical" and centralized imperial society that had replaced the

ancient ideal of the Roman empire as a "commonwealth of cities," it represented a hope of social cohesion that was, in many
ways, as tenuous as it was inspiring.

Christian preaching and, eventually, as we have seen, Christian
theological controversy on the relations of God and humankind,
kept the symbolic expressions of that great hope tuned to a high
pitch. The high-pitched melody of an Early Christian sense of the
joining of God and humanity in the person of Christ, and by mysterious extension, in the persons of the poor, is, for most of us, distant music. It is music from a past whose sheer strangeness con-
tinues to challenge and to excite the historian. But, to be frank,
the hope of solidarity itself, and the recognition of its attendant
burdens, still weighs upon us today. It has remained a fragile aspi-
ration, as much in need of condensation into symbolic forms of
requisite density and imaginative power as it ever was in the
fourth, fifth, and sixth centuries of the Common Era.

Notes

Chapter 1. *"Lover of the Poor"*

1. Pseudo-Athanasius, *Canons* 14, ed. and trans. W. Reidel and W. E. Crum (Amsterdam: Philo Press, 1973), pp. 25–26. See A. Martin, *Athanase d'Alexandrie et l'Église d'Égypte au ive siècle*, Collection de l'école française de Rome 216 (Rome: Palais Farnèse, 1996), pp. 707–763, and "L'image de l'évêque à travers les 'Canons d'Athanase.' Devoirs et réalités," *L'évêque dans la cité du ive au ve siècle. Image et autorité*, ed. E. Rebillard and C. Sotinel, Collection de l'école française de Rome 248 (Paris: de Boccard, 1998), pp. 59–70.

2. *Codex Justinianus* 1.2.12, ed. P. Krüger (Zurich: Weidmann, 1967), p. 13.

3. For Rome, see E. Diehl, *Inscriptiones latinae christianae veteres* (Zurich: Weidmann, 1970), 1:1103.5: "pauperum amator, aelemosinae deditus omnis, cui numquam defuere, unde opus caeleste fecisset." For Gaul, see G. Le Blant, *Inscriptions chrétiennes de la Gaule* (Paris: Imprimerie impériale, 1856), 1:iii. For similar Jewish inscriptions in Rome, see L. V. Rutgers, *The Jews in Late Antique Rome* (Leiden: Brill, 1995), p. 193, for *philopenés* and *philentolos*.

4. Unfortunately, the abundant evidence for Jewish practice, contained largely in rabbinic sources, has yet to be set in a convincing chronological and historical context. Ze'ev Saffrai, *The Jewish Community in the Talmudic Period* (Jerusalem: Zalman Shazar Center, 1995), pp. 62–77 (in Hebrew), represents at least an attempt to do this. The best collection of such references remains H. L. Strack and P. Billerbeck, *Kommentar zum Neuen Testament aus Talmud und Midrasch* (Munich: C. H. Beck, 1928), 4:1, pp. 536–610. Evidence from the Diaspora yields results that appear to challenge the institutional uniformity assumed in the organization of poor relief by the authors of the *Talmud:* compare J. Reynolds and R. Tannenbaum, *Jews and Godfearers at Aphrodisias*, Cambridge Philological Society Supplements 12 (Cambridge: Cambridge Philological Society, 1987), pp. 26–29, on the "plate of the poor" at the synagogue at Aphrodisias, with the criticism of this view by M. H. Williams, "The Jews and Godfearers Inscription from Aphrodisias: A Case of Patriarchal Interference in the early Third Century?" *Historia* 41 (1992): 297–310. On the idiosyncratic organization of synagogues in the Diaspora, see: T. Rajak and D. Noy, "*Archisynagogoi:* Office, Title and Social Status in the Greco-Roman Synagogue, *Journal of Roman Studies*" 83 (1993): 73–93.

5. Julian, *Letter* 22, ed. W. C. Wright, *The Works of the Emperor Julian,*

Loeb Classical Library (London: Heinemann/New York: Putnam, 1953),
1:58–70, printed in Menahem Stern, *Greek and Latin Authors on Jews
and Judaism 2: From Tacitus to Simplicius* (Jerusalem: Israel Academy of
Sciences and Humanities, 1980), no. 482, 549–551.

6. A. von Harnack, *Mission und Ausbreitung des Christentums* (Leipzig: J. C. Hinrichs, 2nd ed. 1906), 1:127–172; trans. J. Moffat, *The Mission
and Expansion of Christianity in the First Three Centuries* (London: William and Norgate/New York: Putnam, 1904–1905), 1:181–249.

7. P. Veyne, *Le pain et le cirque* (Paris: Le Seuil, 1976), pp. 15–273;
abridged trans. *Bread and Circuses* (London: Allen Lane Penguin, 1990),
pp. 5–200. On the crucial issue of food supplies, see P. Garnsey, *Famine
and Food Supply in the Greco-Roman World: Responses to Risk and Crisis* (Cambridge, U.K.: Cambridge University Press, 1988), pp. 82–86.

8. Well summed up by John Ma, *Antiochus III and the Cities of Western Asia Minor* (Oxford, U.K.: Oxford University Press, 2000), p. 241, on
the continued "process of dialogue" between city and giver expected of
the generous.

9. Garnsey, *Famine and Food Supply*, p. 83, and T. W. Gallant, *Risk
and Survival in Ancient Greece* (Stanford, Calif.: Stanford University
Press, 1991), pp. 182–185.

10. Veyne, *Le pain et le cirque*, pp. 539–790; *Bread and Circuses*,
pp. 292–482. For the Hellenistic period, see Ma, *Antiochus III and the Cities of Western Asia*, p. 237, on "the language of euergetism, a language
where power is not spoken of."

11. Y. Tsafrir and G. Foerster, "Urbanism in Scythopolis-Bet Shean in
the Fourth to Seventh Centuries," *Dumbarton Oaks Papers* 51 (1997):
85–146, at p. 118. For Roman Africa, see the case of Thugga (Dougga, Algeria) analyzed in F. Jacques, *Le privilège de la liberté. Politique impériale et
autonomie municipale dans les cités de l'Occident romain (161–244)*,
Collection de l'école française de Rome 76 (Rome: Palais Farnèse, 1984),
pp. 758–760.

12. See P. Brown, *Power and Persuasion in Late Antiquity: Towards a
Christian Empire* (Madison: University of Wisconsin Press, 1992),
pp. 78–86, on this civic ideal as it survived in the Greek literature of the
fourth century C.E.

13. This is vividly illustrated in the case of third-century Oxyrhynchus, where citizens entitled to a corn dole prove their descent from citizens and adduce their place of residence: see *Pap. Oxy.* 2898, *Oxyrhynchus Papyri* 40 (London: British Academy, 1972), pp. 46–47; see R. J.
Rowland, "The 'Very Poor' and the Grain-Dole at Rome and Oxyrhynchus," *Zeitschrift für Papyrologie und Epigraphik* 21 (1976): 69–72.

14. See the revealing case of the donations of queen Laodike, wife of
Antiochus III, in 196/195 B.C.E., for dowries for daughters of the "poor"
citizens of Iasos. Ma, *Antiochus III and the Cities of Western Asia Minor*,
pp. 223–228, with Epigraphical Dossier, no. 26, pp. 329–335, shows how
this gift was instantly reinterpreted, in a fully "civic" sense, by the recipients, as an honor given to the *démos*—there is no mention of the fact that
some were, indeed, "poor." For similar cases, see J. Strubbe, "Armenzorg

in de Grieks-Romeinse wereld," *Tijdschrift voor Geschiedenis* 107 (1994): 163–183, at pp. 165–167.

15. See esp. G. Woolf, "Food, Poverty and Patronage: The Significance of the Epigraphy of the Alimentary Schemes in Early Imperial Italy," *Papers of the British School of Rome* 58 (1990): 197–228. For a further case, recently edited, of an alimentary system in Spain, see now R. S. O. Tomlin, "An Early Third-Century Alimentary Foundation," *Zeitschrift für Papyrologie und Epigraphik* 129 (2000): 287–292.

16. P. Garnsey, *Famine and Food Supply*, pp. 218–243, and "Mass Diet and Nutrition in the City of Rome," *Cities, Peasants and Food in Classical Antiquity* (Cambridge, U.K.: Cambridge University Press, 1998): pp. 226–252; W. Scheidel, "Libertina's Bitter Gains: Seasonal Mortality and Endemic Disease in the Ancient City of Rome," *Ancient Society* 25 (1994): 151–175.

17. C. Virlouvet, *Tessera frumentaria: Les procédés de la distribution du blé public à Rome à la fin de la République et au début de l'Empire*, Bibliothèque des écoles françaises d'Athènes et de Rome 296 (Rome: Palais Farnèse, 1995), pp. 243–362.

18. H. Bolkestein, *Wohltätigkeit und Armenpflege im vorchristlichen Altertum* (Utrecht: A. Oosthoek, 1939).

19. Veyne, *Le pain et le cirque*, pp. 15–183; *Bread and Circuses*, pp. 5–69.

20. E. Patlagean, *Pauvreté économique et pauvreté sociale à Byzance: 4e–7e siècles* (Paris: Mouton, 1977), and "The Poor," *The Byzantines*, ed. G. Cavallo (Chicago: University of Chicago Press, 1997), pp. 15–42.

21. Patlagean, *Pauvreté*, pp. 17–35, 181–196, and 423–432.

22. Patlagean, *Pauvreté*, p. 429.

23. Patlagean, "The Poor," p. 18.

24. Peregrine Horden and Nicholas Purcell, *The Corrupting Sea: A Study of Mediterranean History* (Oxford: Blackwell, 2000), pp. 89–112 and 342–400, esp. 377–383.

25. See S. Demougin, "De l'évergétisme en Italie," *Splendidissima civitas. Études d'histoire romaine en hommage à François Jacques*, ed. A. Chastagnol, S. Demougin, and C. Lepelley (Paris: Bibliothèque de la Sorbonne, 1996), pp. 49–56, on the "surprising" lack of Greek-style euergetism in early imperial Italy; and Jacques, *Le privilège de la liberté*, pp. 704–709, 743, and 750, on failures to complete promises in Roman Africa.

26. Veyne, *Le pain et le cirque*, pp. 295–296; *Bread and Circuses*, 149–150. For Italy, see the younger Pliny's impressive benefactions to Como (about which he wrote extensively) analyzed by R. Duncan-Jones, "The finances of a senator," *The Economy of the Roman Empire* (Cambridge, U.K.: Cambridge University Press, 1974), pp. 17–32, at 29–31; see also C. E. Manning, "*Liberalitas*—the Decline and Rehabilitation of a Virtue," *Greece and Rome* 32 (1985): 73–83.

27. E. Champlin, *Final Judgments: Duty and Emotion in Roman Wills 200 BC–AD 250* (Berkeley: University of California Press, 1991), pp. 155–168.

28. Palladius, *Historia Lausiaca* 68.2–3; trans. R. T. Meyer, Ancient Christian Writers 34 (New York: Newman Press, 1975), 149.

29. Asterius of Amaseia, *Homily 3, Patrologia Graeca* 40:209C, now ed. C. Datema, *Asterius of Amaseia. Homilies I–XIV* (Leiden: Brill, 1970): 35.8.

30. Anne Marie Schimmel, *The Mystical Dimensions of Islam* (Chapel Hill: University of North Carolina Press, 1975), p. 333.

31. *Lives of the Monks of Palestine by Cyril of Scythopolis. Life of Sabas* 62, trans. R. M. Price, Cistercian Studies 114 (Kalamazoo, Michigan: Cistercian Studies, 1991), 173; see Tsafrir and Foerster, Urbanism in Scythopolis—Bet Shean, p. 122.

32. Sulpicius Severus, *Life of Saint Martin* 3.

33. F. Nau, "Histoires des solitaires égyptiens," no. 39, *Revue de l'Orient chrétien* 12 (1907): 172.

34. F. Nau, "Histoires des solitaires égyptiens," no. 214, *Revue de l'Orient chrétien* 13 (1908): 282.

35. Leontius, *Life of John the Almsgiver* 21; trans. E. Dawes and N. H. Baynes, *Three Byzantine Saints* (Oxford: Blackwell, 1948), p. 230. See esp. V. Déroche, *Études sur Léontios de Néapolis*, Studia Byzantina Upsaliensia 3 (Uppsala: Almqvist and Wiksell, 1995), pp. 233–249, 254–264, and 272 n. 7.

36. Keith Wrightson and David Levine, *Poverty and Piety in an English Village: Terling 1525–1700* (Oxford: Clarendon Press, 2nd ed. 1995), p. 185.

37. This is well seen by Valerio Neri, *I Marginali nell'Occidente Tardoantico. Poveri, "infames" e criminali nella nascente società cristiana* (Bari: Edipuglia, 1998), pp. 42 and 72.

38. In general, see Neri, *I Marginali*, pp. 289–417; Brent Shaw, "Bandits in the Roman Empire," *Past and Present* 105 (1984): 3–52, and "War and Violence," *Late Antiquity: A Guide to the Postclassical World*, ed. G. W. Bowersock, Peter Brown, and Oleg Grabar (Cambridge, Mass.: Harvard University at the Belknap Press, 1999), pp. 130–169; Z. Rubin, "Mass Movements in Late Antiquity," *Leaders and Masses in the Roman World. Studies in Honor of Z. Yavetz* (Leiden: Brill, 1995), pp. 129–187. On urban violence, see A. Cameron, *Circus Factions* (Oxford: Clarendon Press, 1975), pp. 271–296, and A. A. Chekalova, *Konstantinopel' v vi. veke. Vosstanie Nika* (Moscow: Nauka, 1986), pp. 69–78. For epigraphic evidence of the circus factions in other cities than Constantinople and for their considerably more peaceable evolution, see now C. Roueché, *Performers and Partisans at Aphrodisias*, Journal of Roman Studies Monographs 6 (London: Society for the Promotion of Roman Studies, 1992), pp. 83–128.

39. See *Anonymus de rebus bellicis* 2.3, *A Roman Reformer and Inventor*, ed. E. A. Thompson (Oxford: Clarendon Press, 1952), p. 94, for what may be unrest in the Eastern empire in the 360s; and Chekalova, *Konstantinopel'*, pp. 79–88 and 123–134, on the upper-class background of the Nika Riot of 532.

40. For the control of able-bodied beggars in Rome, see *Codex Theodosianus* 14.18.1 (382 C.E.) with Neri, *Marginali*, pp. 135–138, and J. Rougé, "A propos des mendiants au ive siècle," *Cahiers d'Histoire* 20 (1975):

339–346. Such concerns did influence poor relief in Armenia; see pp. 42–43 in this volume. But they are minor compared with the constant preoccupation with the dangerous poor, documented in P. Slack, *Poverty and Policy in Tudor and Stuart England* (London: Routledge, 1988), pp. 91–112, and J.-P. Gutton, *La société et les pauvres. L'exemple de la généralité de Lyon 1534–1789* (Paris: Belles Lettres, 1971), pp. 86–97 and 225–247. Ruth Mellinkoff, *Outcasts. Signs of Otherness in Northern European Art of the Late Middle Ages*, 2 vols. (Berkeley: University of California Press, 1991), 1:113–194, provides a gripping visual survey.

41. C. E. Bosworth, *The Medieval Islamic Underworld; The Banū Sāsān in Arabic Society and Literature*, 2 vols. (Leiden: Brill, 1976), 1:1–47.

42. John Chrysostom, *Homily 66 on Matthew 3: Patrologia Graeca* 58:630.

43. David Cannadine, "Beyond Class? Social Structure and Social Perception in Modern England," *Proceedings of the British Academy* 97 (1998): 95–118, at p. 99.

44. B. Geremek, *The Margins of Society in Late Medieval Paris* (Cambridge, U.K.: Cambridge University Press, 1987), pp. 193–194; John Henderson, *Piety and Charity in Late Medieval Florence* (Oxford: Clarendon Press, 1994), p. 323 (10 percent received alms at Orsanmichele in 1357). The proportions fluctuated widely (as much as 25 percent in 1347), mainly as a result of immigration from the countryside: see p. 295. For the early modern period, see Slack, *Poverty and Policy*, pp. 4, 72, and 179, and Gutton, *La société et les pauvres*, p. 10.

45. William Booth, *In Darkest England and the Way Out* (London: Salvation Army, 1890), p. 31.

46. Slack, *Poverty and Policy*, pp. 38–40.

47. Gutton, *La société et les pauvres*, p. 10.

48. These, at least, are the conclusions I would draw from the prolonged and tenacious arguments of Horden and Purcell, *The Corrupting Sea*, notably on pp. 175–182, 201–208 and 230; and 266–278 and 377–391.

49. Aldo Schiavone, *La storia spezzata. Roma antica e Occidente moderno* (Rome/Bari: Laterza, 1996), p. 75; trans. *The End of the Past: Ancient Rome and the Modern West* (Cambridge, Mass.: Harvard University Press, 2000), p. 69.

50. Bolkestein, *Wohltätigkeit und Armenpflege*, p. 484.

51. Harnack, *Mission und Ausbreitung des Christentums*, 2:5–262, *Mission and Expansion*, 2:2–337, remains the best single collection of evidence. See also R. Lane-Fox, *Pagans and Christians* (New York: A. Knopf, 1987), pp. 265–335. The sociological approach of R. Stark, *The Rise of Christianity* (Princeton, N.J.: Princeton University Press, 1996), adds little but has provoked debate: see "Robert Stark's *The Rise of Christianity*: A Discussion," *Journal of Early Christian Studies* 6 (1998): 162–267, and esp. K. Hopkins, "Christian Number and Its Implications," pp. 185–226, which provides a refreshingly novel approach.

52. See D. Flusser, "Blessed are the Poor in Spirit . . . ," *Israel Exploration Journal* 10 (1960): 1–13, and, in general, s.v. *ploutos* and *ptôchos, Theological Dictionary of the New Testament,* ed. G. Kittel (Grand Rapids, Mich.: Eerdmans, 1968), 6:318–332 and 885–915.

53. Well seen by R. Rosenzweig, *Solidarität mit den Leidenden im Judentum,* Studia Judaica 10 (New York: de Gruyter, 1978), p. 79.

54. Romans 15:26 and Galatians 2:10, with I Corinthians 16:1 and 2 Corinthians 8:4 and 9:1–12. See L. Keck, "The Poor among the Saints in Jewish Christianity and Qumran," *Zeitschrift für neutestamentliche Wissenschaft* 57 (1966): 54–78.

55. See E. Bruck, "Ethics vs. Law: Saint Paul, the Fathers of the Church and the 'Cheerful Giver' in Roman Law," *Traditio* 2 (1944): 97–121.

56. See esp. s.v. *'ebyôn, Theological Dictionary of the Old Testament,* ed. G. J. Botterweck and H. Ringgren; trans. J. T. Willis (Grand Rapids, Mich.: Eerdmans, 1974), 1:27–41. See chapter 2 in this volume, pp. 69–70.

57. G. Theissen, *Sociology of Early Palestinian Christianity* (Philadelphia: Fortress Press, 1978); but now see J. A. Draper, "Weber, Theissen and 'Wandering Charismatics' in the *Didache,*" *Journal of Early Christian Studies* 6 (1998): 541–576.

58. Wayne A. Meeks, *The First Urban Christians* (New Haven, Conn.: Yale University Press, 1983); G. Theissen, *The Social Setting of Pauline Christianity* (Philadelphia: Fortress Press, 1982).

59. See esp. now G. Schöllgen, *Die Anfänge der Professionalisierung des Klerus und das kirchliche Amt in der Syrischen Didaskalie,* Jahrbuch für Antike und Christentum, Ergänzungsband 26 (Münster: Aschendorff, 1998).

60. See O. Wischmeyer, *Die Kultur des Buchs Jesus Sirach,* Beiheft der Zeitschrift für neutestamentliche Wissenschaft 77 (Berlin: de Gruyter, 1995), pp. 64–65 and 259–265.

61. See esp. E. P. Sanders, *Judaism. Practice and Belief 63* BCE–66 CE (London: S.C.M., 1992), p. 383; for a vivid evocation of the role of civic priests in Asia Minor, see Lane-Fox, *Pagans and Christians,* pp. 46–89; see also D. Gordon, "The Veil of Power: Emperors, Sacrificers and Benefactors," *Pagan Priests: Religion and Power in the Ancient World,* ed. M. Beard and J. North (Ithaca, N.Y.: Cornell University Press, 1990), pp. 201–255.

62. Sanders, *Judaism: Practice and Belief,* p. 405.

63. Eusebius, *Ecclesiastical History* 3.20.1–3; trans. A. C. McGiffert, *Library of the Nicene and Post-Nicene Fathers* (Grand Rapids, Mich.: Eerdmans, 1979), 1:149.

64. Hesiod, *Works and Days,* lines 303 ff. For a vivid reminder of the difference in physical conditions between a peasant and a member of the leisured classes, see the archaeo-medical report on the marks of acute physical stress found on the bodies in graves at a late antique villa complex in southern Italy and the absence of such marks on the bodies of the privileged few who were buried within the villa chapel: G. Volpe, *San Giusto: Le ville, le ecclesiae* (Bari: Edipuglia, 1998), pp. 234–236.

65. Lucian, *The Dream, or Lucian's Career* 9, trans. A. M. Harmon, *Lu-*

cian, Loeb Classical Library (Cambridge, Mass.: Harvard University Press, 1969), 3:223.

66. W. Shakespeare, *Midsummer Night's Dream*, Act 5, scene 1.

67. Hermas, *The Shepherd* 50, Similitude 2, ed. R. Joly, *Hermas. Le Pasteur*, Sources chrétiennes 53 bis (Paris: Le Cerf, 1968), pp. 214–218. Compare *b. Hullin* 92a, trans. I. Epstein, *The Babylonian Talmud* (London: Soncino, 1935), p. 516, cited in L. Levine, *The Rabbinic Class in Late Antiquity* (Jerusalem: JTSA, 1987), pp. 115–116. The extent to which the rabbis were dependent on the financial support of others is uncertain, because the social composition of the rabbinate itself remains unclear: see C. Hezser, *The Social Structure of the Rabbinic Movement in Roman Palestine*, Texte und Studien zum Antiken Judentum 66 (Tübingen: Mohr/Siebeck, 1998): 263–266. Some cases of support exist, as do examples of tension on the issue: see F. Avemarie, *Tora und Leben*, Texte und Studien zum Antiken Judentum 55 (Tübingen: Mohr/Siebeck, 1996), pp. 418–430, and R. Kamlin, *The Sage in Jewish Society in Late Antiquity* (London and New York: Routledge, 1999), pp. 29–35.

68. For a survey of pagan religious entrepreneurs, see Schöllgen, *Die Anfänge der Professionalisierung des Klerus*, pp. 21–33. On Paul see R. E. Hock, *The Social Context of Paul's Ministry: Tentmaking and Apostleship* (Philadelphia: Fortress Press, 1980), pp. 52–65, and G. Theissen, "Legitimation and Sustenance: An Essay on the Sociology of Early Christian Missions," *The Social Setting of Pauline Christianity*, pp. 27–67.

69. 1 Corinthians 9:1–14.

70. 2 Thessalonians 3:7–10.

71. Lucian, *The Passing of Peregrinus* 11–13, trans. Harmon, *Lucian* 2:12–14.

72. Basil of Caesarea, *Letter* 169, ed. R. J. Deferrari, Loeb Classical Library (Cambridge, Mass.: Harvard University Press, 1962), 2:438–439.

73. For a sympathetic study of one such creator of a cult accused of fraudulence and avarice, see Lane-Fox, *Pagans and Christians*, pp. 241–250, on Alexander of Abonouteichos (Inebolu, Turkey). An *agyrtés*, a religious beggar, of the Syrian goddess Atargatis collected forty sacks on twenty journeys, with which to build a votive statue at Kefr Haouar: *Bulletin de Correspondence Héllénique* 21 (1897): 60–61.

74. Schöllgen, *Die Anfänge der Professionalisierung des Klerus*, pp. 116–134.

75. Cyprian, *Letters* 12.2 2 and 14.2.1, ed. W. Hartel, *Corpus Scriptorum Ecclesiasticorum Latinorum* 3:2 (Vienna: Gerold, 1871), pp. 503–504 and 510; trans. Graeme Clarke, *The Letters of St. Cyprian*, Ancient Christian Writers 43 (New York: Newman Press, 1984), pp. 82 and 88.

76. Cyprian, *Letter* 14.2, p. 511; trans. Clarke *Letters 1*, pp. 88–89.

77. Cyprian, *Letter* 7.2, p. 485; trans. Clarke, p. 67.

78. Cyprian, *Letter* 41.1.2, p. 587; trans. Clarke, *Letters 2*, p. 59, see also p. 205.

79. Cyprian, *Letter* 2.2.2, pp. 468–469; trans. Clarke, *Letters 1*, pp. 53–54.

80. Cyprian, *Letter* 62.4–5, pp. 700–701; trans. Clarke, *Letters 3*, Ancient Christian Writers 46 (New York: Newman Press, 1986), pp. 277–286.
81. G. Schöllgen, *Ecclesia Sordida? Zur Frage der sozialen Schichtung frühchristlicher Gemeinden am Beispiel Karthagos zur Zeit Tertullians*, Jahrbuch für Antike und Christentum: Ergänzungsband 12 (Münster in Westfalen: Aschendorff, 1984).
82. Clarke, *Letters 1*, p. 163.
83. Eusebius, *Ecclesiastical History* 6.43.11; trans. McGiffert, p. 288. Compare R. Duncan-Jones, *The Economy of the Roman Empire*, pp. 277–283.
84. Optatus of Milevis, *On the Schism of the Donatists:* Appendix 1, *Gesta apud Zenophilum*, ed. J. Ziwsa, *Corpus Scriptorum Ecclesiasticorum Latinorum* 26 (Vienna: Tempski, 1882), pp. 185–186; also in H. von Soden, *Urkunden zur Entstehungsgeschichte des Donatismus* (Berlin: de Gruyter, 1950), pp. 40–41; trans. M. Edwards, *Optatus: Against the Donatists* (Liverpool: Liverpool University Press, 1997), p. 154.
85. Eusebius, *Ecclesiastical History* 6.43.18, trans. McGiffert, p. 289, shows that to be able to make this division was part of what constituted the office of a bishop. See now Schöllgen, *Die Anfänge der Professionalisierung des Klerus*, pp. 55–56 and T. Mathews, "An Early Roman Chancel Arrangement and its Liturgical Uses," *Rivista di archeologia cristiana* 38 (1962): 73–95.
86. Lane-Fox, *Pagans and Christians*, p. 623.
87. Optatus of Milevis, Appendix 1: *Gesta apud Zenophilum*, ed. Ziwsa, p. 187, von Soden, p. 42; trans. Edwards, pp. 166–167. The sum offered by Lucilla was large compared with other sums that usually circulated in the African church. In Cirta, a future priest offered twenty sacks of coins *(folles)* for his ordination. This evidence is now excellently studied by Y. Duval, *Chrétiens d'Afrique à l'aube de la paix constantinienne* (Paris: Institut d'Études Augustiniennes, 2000), pp. 169–173 and 408–420.
88. Eusebius, *Ecclesiastical History* 10.6.1; trans. McGiffert, p. 382.
89. Santo Mazzarino, *Aspetti sociali del quarto secolo* (Rome: Bretschneider, 1951), pp. 217–269, was decisive. See now J. M. Carrié, "Les distributions alimentaires dans les cités de l'empire romain tardif," *Mélanges d'Archéologie et d'Histoire de l'École française de Rome: Antiquité* 87 (1975): 995–1101, and Jean Durliat, *De la ville antique à la ville byzantine. Le problème des subsistances*, Collection de l'école française de Rome 136 (Rome: Palais Farnèse, 1990).
90. Durliat, *De la ville antique à la ville byzantine*, pp. 37–137, with S. Barnish, "Pigs, Plebeians and *Potentes*," *Papers of the British School of Rome* 55 (1987): 157–185; and N. Purcell, "The Populace of Rome in Late Antiquity: Problems of Classification and Historical Description," *The Transfomations of Vrbs Roma in Late Antiquity*, ed. W. V. Harris, Journal of Roman Archaeology: Supplementary Series 33 (Portsmouth, R.I.: Journal of Roman Archaeology, 1999), pp. 135–161.
91. Durliat, *De la ville antique à la ville byzantine*, pp. 185–278.
92. See esp. C. Lepelley, *Les cités de l'Afrique romaine au Bas-Empire* (Paris; Études augustiniennes, 1979), 1:59–120, and R. MacMullen, *Cor-*

ruption and the Decline of Rome (New Haven, Conn.: Yale University Press, 1988), pp. 29–34.

93. See esp. C. Roueché, *Aphrodisias in Late Antiquity,* Journal of Roman Studies Monographs 5 (London: Society for the Promotion of Roman Studies, 1989), pp. xxii–xxiii and 68–70, and L. Robert, "Épigrammes du Bas-Empire," *Hellenica* 4 (1948): 35–114.

94. L. Robert, *Hellenica* 11–12 (1960): 569–572.

95. A. Ovadiah and S. Mucznik, "The Mosaic Pavement of Kissufim, Israel," *Mosaïque. Recueil d'hommages à Henri Stern* (Paris. Éditions Recherche sur les civilisations, 1983), pp. 273–280. The mosaic is now illustrated in *Cradle of Christianity*, eds. Y. Israeli and D. Mevorah (Jerusalem: The Israel Museum, 2000), pp. 86–87. Compare the illustration in the *Calendar of 354* of the consular *sparsio*—the scattering of money—of Constantius II: H. Stern, *Le Calendrier de 354*, Institut français d'archéologie de Beyrouth: Bibliothèque archéologique et historique 55 (Paris: P. Geuthner, 1953), pp. 155–157 and plate XIV.

96. W. Tabbernee, *Montanist Inscriptions and Testimonies*, Patristic Monographs Series 16 (Macon, Georgia: Mercer University Press, 1997), pp. 414–419, from Phrygia.

97. Brown, *Power and Persuasion*, pp. 17–20, and "The World of Late Antiquity Revisited," *Symbolae Osloenses* 72 (1997): 5–90, at pp. 24–26; see now esp. C. Kelly, "Emperors, Government and Bureaucracy," *Cambridge Ancient History XIII*, ed. A. Cameron and P. Garnsey (Cambridge, U.K.: Cambridge University Press, 1998), pp. 138–183.

98. Best reviewed in T. D. Barnes, *Constantine and Eusebius* (Cambridge, Mass.: Harvard University Press, 1981), p. 50, with reference to the *Syro-Roman Law Book* 117, *Fontes Iuris Romani Anteiustiniani*, ed. S. Riccobono (Florence: G. Barberà, 1968), 2:1, p. 794.

99. See esp. *Codex Theodosianus* 16.2.1–16, from 313 to 361 A.D. See F. Vittinghoff, "Staat, Kirche und Dynastie beim Tod des Konstantins" and K. L. Noethlichs, "Kirche, Reich und Gesellschaft in der Jahrhundertmitte," *L'Église et l'Empire au ive. siècle*, ed. A. Dihle, Entretiens de la Fondation Hardt 34 (Geneva: Fondation Hardt, 1989), pp. 1–28 and 251–294. I am told by Professor Barnes that the dating and sequence of these laws remain uncertain and would merit further examination.

100. A. H. M. Jones, *The Later Roman Empire 284–602* (Oxford: Blackwell, 1964), 2:906–909. For Egypt, see Martin, *Athanase d'Alexandrie*, pp. 653–662, and R. Bagnall, *Egypt in Late Antiquity* (Princeton, N.J.: Princeton University Press, 1993), pp. 283–286.

101. See now R. Lizzi, "The Bishop, Vir Venerabilis: Fiscal Privileges and Status Definition in Late Antiquity," *The Thirteenth International Congress in Patristic Studies (Oxford, 16–21 August 1999)*—forthcoming.

102. See esp. *Cod. Theod.* 16.2.7 (330); 2.15 (360); 12.1.49 (361); Basil, *Ep.* 104, ed. Deferrari, 2:196.

103. See, e.g., Basil, *Ep.* 237, Deferrari, 4:408, on the activities of Demosthenes, Vicar of Pontus, the supporter of his opponents, "nit-picking," and withdrawing the exemptions of Basil's clergy in 374–375.

104. R. M. Grant, *Early Christianity and Society* (New York: Harper

and Row, 1977), pp. 44–65; and M. Weinfeld, *Social Justice in Ancient Israel and in the Ancient Near East* (Jerusalem: Magnes Press/ Minneapolis: Fortress, 1995), pp. 16–17 and 79–80.

105. *Cod. Theod.* 16.2.16 (361); trans. C. Pharr, *The Theodosian Code* (Princeton, N.J.: Princeton University Press, 1952), p. 443.

106. *Jerusalem Talmud: Schebith* 4.3; trans. M. Schwab, *Le Talmud de Jérusalem* (Paris: Maisonneuve and Larose, 1972), 2:359.

107. *Cod. Theod.* 16.8.2 and 4 (330/331) and 16.8.13 (397), also in A. Linder, *The Jews in Roman Imperial Legislation* (Detroit: Wayne State University Press, 1987), pp. 132–138 and 201–204. See now M. Jacobs, *Die Institution des jüdischen Patriarchen*, Texte und Studien zum Antiken Judentum 52 (Tübingen: Mohr/Siebeck, 1995), pp. 274–284.

108. Jacobs, *Die Institution des jüdischen Patriarchen*, pp. 154–157, on exemption from the *aurum coronarium*.

109. *Cod.Theod.* 16.2.6 (326), trans. Pharr, p. 441.

110. *Cod. Theod.* 16.2.6 (326), trans. Pharr, p. 441. See R. Delmaire, *Largesses sacrées et res privata*, Collection de l'École française de Rome 121 (Rome: Palais Farnèse, 1989), pp. 362–364.

111. Eusebius of Caesarea, *Commentary on Isaiah*, ed. J. Ziegler, Die griechischen christlichen Schriftsteller: Eusebius Werke 9 (Berlin: Akademie Verlag, 1975), p. 316: see M. J. Hollerich, *Eusebius' Commentary on Isaiah: Christian Exegesis in the Age of Constantine* (Oxford, U.K.: Clarendon Press, 1999), pp. 21–22. Sozomen, *Ecclesiastical History* 5.5 3, ed. J. Bidez and G. C. Hansen, Die griechischen christlichen Schriftsteller 50 (Berlin: Akademie-Verlag, 1960), p. 199; trans. C. D. Hartranft, *Library of the Nicene and Post-Nicene Fathers* (Grand Rapids, Mich.: Eerdmans, 1979), 2:329.

112. Durliat, *De la ville antique à la ville byzantine*, pp. 354–355, 365–375, and 552 n. 155.

113. Athanasius, *Apologia contra Arianos* 18.2: see T. D. Barnes, *Athanasius and Constantius: Theology and Politics in the Constantinian Empire* (Cambridge, Mass.: Harvard University Press, 1993), pp. 37 and 178.

114. E. Kislinger, "Kaiser Julian und die (christlichen) Xenodochien," *Byzantios. Festschrift für Herbert Hunger zum 70. Geburtstag*, ed. W. Hörander et al. (Vienna: E. Beevar, 1984), pp. 171–184; T. Sternberg, *Orientalium More Secutus. Räume und Institutionen der Caritas des 5. bis 7. Jahrhunderts in Gallien*, Jahrbuch für Antike und Christentum, Ergänzungsband 16 (Münster: Aschendorff, 1991), pp. 147–193; K. Mentzou-Meimari, "Eparkhiaka evagé idrymata mekhri tou telous tés eikonomakhias," *Byzantina* 11 (1982): 243–308, lists 59 *xenodocheia*, 45 hospitals, and 22 *ptôcheia* (poor houses) founded outside Constantinople between the fourth and the eighth centuries, and 40 *xenodocheia* founded in Constantinople itself; see also J. P. Thomas, *Private Religious Foundations in the Byzantine Empire*, Dumbarton Oaks Studies 24 (Washington, D.C.: Dumbarton Oaks, 1987).

115. Y. Magen, *The Monastery of Martyrius at Ma'ale Adummim* (Jerusalem: Israel Antiquities Authority, 1993), pp. 5–60.

116. Epiphanius, *Panarion* 75.1: *Patrologia Graeca* 42:504C; trans. F. Williams, *The Panarion of Epiphanius of Salamis*, Nag Hammadi Studies 36 (Leiden: Brill, 1994), p. 91.

117. Patlagean, *Pauvreté*, pp. 193–195; T. S. Miller, *The Birth of the Hospital in the Byzantine Empire* (Baltimore, Md.: Johns Hopkins University Press, 1985; reprint 1997), pp. 30–136.

118. E.g. Linda Martz, *Poverty and Welfare in Habsburg Spain: The Example of Toledo* (Cambridge, U.K.: Cambridge University Press, 1983), pp. 185–187; and Ömer Barkan, "Edirne civarındaki bazı imäret tesisleri- nin yıllık bilânçoları" (The yearly accounts of some soup-kitchens in Edirne and its neighborhood), *Türk Târih Kurumu: Belgeler* 1 (1964): 236–262, at pp. 242–247.

119. F. Van Ommeslaeghe, "Jean Chrysostome et Eudoxie," *Analecta Bollandiana* 97 (1979): 131–159, at p. 151. See also Patlagean, *Pauvreté*, pp. 110–111, and M. Avi-Yonah, "The Bath of the Lepers at Scythopolis," *Israel Exploration Journal* 13 (1963): 325–326.

120. Sternberg, *Orientalium More Secutus*, pp. 177–180.

121. The earliest certain references known to me are in the *Chronicon Paschale*, which draws on Arian sources and so reflects what was either taken for granted or admired under Constantius II: *Chronicon Paschale 284–628 AD*, trans. M. and M. Whitby (Liverpool: Liverpool University Press, 1989), 26 (350 C.E.) and 35 (360 C.E.). It is significant that, in Rome, the gifts of the consul Gallicanus to the church of Saints Peter, Paul and John the Baptist, made under Constantine, contain no mention of a *xeno- docheion*; the later fourth-century legend does do so: see s.v. Gallicanus, *Prosopographie chrétienne du Bas Empire 2: Italie*, part 1, ed. C. Pietri and L. Pietri (Rome: École française de Rome, 1999), pp. 883–884.

122. Paulinus, *Poem* 21.384–386, ed. W. Hartel, *Corpus Scriptorum Ec- clesiasticorum Latinorum* 30:2 (Vienna: Tempsky, 1894), pp. 170–171; trans. P. G. Walsh, *The Poems of St. Paulinus of Nola*, Ancient Christian Writers 40 (New York: Newman Press, 1975), p. 185.

123. Basil, *Ep.* 143, Deferrari, 2:346.

124. *Studia Pontica 3*, ed. J. G. C. Anderson, F. Cumont, and H. Gré- goire (Brussels: H. Lamertin, 1910), no. 68a, pp. 88–89.

125. Sternberg, *Orientalium More Secutus*, p. 138 n.223.

126. G. W. Bowersock, "The Rich Harvest of Near Eastern Mosaics," *Journal of Roman Archaeology* 11 (1998): 693–688, at p. 696. It is illus- trated in *Late Antiquity: A Guide to the Postclassical World*, plate 8.

127. Sozomen, *Ecclesiastical History* 6.34.9, ed. Bidez and Hansen, p. 291; trans. Hartranft, p. 371.

128. See esp. J. Gribomont, "Le monachisme au iv siècle en Asie Mi- neure: de Gangres au Messalianisme," *Studia Patristica 1: Texte und Un- tersuchungen 64* (Berlin: Akademie Verlag, 1957), pp. 400–415; "Un aristo- crate révolutionnaire, évêque et moine: Basile de Césarée," *Augustinianum* 17 (1977): 179–191; and "Saint Basile et le monachisme enthousiaste," *Irénikon* 53 (1980): 123–144.

129. On this hotly disputed person, see the summary of W. D. Haus-

child, s.v. Eustathius von Sebaste, *Theologische Real-Enzyklopädie* 10 (Berlin: de Gruyter, 1982), pp. 547–550; and P. Rousseau, *Basil of Caesarea* (Berkeley: University of California Press, 1994), pp. 233–245.

130. After much uncertainty (and the possibility of a date as late as 355), the date of the council has been confirmed, for 343, by A. Laniado, "Note sur la datation conservée en syriaque du concile de Gangres," *Orientalia Christiana Periodica* 61 (1995): 195–199.

131. *Council of Gangra, Letter to the bishops of Armenia* and *Canons* 3, 13 and 17, in J. D. Mansi, *Sacrorum Conciliorum nova et amplissima collectio* (Florence, 1762), 2:1095–1106; trans. H. R. Percival, *The Seven Ecumenical Councils*, Library of the Nicene and Post-Nicene Fathers 14 (Grand Rapids, Mich.: Eerdmans, 1972), pp. 91–101, and by O. L. Yarborough in *Ascetic Behavior in Greco-Roman Antiquity: A Sourcebook*, ed. V. L. Wimbush (Minneapolis: Fortress, 1990), pp. 448–456.

132. Rousseau, *Basil of Caesarea*, pp. 61–92.

133. For an instructive example of the formation and transmission of one such "negative identikit," see K. Fitschen, *Messalianismus und Antimessalianismus. Ein Beispiel ostkirchlicher Kirchengeschichte*, Forschungen zur Kirchen-und Dogmengeschichte 71 (Göttingen: Vandenhoek and Ruprecht, 1998). For less savory accusations, see T. D. Barnes, "The Crimes of Basil of Ancyra," *Journal of Theological Studies*, n.s. 47 (1996): 550–554.

134. Gribomont, "Saint Basile et le monachisme enthousiaste," pp. 132–133.

135. Epiphanius, *Panarion* 75.1–3: *Patrologia Graeca* 42:504A–506C, trans. Williams, *The Panarion of Epiphanius*, pp. 491–492.

136. This was suggested by G. Dagron in his innovative study, "Les moines et la ville. Le monachisme à Constantinople jusqu'au concile de Chalcédoine," *Travaux et Mémoires* 4 (1970): 229–276, at pp. 246–253.

137. Socrates, *Ecclesiastical History* 4.16.7–8, ed. G. C. Hansen, Die griechischen christlichen Schriftsteller n.s. 1 (Berlin: Akademie-Verlag, 1995), p. 295; trans. A. C. Zenos, *Library of the Nicene and Post-Nicene Fathers* (Grand Rapids, Mich.: Eerdmans, 1979), 2:104.

138. Sozomen, *Ecclesiastical History* 4.20.2 and 27.4.2, pp. 170 and 184, trans. Hartranft, pp. 315 and 322, has been interpreted in a different manner from Dagron by H. C. Brennecke, *Studien zur Geschichte der Homöer*, Beiträge zur historischen Theologie 73 (Tübingen: J. C. B. Mohr, 1988), pp. 61–62.

139. Sozomen, *Ecclesiastical History* 4.27.4, p. 184; trans. Hartranft, p. 322.

140. W. H. C. Frend, "The Church in the Reign of Constantius II," *L'Église et l'Empire au ive. siècle*, p. 111.

141. Gribomont, Saint Basile et le monachisme enthousiaste, p. 127.

142. Basil, *Homily 8: On Famine and Drought: Patrologia Graeca* 31:309B, now carefully analyzed by S. Holman, "The Hungry Body: Famine, Poverty and Basil's *Hom. 8*," *Journal of Early Christian Studies* 7 (1999): 337–363. The principal accounts of the famine are the posthumous pane-

gyric of Basil's friend Gregory Nazianzen and the defense of Basil by his brother, Gregory of Nyssa: Gregory of Nazianze, *Oratio* 43.34–36, ed. J. Bernardi, *Grégoire de Nazianze: Les Discours*, Sources chrétiennes 384 (Paris: Le Cerf, 1992), pp. 200–206, trans.C. G. Browne and J. E. Swallow, *Library of the Nicene and Post-Nicene Fathers* (Grand Rapids, Mich.: Eerdmans, 1974), 7:406–408; Gregory of Nyssa, *Against Eunomius* 1.103: *Patrologia Graeca* 45:281C, ed. W. Jaeger, *Contra Eunomium* (Leiden: Brill, 1960), p. 57. See now Rousseau, *Basil of Caesarea*, pp. 133–189. The reader should know that the chronology of the letters of Basil (on which we depend for so much knowledge of his life and activities) remains uncertain: see the chronological arguments in the commentaries of W. D. Hauschild, *Basilius von Cäsarea, Briefe 1–3*, Bibliothek der griechischen Literatur 32, 3, and 37, respectively (Stuttgart: A. Hiersemann, 1973, 1990, and 1993). Not all the datings proposed by Hauschild are convincing. I would prefer the conclusions of R. Van Dam, "Governors of Cappadocia during the fourth century," *Medieval Prosopography* 17 (1996): 7–93.

143. Garnsey, *Famine and food supply*, pp. 22–23.

144. S. Faroqhi, *Men of Modest Substance: Houseowners and House Property in Seventeenth-Century Ankara and Kayseri* (Cambridge, U.K.: Cambridge University Press, 1987), p. 208.

145. B. E. Daley, "Building a New City: The Cappadocian Fathers and the Rhetoric of Philanthropy," *Journal of Early Christian Studies* 7 (1999): 431–461, at p. 459.

146. Basil, *On that Passage of Luke: "I shall pull down my barns . . ."* 3: *Patrologia Graeca* 31:265D. This sermon was used by Louis Robert to throw light on the epigraphic language of euergetism: *Hellenica* 11–12 (1960): 569–570.

147. Basil, *Homily 7: On the Rich* 4:289C.

148. Gregory of Nyssa, *Against Eunomius* 1.103: *Patrologia Graeca* 45:281C, ed. Jaeger, p. 57.

149. Basil, *Ep.* 94, Deferrari, 2:148. On the date, see Van Dam, Governors of Cappadocia, pp. 53–54.

150. Gregory of Nazianze, *Oratio* 43.63, pp. 260–264; trans. Browne and Swallow, p. 416. B. Gain, *L'Église de Cappadoce d'après la correspondance de Basile de Césarée*, Orientalia Christiana Analecta 225 (Rome: Institutum Pontificium Studiorum Orientalium, 1985), p. 277, compares it to a major institution in early nineteenth-century Turin, the *Maison de la Providence Divine*. The comparison greatly exaggerates the scale of the *Basileias* and of other late Roman poorhouses compared with the substantial foundations of early modern Europe, in which the government and upper classes of entire cities were involved: see S. Cavallo, *Charity and Power in Early Modern Italy: Benefactors and Their Motives in Turin, 1541–1789* (Cambridge, U.K.: Cambridge University Press, 1995).

152. Daley, *Building a New City*, p. 443.

153. Éphrem de Nisibe, *Memré sur Nicomédie* III, lines 217–218, ed. C. Renoux, *Patrologia Orientalis* 37 (Turnhout: Brepols, 1975), pp. 20–21; compare Basil, *Homily on Luke, "I shall destroy,"* 276C–277A.

154. N. Lenski, rev. of P. Rousseau, *Basil of Caesarea, Bryn Mawr Classical Review* 7 (1996): 438–444, at pp. 441–442, referring to Jerome, *Chronicle*, ad ann. 370. Note that the famine caused massive migration from Phrygia: Socrates, *Ecclesiastical History* 4.16.7–8, p. 245; trans. Zenos, p. 104.

155. Eraclius, successor of Augustine at Hippo, built a *memoria* of the martyr Stephen: Augustine, *Sermon* 356.7. At Ephesus, Bassianus built a *ptôcheion* with seventy beds, only to be rewarded for his pains by being nominated by his elderly and jealous superior, Memnon, to faraway Theodosiopolis (Erzerum, eastern Turkey)!: *Council of Chalcedon*, Mansi, *Sacrorum conciliorum . . . collectio*, 7:277B.

156. On Demosthenes "the cook," see Gregory of Nyssa, *Contra Eunomium* 1.139:293B, ed. Jaeger, p. 69 and s.v. Demosthenes 1, *Prosopography of the Later Roman Empire 1*, ed. A. H. M. Jones, J. R. Martindale, and J. Morris (Cambridge, U.K.: Cambridge University Press, 1971), p. 249.

157. Theodoret, *Ecclesiastical History* 4.19.13, ed. L. Parmentier and G. C. Hansen, Die griechischen christlichen Schriftsteller n.s. 5 (Berlin: Akademie-Verlag, 1998), p. 245; trans. B. Jackson, *Library of the Nicene and Post-Nicene Fathers* (Oxford: James Parker, 1892), p. 120. The reader should note that the overall nature of Basil's relations with Valens (which were marked by collaboration rather than by confrontation at this period) is proven, independent of my present chronological arguments: see Brennecke, *Geschichte der Homöer*, pp. 212–228.

158. N. Garsoian, "Nersês le Grand, Basile de Césarée et Eustathe de Sébaste," *Revue des études arméniennes* n.s. 17 (1983): 145–169; now in *Armenia between Byzantium and the Sasanians* (London: Variorum, 1985).

159. P'awstos Buzand, *Buzandaran Patmut'iwnk' (Histories)* 4.4, ed. K. Patkanean (St. Petersburg, 1883; repr. Delmar, N.Y.: Caravan Books, 1984), p. 65; trans. N. Garsoian, *The Epic Histories Attributed to P'awstos Buzand* (Cambridge, Mass.: Harvard University Press, 1989), p. 113.

160. On the background of P'awstos, see Garsoian, *Epic Histories*. On the Armenian notion of an "order of the kingdom," maintained by good kings and *katholikoi* and turned upside down by bad kings, see N. Garsoian, "The Two Voices of Armenian Historiography: The Iranian Index," *Studia Iranica* 25 (1996): 7–43; now in *Church and Culture in Early Medieval Armenia* (Aldershot: Variorum, 1999) and J. Russell, *Zoroastrianism in Armenia* (Cambridge, Mass.: Harvard University Press, 1987), pp. 126–130; see also A. and J.-P. Mahé, *Histoire de l'Arménie de Moïse de Khoréne* (Paris: Gallimard, 1993), p. 57. It may even be possible to detect, in P'awstos' account of Nersês, a trace of a highly specific form of poor relief, the provision of linen burial shrouds: see *Epic Histories* 4.4, Garsoian, p. 109, where *patans* (dismissed by Garsoian, p. 272 n.22, as a misreading, and translated "shelters") could, indeed, mean "shrouds." See *Apophthegmata Patrum*, Ammonas 8: *Patrologia Graeca* 65:121BC, where linen shrouds are provided by a monk as an act of charity to a dying woman.

161. Movsês Khorenac'i, *Antiquities* 3.27, ed. and trans. Le Vaillant de

Florival, *Histoire d'Arménie de Moise de Khoren* (Venice: Typographie arménienne de Saint-Lazaire, 1836), p. 60; trans. R. W. Thomson, *History of the Armenians* (Cambridge, Mass.: Harvard University Press, 1978), p. 282. See N. Pigulevskaia, *Goroda Irana v rannem srednovekovi* (Moscow: Nauk, 1956), pp. 268–272; trans. *Les villes de l'État iranien aux époques parthe et sasanide* (Paris: Mouton, 1963), pp. 187–189.

162. P'awstos Buzand, *Histories* 4.4, p. 58; trans. Garsoian, p. 109. See N. Garsoian, "Sur le titre de *Protecteur des pauvres*," *Revue des études arméniennes* n.s. 15 (1981): 21–32, at p. 26.

163. P'awstos Buzand, *Histories* 4.4, p. 65; trans. Garsoian, p. 113.

164. Movsês Khorenac'i, *Antiquities* 3.20, pp. 42–43; trans. Thomson, p. 274.

165. A. E. Redgate, *The Armenians* (Oxford: Blackwell, 1998), pp. 116–122.

166. In this, Garsoian, "Nersês le Grand," pp. 165–166, follows the suggestions of Dagron, "Les moines et la ville," pp. 246–253.

167. On the role of royal estates in the endowments of Nersês, see esp. P'awstos, *Epic Histories* 4.14 and 5.31, pp. 97 and 194; trans. Garsoian, pp. 139–140 and 212–213. On the tax-exemption granted to King Arshak (Arsaces) by Constantius II for his own estates, equated, in this privilege, to estates of the church, see *Cod. Theod.* 11.1.1 (360).

Chapter 2. *"Governor of the Poor"*

1. W. E. Crum, *Der Papyruscodex saec. vi–vii der Phillippsbibliothek in Cheltenham*, Schriften der Wissenschaftlichen Gesellschaft in Strassburg 18 (Strassburg: K. J. Trübner, 1915), pp. 9.15 (Coptic) and 61 (trans.). See L. Cracco-Ruggini, "Vescovi e miracoli," *Vescovi e pastori in epoca Teodosiana*, Studia Ephemeredis Augustinianum 58 (Rome: Institutum Pontificium Augustinianum, 1997), pp. 16–35.

2. Gregory of Tours, *Histories* 8.12, trans. L. Thorpe, *The History of the Franks* (London: Penguin, 1974), p. 443.

3. Ferrandus, *Life of Fulgentius* 12.25: *Patrologia Latina* 65:130A.

4. G. Himmelfarb, *The Idea of Poverty. England in the Early Industrial Age* (New York: Vintage, 1983), p. 523.

5. Petrus Chrysologus, *Sermon* 14.2.19, ed. A. Olivár, *Corpus Christianorum* 24 (Turnhout: Brepols, 1975), p. 88.

6. C. Pietri, "Les pauvres et la pauvreté dans l'Italie de l'empire chrétien (ive siècle)," *Miscellanea Historiae Ecclesiasticae* 6, Bibliothèque de la Revue d'Histoire Ecclésiastique 67 (Brussels: Nauwelaerts, 1983), pp. 267–300, at pp. 277–279; now in *Christiana Respublica: Éléments d'une enquête sur le christianisme antique*, Collection de l'école française de Rome 234 (Rome: Palais Farnèse, 1998), 2:835–868, at pp. 845–847.

7. G. Himmelfarb, The Culture of Poverty, *The Victorian City*. ed. H. J. Dyers and M. Wolff (London: Routledge and Kegan Paul, 1973), 2:726.

8. The classic (but by no means the only) statement of this view is

G. E. M. de Ste Croix, *The Class Struggle in the Ancient Greek World* (London: Duckworth, 1981), pp. 453–503: see B. Shaw, "Anatomy of the Vampire Bat," *Economy and Society* 13 (1984): 208–249.

9. M. M. Fox, *The Life and Times of Saint Basil the Great as Revealed in His Works* (Washington, D.C.: Catholic University of America, 1939), p. 31. For a characteristic use of the sermons of the Cappadocian Fathers to support this view, see P. Gruszka, "Die Stellungnahme der Kirchenväter Kappadoziens zu der Gier um Gold, Silber und andere Luxuswaren im täglichen Leben der Oberschichten des 4. Jhts.," *Klio* 63 (1981): 661–668. R. Teja, *Organización económica y social de Capadocia en el siglo iv. según los padres capadocios,* Acta Salmanticensia: Filosofía y letras 78 (Salamanca: Universidad de Salamanca, 1974), is more differentiated, but still remains dependent on the perspective of the Christian sources.

10. A. Wallace-Hadrill, "The Social Spread of Roman Luxury: Sampling Pompeii and Herculanum," *Papers of the British School of Rome* 58 (1990): 145–192, at p. 147.

11. A. S. Esmonde-Cleary, *The Ending of Roman Britain* (London: Batsford, 1989), p. 116.

12. P. Garnsey and C. Humfress, *The Evolution of the Late Antique World* (Cambridge: Orchard Academic, 2000), pp. 81–93, cited at p. 82. See also P. Brown, "The Study of Elites in Late Antiquity," *Arethusa* 33 (2000): 321–346.

13. See esp. C. R. Whittaker and P. Garnsey, "Rural Life in the Later Roman Empire," *Cambridge Ancient History 13: The Late Empire* A.D. *337–425,* ed. Averil Cameron and P. Garnsey (Cambridge, U.K.: Cambridge University Press, 1998), pp. 277–311; P.-L. Gatier, "Villages du Proche Orient protobyzantine (4ème-7ème s.). Étude régionale," *The Byzantine and Early Islamic Near East 2: Land Use and Settlement Patterns,* ed. G. R. D. King and Averil Cameron (Princeton, N.J.: Darwin Press, 1994), pp. 17–48; C. Foss, "Syria in Transition, A.D. 550–750: An Archaeological Approach," *Dumbarton Oaks Papers* 51 (1997): 189–269; Y. Hirschfeld, "Farms and Villages in Byzantine Palestine," *Dumbarton Oaks Papers* 51 (1997): 33–71, and "Habitat," *Late Antiquity: A Guide to the Postclassical World,* ed. G. W. Bowersock, P. Brown, and O. Grabar (Cambridge, Mass.: Harvard University at the Belknap Press, 1999), pp. 258–272; R. Bagnall, *Egypt in Late Antiquity* (Princeton, N.J.: Princeton University Press, 1993), pp. 45–147; M. Kaplan, *Les hommes et la terre à Byzance du vie au xie siècle* (Paris: Publications de la Sorbonne, 1992), pp. 89–134.

14. A. Mandouze with A. M. de la Bonnardière, *Prosopographie de l'Afrique chrétienne* (Paris: CNRS, 1982); and the late Charles Pietri and Luce Pietri, *Prosopographie de l'Italie chrétienne (313–604)* (Rome: École française de Rome, 1999). See esp. C. Pietri, "Aristocratie et société cléricale dans l'Italie chrétienne au temps d'Odoacre et de Théodoric," *Mélanges de l'école française de Rome: Antiquité* 93 (1981): 417–461, now in *Christiana Respublica,* 2:1007–1057; C. Sotinel, "Le recrutement des

évêques en Italie aux ive et ve siècles and A. Cecconi, Vescovi e maggiorenti cristiani nell'Italia centrale fra iv e v secolo," *Vescovi e pastori in epoca Teodosiana,* pp. 193–204 and 205–244, and C. Sotinel, "Le personnel épiscopal. Enquête sur la puissance de l'évêque dans la cité," *L'évêque dans la cité du ive au ve siècle. Image et autorité* , ed. C. Sotinel and E. Rebillard, Collection de l'école française de Rome 248 (Rome: École française de Rome, 1998), pp. 103–126. See now E. Rebillard, "La 'conversion' de l'empire romain selon Peter Brown," *Annales* 54 (1999): 813–823, at pp. 822–823, for the implications of this work for our interpretation of the activity of the few better-known, upper-class bishops (such as Ambrose) in the fourth and fifth centuries.

15. *Syro-Roman Law Book* 116, trans. J. Furlani, *Fontes Iuris Romani Antejustiniani,* ed. S. Riccobono (Florence: G. Barberà, 1968), 2:1, p. 794.

16. R. Kaster, *Guardians of Language: The Grammarian and Society in Late Antiquity* (Berkeley: University of California Press, 1988), p. 133. Compare Bagnall, *Egypt in Late Antiquity,* pp. 225–229.

17. K. Hopkins, "Christian Number and Its Implications," *Journal of Early Christian Studies* 6 (1998): 185–226, at pp. 210–211.

18. See esp. A. H. M. Jones, *The Later Roman Empire* (Oxford: Blackwell, 1964), 2:904–914, on the unequal distribution of wealth and of numbers of the clergy in major cities compared with other towns. E. Patlagean, *Pauvreté économique et pauvreté sociale à Byzance: 4e–7e siècles* (Paris: Mouton, 1977), pp. 156–235, remains fundamental. See also *Roma: Politica, Economia, Paesaggio Urbano. Società romana e impero tardoantico* 2, ed. A. Giardina (Bari: Laterza, 1986); and N. Purcell, "The Populace of Rome in Late Antiquity: Problems of Classification and Historical Description," *The Transfomations of Vrbs Roma in Late Antiquity,* ed. W. V. Harris, Journal of Roman Archaeology: Supplementary Series 33 (Portsmouth, R.I.: Journal of Roman Archaeology, 1999), pp. 135–161, and F. Marazzi, "Rome in Transition: Economic and Political Changes in the Fourth and Fifth Centuries," *Early Medieval Rome and the Christian West: Essays in Honour of Donald A. Cullough,* ed. J. M. H. Smith (Leiden: Brill, 2000), pp. 21–41.

19. Foss, "Syria in Transition," pp. 258–268; H. Kennedy, "From Polis to Madina: Urban Change in Late Antique and Early Islamic Syria," *Past and Present* 106 (1985): 3–27; M. Whittow, "Ruling the Late Roman and Early Byzantine City: A Continuous History," *Past and Present* 129 (1990): 3–29; *Towns in Transition: Urban Evolution in Late Antiquity and the Early Middle Ages,* ed. N. Christie and S. T. Loseby (Aldershot: Scolar Press, 1996).

20. T. Sternberg, *Orientalium More Secutus. Räume und Institutionen der Caritas des 5. bis 7. Jahrhunderts in Gallien,* Jahrbuch für Antike und Christentum: Ergänzungsband 16 (Münster in Westfalen: Aschendorff, 1991), pp. 194–286.

21. Sulpicius Severus, *Dialogues* 2.10, trans. F. R. Hoare, *The Western Fathers* (New York: Harper Row, 1965): 115.

22. Patlagean, *Pauvreté,* pp. 322–340. See also Gregory of Tours, *Life of*

the Fathers 15.1–3, trans. E. James (Liverpool University Press, 1985),
p. 104. Senoch, a hermit near Loches in the Touraine, ransomed 200 persons over a lifetime from the alms he received; Palladius, *Lausiac History*
45.3: Philoromus, a hermit in Galatia, made 250 *solidi* from his trade, as a
calligrapher, to give in alms; Eutropius, *de similitudine carnis peccati, Patrologia Latina: Supplementum* 1:555: describes a hospital founded in a
villa in northern Spain; Gregory of Nyssa, *Life of Macrina* 12 and 26, ed. P.
Maraval, *Sources chrétiennes* 178 (Paris: Le Cerf, 1971), pp. 184 and 232:
famine relief and the taking in of children at the rural monastery at An-
nesi (Kaleköy, Amasya/Amaseia, Turkey).
     23. See esp. G. Scholten, "Der Chorbischof bei Basilius," *Zeitschrft für
Kirchengeschichte* 103 (2992): 149–173.
     24. H. Kennedy, "The Last Century of Byzantine Syria: A Reinterpreta-
tion," *Byzantinische Forschungen* 19 (1985): 141–184; C. Pietri, "Chiesa e
communità locali nell'Occidente cristiano (iv-vi d.C.): l'esempio di Gal-
lia," *Le Merci, gli Insediamenti. Società romana e impero tardoantico* 3,
ed. A. Giardina (Bari: Laterza, 1986), pp. 761–795; and F. R. Trombley,
"Monastic Foundations in Sixth-Century Anatolia and Their Role in the
Social amd Economic Life of the Region," *Byzantine Saints and Monasteries,* ed. N. M. Vaporis (Brookline, Mass.: Hellenic College Press, 1985),
pp. 45–59.
     25. E. Wipszycka, "L'attività carititativa dei vescovi egiziani," *L'évêque
dans la cité,* pp. 71–80.
     26. P. Horden and N. Purcell, *The Corrupting Sea: A Study of Mediter-
ranean History* (Oxford: Blackwell, 2000), pp. 377–383.
     27. S. Keay, "Tarraco in Late Antiquity," *Towns in Transition,*
pp. 18–44, at 32.
     28. J. Patrich, "The Warehouse Complex and Governor's Palace," *Cae-
sarea Papers* 2, ed. K. G. Holum, A. Raban, and J. Patrich (Portsmouth,
R.I.: Journal of Roman Archaeology, 1999), pp. 71–107.
     29. A. Laniado, *Recherches sur les notables municipaux dans l'empire
protobyzantin* (Paris: de Boccard, forthcoming).
     30. Foss, "Syria in Transition," p. 233.
     31. See chapter 1 in this volume, pp. 27–28, and G. Dagron, *La nais-
sance d'une capitale. Constantinople et ses institutions de 330 à 451*
(Paris: Presses Universitaires de France, 1974), pp. 533–541, on the less
democratic, household-based nature of entitlement in Constantinople; see
now Garnsey and Humfress, *Evolution of the Late Antique World,*
pp. 107–111.
     32. P. Brown, *Power and Persuasion in Late Antiquity: Towards a
Christian Empire* (Madison, Wis.: University of Wisconsin Press, 1992),
pp. 25–33 and 51–54.
     33. D. Grodzynski, "Pauvres et indigents, vils et plebéiens," *Studia et
Documenta Historiae et Juris* 53 (1987): 140–218; and Garnsey and Humfress, *Evolution of the Late Antique World,* pp. 86–93.
     34. Basil, *Regula fusius tractata* 22: *Patrologia Graeca* 31:980C.
     35. On the *corpora,* see now L. Cracco Ruggini, s.v. Guilds, *Late An-*

tiquity, pp. 479–481; on free labor, see Purcell, "The populace of Rome in Late Antiquity," *Transformations of Vrbs Roma*, pp. 142–146 and 152–156. In general, see P. Garnsey and C. R. Whittaker, "Trade, Industry and the Urban Economy," *Cambridge Ancient History 13*, pp. 312–337.

36. C. Roueché, *Aphrodisias in Late Antiquity*, Journal of Roman Studies Monographs 5 (London: Society for the Promotion of Roman Studies, 1989), pp. 218–226; and *Performers and Partisans in Aphrodisias*, Journal of Roman Studies Monographs 6 (London: Society for the Promotion of Roman Studies, 1992), pp. 129–140.

37. A. H. M. Jones, "Church Finances in the 5th and 6th Centuries," *Journal of Theological Studies*, n.s. 11 (1960): 84–94; E. Wipszycka, *Les ressources et les activités économiques des églises en Égypte du ive au viiie siècle*, Papyrologica Bruxelliensia 10 (Brussels: Fondation Égyptologique Reine Élizabeth, 1972), pp. 34–56 and 64–92; C. Pietri, "Évergétisme et richesses ecclésiastiques dans l'Italie du ive au ve siècle," *Ktéma* 3 (1978): 317–337 in *Christiana Respublica*, 2:813–833.

38. C. Thomas, *Christianity in Roman Britain* (Berkeley: University of California Press, 1981), pp. 113–119; J. P. Caillet, *L'évergétisme monumental chrétien en Italie*, Collection de l'école française de Rome 175 (Rome: Palais Farnèse, 1993); and see, in this volume, chapter 1, n. 95, p. 121.

39. F. Lifshitz, *Donateurs et fondateurs dans les synagogues juives*, Cahiers de la Revue Biblique 7 (Paris: J. Gabalda, 1967); and now L. Roth-Gerson, *The Greek Inscriptions from the Synagogues in Eretz-Israel* (in Hebrew) (Jerusalem: Magnes Press, 1987), and J. Naveh, *On Stone and Mosaic: Aramaic and Hebrew Inscriptions in the Time of the Second Temple, Midrash and Talmud* (in Hebrew) (Jerusalem: Magnes Press, 1992).

40. *Life of Saint Melania* 21, ed. D. Gorce, *Vie de sainte Mélanie*, Sources chrétiennes 90 (Paris: Le Cerf, 1962), p. 172; trans. E. Clark, *Life of Saint Melania the Younger* (New York: Edwin Mellen Press, 1984), p. 44.

41. Augustine, *Letter* 126.7: see A. Cecconi, "Un evergete mancato: Piniano ad Ippona," *Athenaeum* n.s. 60 (1988): 371–389.

42. TB: *Baba Bathra* 9a, trans. I. Epstein, *The Babylonian Talmud* (London: Soncino, 1935), 11:42.

43. *Didache* 1, trans. J. B. Lightfoot, *The Apostolic Fathers* (Grand Rapids, Mich.: Baker Book House, 1956), p. 123.

44. Augustine, *Enarratio in Psalm 102* 12.

45. P. Veyne, *Le pain et le cirque* (Paris: Le Seuil, 1976), p. 286; trans. *Bread and Circuses* (London: Allen Lane Penguin, 1990), p. 146.

46. Augustine, *Letter* 22*.2, ed. and trans. *Oeuvres de Saint Augustin 46B: Lettres 1*–29**, Bibliothèque augustinienne (Paris: Études augustiniennes, 1987), p. 348; trans. R. Eno, *Letters of Saint Augustine VI (1*–29*)*, Fathers of the Church (Washington, D.C.: Catholic University Press, 1989), p. 157. See F. Jacques, "Le défenseur de la cité d'après la Lettre 22* de Saint Augustin," *Revue des études augustiniennes* 32 (1986): 56–73.

47. Basil, *Letter* 110, ed. R. J. Deferrari, *Saint Basil. The Letters*, Loeb Classical Library (Cambridge, Mass.: Harvard University Press, 1962), 2:210–212.

48. L. Cracco Ruggini, "Le associazioni professionali nel mondo romano-bizantino," *Settimane di Studio sull'Alto Medio Evo* 18 (Spoleto: Centro di Studi sull'Alto Medio Evo, 1971), pp. 59–193, at 171.

49. Gregory of Nazianze, *Oration* 43.57., trans. C. G. Browne and J. E. Swallow, *Library of the Nicene and Post-Nicene Fathers* (Grand Rapids, Mich.: Eerdmans, 1974), 7:413.

50. *Pap. London* 1915, ed. H. I. Bell, *Jews and Christians in Egypt* (London: Egypt Exploration Fund, 1924), pp. 72–76.

51. Acts 6:1, 9:39; I Tim. 5:16; James 1:27.

52. J. U. Krause, *Witwen und Waisen im römischen Reich*, vols. 1 and 2 (Heidelberg: F. Steiner, 1994 and 1995), with *Witwen und Waisen im frühen Christentum* (Heidelberg: F. Steiner, 1995) are comprehensive studies; see the same author's "La prise en charge de veuves par l'Église dans l'Antiquité tardive," *La fin de la cité antique et le début de la cité médiévale*, ed. C. Lepelley (Bari: Edipuglia, 1996), pp. 115–126. But see the criticisms of G. Schöllgen in *Zeitschrift für antikes Christentum* 1 (1997): 137–140—not all the widows who were supported by the church belonged to the more restricted "order of widows." See now also T. A. J. McGinn, "Widows, Orphans and Social History," *Journal of Roman Archaeology* 12 (1999): 617–632.

53. J. Henderson, *Piety and Charity in Late Medieval Florence* (Cambridge, U.K.: Cambridge University Press, 1994), p. 266.

54. See esp. now G. Schöllgen, *Die Anfänge der Professionalisierung des Klerus und das kirchliche Amt in der Syrischen Didaskalie*, Jahrbuch für Antike und Christentum, Ergänzungsband 26 (Münster: Aschendorff, 1998), pp. 151–171, and J. Bremmer, "Pauper or Patroness? The Widow in the Early Church," *Between Poverty and the Pyre, Moments in the History of Widowhood*, eds. J. Bremmer and L. van den Bosch (London: Routledge, 1995), pp. 31–57.

55. Palladius, *Dialogus de vita Johannis Chrysostomi* 5: *Patrologia Graeca* 47:20. For enrollment in the "order of widows" as a bribe, see Theophilus of Alexandria, *Letter to the Bishops of Palestine*, in Jerome, *Letter* 92.1: *Patrologia Latina* 22:766.

56. E.g. Basil, *Letters* 84 and 108, ed. Deferrari, Loeb Classical Library, 2:104 and 207. B. Gain, *L'Église de Cappadoce d'après la correspondance de Basile de Césarée*, Orientalia Christiana Analecta 225 (Rome: Institutum Pontificium Studiorum Orientalium, 1985), p. 273, finds the absence of reference to the poor in Basil's correspondence "curious." In fact, the choice to preserve these letters shows the need of future readers for models of appeals to officials for widows, as a privileged and influential group among the "poor."

57. Veyne, *Le pain et le cirque*, p. 65; trans. *Bread and Circuses*, p. 32.

58. G. Dagron, *Constantinople imaginaire* (Paris: Presses Universitaires de France, 1984), p. 280. I owe this suggestion and the succeeding reference to Procopius to the kindness of Dr. A. Laniado.

59. Procopius, *The Secret History* 29.5, ed. H. B. Dewing, *Procopius*, Loeb Classical Library (Cambridge, Mass.: Harvard University Press, 1954), 6:342.

60. Gregory the Great, *Letter* 1.44, ed. D. Norberg, *Corpus Christianorum* 140 (Turnhout: Brepols, 1972), p. 58. See, in general, R. A. Markus, *Gregory the Great and his World* (Cambridge, U.K.: Cambridge University Press, 1997), pp. 120–121.

61. Gregory the Great, *Letter* 1.39, p. 44.

62. Gregory the Great, *Letter* 7.23, p. 476.

63. John the Deacon, *Life of Gregory* 2.30: *Patrologia Latina* 75:98A.

64. John the Deacon, *Life of Gregory* 2.28:97C.

65. E.g. *Talmud Yerushalmi* Pe'ah 8 and 9, trans. M. Schwab, *Le Talmud de Jérusalem* (Paris: Maisonneuve, 1972), 1:114–117. For a similar Christian anecdote, see F. Nau, "Histoires de solitaires d'Égypte, no. 287," *Revue de l'Orient chrétien* 13 (1908): 375.

66. Pelagius, *Letter* 14: *Patrologia Latina* 69:408A.

67. P. Garnsey, *Ideas of Slavery from Aristotle to Augustine* (Cambridge, U.K.: Cambridge University Press, 1996), pp. 189–235; and Garnsey and Humfress, *Evolution of the Late Antique World*, pp. 204–207.

68. See R. MacMullen, "Late Roman Slavery," *Historia* 36 (1987): 359–382, now in *Changes in the Roman Empire. Essays in the Ordinary* (Princeton, N.J.: Princeton University Press, 1990), pp. 236–248, contested by R. Samson, "Rural Slavery, Inscriptions, Archaeology and Marx," *Historia* 38 (1989): 99–110.

69. P. Bonnassie, *From Slavery to Feudalism in South-west Europe* (Cambridge, U.K.: Cambridge University Press, 1991), pp. 1–103; and R. Samson, "Slavery, the Roman Legacy," *Fifth Century Gaul: A Crisis of Identity?* ed. J, Drinkwater and H. Elton (Cambridge, U.K.: Cambridge University Press, 1992), pp. 218–227. See now H. Greiser, *Sklaverei in spätantiken und frühmittelalterlichen Gallien (5.–7. Jht.)* (Stuttgart: F. Steiner, 1997).

70. O. Hufton, *The Poor in Eighteenth Century France, 1750–1789* (Oxford, U.K.: Oxford University Press, 1974), pp. 11–12, 107–117, and 329.

71. W. V. Harris, "Demography, Geography and the Supply of Slaves," *Journal of Roman Studies* 89 (1999): 62–74, at pp. 73–74.

72. Augustine, *Sermon Mayence* 12/*Sermon Dolbeau* 5.12.258, ed. F. Dolbeau, *Revue des études augustiniennes* 39 (1993): 82; now in F. Dolbeau, *Vingt-Six Sermons au Peuple d'Afrique* (Paris: Institut d'Études Augustiniennes, 1996), p. 444, trans. E. Hill, *Sermons III/11: Newly Discovered Sermons*, The Works of Saint Augustine: A Translation for the 21st Century (Hyde Park, N.Y.: New City Press, 1997), pp. 110–111.

73. H. Langenfeld, *Christianisierungspolitik und Sklavengesetzgebung der römischen Kaiser von Konstantin bis Theodosius II*, Antiquitas 1:26 (Bonn: Habelt, 1977).

74. M. Ducloux, *Ad Ecclesiam confugere. Naissance du droit d'asile dans les églises* (Paris: de Boccard, 1994). On the admission of slaves to monasteries, see, e.g., Basil, *Regula fusius tractata* 11: *Patrologia Graeca* 31:948AC.

75. J. R. Russell-Wood, *Fidalgos and Philanthropists. The Santa Casa da Misericórdia of Bahia, 1550–1755* (London: MacMillan, 1968); and I. dos Guimarâes Sá, *Quando o rico se faz pobre. Misericórdias, caridade e*

poder no império português, 1500–1800 (Lisbon: Comissâo nacional para as Comemoraçôes dos Descobrimentos, 1977).

76. C. Roueché, "The Ages of Man," *Ktéma* 18 (1993): 159–169; and T. Parker, "Out of Sight, Out of Mind: Elderly Members of the Roman Family," *The Roman Family in Italy: Status, Sentiment, Space,* ed. B. Rawson and P. Weaver (Canberra: Humanities Research Center, and Oxford: Clarendon Press, 1997), pp. 123–148.

77. *Pap. London* 1915, ed. Bell, *Jews and Christians,* pp. 73 and 75.

78. *Pap. Oxy.* 1205, *Oxyrhynchus Papyri* 9, ed. A. S. Hunt (London: Egypt Exploration Fund, 1912), pp. 239–242.

79. W. Klingshirn, "Charity and Power: The Ransoming of Captives in Sub-Roman Gaul," *Journal of Roman Studies* 75 (1985): 95–102; E. A. Thompson, *Who was Saint Patrick?* (Woodbridge, Surrey: Boydell Press, 1985), pp. 95–102; T. Sternberg, "Aurum Utile. Zu einem Topos vom Vorrang der Caritas über Kirchenschätze seit Ambrosius," *Jahrbuch für Antike und Christentum* 39 (1996): 128–148.

80. Augustine, *Letter* 10*.5, pp. 174–176; trans. Eno, pp. 78–79.

81. Augustine, *Letter* 24*, ed. pp. 382–386; trans. Eno, pp. 172–174. See esp. M. Humbert, "Enfants à louer et à vendre" and C. Lepelley, "Liberté, colonat et esclavage," *Les Lettres de Saint Augustin découvertes par Johannes Divjak* (Paris: Études augustiniennes, 1983), pp. 189–204 and 329–342.

82. Gregory the Great, *Letter* 1.73, p. 81.

83. Augustine, *Sermon Mayence 40/ Sermon Dolbeau 11,* 13.291, ed. F. Dolbeau, *Revue bénédictine* 102 (1992): 78; *Sermons au Peuple d'Afrique,* p. 65, with comment on p. 65/58; trans. Hill, p. 85.

84. Augustine, *Sermon* 41.7.

85. Augustine, *Sermon* 25.8.8.

86. T. Shanin, *The Awkward Class* (Oxford, U.K.: Oxford University Press, 1972), pp. 114–115—on the *kulaks* of pre-revolutionary Russia.

87. Augustine, *Sermon* 9.6.8.

88. Augustine, *Letter* 26*.1.13, ed. p. 390; trans. Eno, p. 179.

89. Firmicus Maternus, *Mathesis* 6.31.13; trans. J. R. Bram, *Ancient Astrology: Theory and Practice* (Park Ridge, N.J.: Noyes Press, 1975), p. 211.

90. Augustine, *Letter* 20*.2, ed. p. 294; trans. Eno, p. 134.

91. Augustine, *Letter* 20*.6, ed. p. 302; trans. Eno, p. 137.

92. Augustine, *Sermon* 356.10; see s.v. Leporius, *Prosopographie de l'Afrique chrétienne,* pp. 634–635.

93. P. Horden, Introduction, *The Locus of Care: Families, Communities, Institutions and the Provision of Welfare since Antiquity,* ed. P. Horden and R. Smith (London/New York: Routledge, 1998), p. 21.

94. John Chrysostom, *Homilies on Matthew* 66 (67).3: *Patrologia Graeca* 58:630, trans. G. Prevost, *Library of the Nicene and Post-Nicene Fathers* (Grand Rapids, Mich.: Eerdmans, 1978), 10:407 (for Antioch); Leontius, *Life of John the Almsgiver* 2, trans. E. Dawes and N. H. Baynes, *Three Byzantine Saints* (Oxford: Blackwell, 1948), p. 211 (for Alexandria);

Mark the Deacon, *Vie de Porphyre* 94, eds. H. Grégoire and M.-A. Kugener (Paris: Belles Lettres, 1930), p. 73 (for Gaza). These are the only direct statistics that we have. On the poor rolls, the *matricula*, see M. Rouche, "La matricule des pauvres," *Études sur l'histoire de la pauvreté*. Publications de la Sorbonne. Études 8 (Paris: Sorbonne, 1974), pp. 83–109, with corrections and additions in Sternberg, *Orientalium More Secutus*, pp. 105–145, and Brown, *Power and Persuasion*, p. 98, n.144. For an excellent survey, see now Garnsey and Humfress, *Evolution of the Late Antique World*, pp. 119–125.

95. John Chrysostom, *Homilies on Acts* 45.4; *Patrologia Graeca* 60:319; trans. J. Walker, *Library of the Nicene and Post-Nicene Fathers* (Grand Rapids, Mich.: Eerdmans, 1975), 11:276. See O. Plassman, *Die Almosen bei Johannes Chrysostomus* (Münster in Westfalen: Aschendorff, 1961).

96. Gregory of Tours, *Life of the Fathers* 8.9, trans. James, p. 74. See also *Council of Chalcedon: Canon* 11, J. J. Mansi, *Sacrorum Conciliorum Nova et Amplissima Collectio* (Florence, 1762), 7:364AB; and J. Flemming, *Akten der ephesinischen Synode vom Jahre 449*, Abhandlungen der königlichen Gesellschaft der Wissenschaften zu Göttingen, Philol.-Hist. Klasse 15:1 (1917): 82.17, trans. 83.25.

97. W. E. Crum, *Coptic Ostraca from the Collections of the Egypt Exploration Fund, the Cairo Museum and Others* (London: Egypt Exporation Fund, 1902), no. 17, p. 13. This ostracon is illustrated in F. D. Friedman, *Beyond the Pharaohs. Egypt and the Copts in the 2nd to 7th centuries* A.D. (Providence, R.I.: Rhode Island School of Design, 1989), no. 136, p. 223.

98. Crum, *Coptic Ostraca*, no. 75, p. 14.

99. Crum, *Coptic Ostraca*, no. 67, p. 49.

100. Crum, *Coptic Ostraca*, no. 255, p. 64.

101. Crum, *Coptic Ostraca*, no. 52, p. 47.

102. Crum, *Coptic Ostraca*, no. 51, p. 35.

103. See, in general, J. Lamoreaux, "Episcopal Courts in Late Antiquity," *Journal of Early Christian Studies* 3 (1995): 143–167; and Garnsey and Humfress, *Evolution of the Late Antique World*, pp. 72–77.

104. *Constitutio Sirmondiana* 1 (333) and *Codex Theodosianus* 1.27.1 and 2, trans. C. Pharr, *The Theodosian Code* (Princeton, N.J.: Princeton University Press, 1952), pp. 477 and 31–32, respectively. See Barnes, *Constantine and Eusebius* (Cambridge, Mass.: Harvard University Press, 1981), pp. 51 and 312. On this delicate issue, the best study remains W. Selb, "Episcopalis audientia von der Zeit Konstantins bis zu Novelle XXXV Valentinians III," *Zeitschrift der Savigny-Stiftung für Rechtsgeschichte* 84 (1967): 162–217—whose legal interpretation is to be preferred to that of Lamoreaux, "Episcopal Courts."

105. J. M. Carrié, "Les gouverneurs romains à l'époque tardive," and C. Roueché, "The functions of the governors in late antiquity: Some observations," in *Les gouverneurs de province dans l'antiquité tardive: Antiquité tardive* 6 (1998): 17–30 and 31–36, respectively, emphasize the

weight of judicial functions dealt with by governors. See now H. A. Drake, *Constantine and the Bishops* (Baltimore, Md.: Johns Hopkins University Press, 2000), pp. 322–352.

106. Julian, *Letter* 41, ed. and trans. W. C. Wright, Loeb Classical Library (Cambridge, Mass.: Harvard University Press, 1953), 3:128–134.

107. Augustine, *Enarratio in Ps.* 46 5.

108. Augustine, *Letter* 247.2.

109. Augustine, *Letter* 24*.1, p. 384; trans. Eno, p. 173.

110. Augustine, *de opere monachorum* 29.37; and Possidius, *Life of Augustine* 19, trans. Hoare, *Western Fathers*, p. 218.

111. J. C. Picard, "La fonction des salles de réception dans le groupe épiscopal de Génève," *Rivista di archeologia cristiana* 65 (1989): 87–104. I owe this reference to Dr. Barbara Polci of the University of East Anglia.

112. Sulpicius Severus, *Dialogues* 2.1: *Patrologia Latina* 20:201C, trans. Hoare, *Western Fathers*, p. 102.

113. *Life of Epiphanius of Salamis* 55: *Patrologia Graeca* 41:93A; Socrates, *Ecclesiastical History* 7.37.17, ed. G. C. Hansen, Die griechischen christlichen Schriftsteller, n.s. 1 (Berlin: Akademie-Verlag, 1995), p. 387.

114. Socrates, *Ecclesiastical History* 2.42.5, ed. Hansen, p. 179; see T. D. Barnes, "The Crimes of Basil of Ancyra," *Journal of Theological Studies* n.s. 47 (1996): 550–554, at pp. 553–554.

115. Possidius, *Life of Augustine* 19.4, trans. Hoare, *Western Fathers*, p. 218.

116. S.v. *'ebyôn*, *Theologisches Wörterbuch des Alten Testaments*, ed. G. J. Botterweck and H. Ringgren (Stuttgart: W. Kohlhammer, 1973), 1:27–43; trans. J. T. Willis, *Theological Dictionary of the Old Testament* (Grand Rapids, Mich.: Eerdmans, 1974), 1:27–41; with M. E. Polley, *Amos and the Davidic Empire* (Oxford, U.K.: Oxford University Press, 1989), pp. 112–138; and now esp. M. Weinfeld, *Social Justice in Ancient Israel and in the Ancient Near East* (Jerusalem: Magnes Press/Minneapolis: Fortress, 1995).

117. Weinfeld, *Social Justice in Ancient Israel*, pp. 46 and 182–188.

118. F. C. Fensham, "Widows, Orphans and the Poor in Ancient Near Eastern Legal and Wisdom Literature," *Journal of Near Eastern Studies* 21 (1962): 129–139.

119. S. N. Kramer, *History Begins at Sumer* (London: Thames and Hudson, 1958), pp. 77–79.

120. *Code of Hammurabi* 24.1–8, cited by Weinfeld, *Social Justice in Ancient Israel*, p. 193.

121. N. Yoffee, The Collapse of Ancient Mesopotamian Society and Civilization, *The Collapse of Ancient Societies and Civilizations*, ed. N. Yoffee and G. C. Cowgill (Tucson: Arizona University Press, 1991), pp. 44–68, at 52.

122. J. Gray, "Social Aspects of Canaanite Religion," *Vetus Testamentum: Supplement* 15 (1966): 170–192, at pp. 172–173.

123. S.v. *'ebyôn*, *Theological Dictionary of the Old Testament*, p. 30.

124. Jerome, *Commentary on Isaiah* 2.5: *Patrologia Latina* 24:75C.

125. Brown, *Power and Persuasion*, pp. 103–113. See now R. Lizzi, "I vescovi e i *potentes* della terra: Definizione e limite del ruolo episcopale nelle due *partes imperii* tra iv e v secolo d.C.," *L'Évêque et la cité*, pp. 81–104.

126. N. McLynn, *Ambrose of Milan: Church and Court in a Christian Capital* (Berkeley: University of California Press, 1994), pp. 315–330.

127. P. Delmaire and C. Lepelley, "Du nouveau sur Carthage," *Opus* 2 (1983): 473–487.

128. Augustine, *Letter* 15*.2, ed. pp. 254–266, trans. Eno, p. 115.

129. Augustine, *Letter* 20*.11, ed. p. 310; trans. Eno, p. 139.

130. Augustine, *On Lying* 13.23.

131. Augustine, *Letter* 22*.7, ed. p. 354; trans. Eno, p. 158.

132. Synesius, *Letter* 67, trans. A. Fitzgerald, *The Letters of Synesius of Cyrene* (Oxford, U.K.: Oxford University Press, 1926), p. 151.

133. Crum, *Papyruscodex*, p. 9.8 (Coptic); trans. p. 61.

134. M. Çetin Şahin, *Die Inschriften von Stratronikeia*, Inschriften griechischer Städte aus Kleinasien 22:1 (Bonn: R. Habelt, 1982), no. 1204, pp. 166–167.

135. E.g. E. Le Blant, *Inscriptions chrétiennes de la Gaule* (Paris: Imprimerie impériale, 1956), 1:48, no. 402, and 98, no. 425.

136. Gregory of Tours, *Histories* 5.42, trans. Thorpe, *History of the Franks*, pp. 306–307.

3. "Condescension"

1. A. von Harnack, *Mission und Ausbreitung des Christentums* (Leipzig: J. C. Hinrichs, 1906, 2nd ed.), 1:127–172; trans. J. Moffat, *The Mission and Expansion of Christianity in the First Three Centuries* (London: William Norgate/New York: Putnam, 1904), 1:181–249.

2. Augustine, *Confessions* 5.13.23.

3. Well described by K. Wrightson and D. Levine, *Poverty and Piety in an English Village: Terling 1525–1700* (Oxford: Clarendon Press, 1995, 2nd ed.), pp. 197–211. See also P. Slack, *Poverty and Policy in Tudor and Stuart England* (London: Longmans, 1988), pp. 37–90.

4. J. Iliffe, *The African Poor: A History* (Cambridge, U.K.: Cambridge University Press, 1987), pp. 9–29.

5. Slack, *Poverty and Policy*, pp. 113–161.

6. N. Z. Davis, "Gregory Nazianzen in the Service of Humanist Social Reform," *Renaissance Quarterly* 20 (1967): 455–464 (for Lyons); for Russia, see P. Pascal, *Avvakum et les débuts du Raskol* (Paris: Mouton, 1963), pp. 23, 39, and 47, with A. N. Robinson, *Bor'ba idei v russkoi literature xvii veka* (Moscow: Nauk, 1974), pp. 246–277. I am grateful to Dr. Olga Strahov for her help, and for having drawn to my attention the *Slovo o milosti, The Oration on Charity* of Epifanii Slavinetskii; see A. S. Eleonksaia, Sotsial'no-utopicheskii tratat xvii veka, *Germenevtika drevnerusskoi literatury* (Moscow: Nauk, 1989), 2:179–191.

7. G. Dagron, "'Ainsi rien n'échappera à la réglementation.' État, église, corporations, confréries: à propos des inhumations à Constantinople (ive–xe siècles)," *Hommes et richeses dans l'Empire byzantin 2*, ed. V. Kravari and others (Paris: P. Lethielleux, 1991), pp. 155–198. See now E. Rebillard, "Les formes de l'assistance funéraire dans l'empire romain et leur évolution dans l'antiquité tardive," *Antiquité tardive* 7 (1999): 269–282.

8. See chapter 1, pp. 28–29, in this volume.

9. A. Natali, "Église et évergétisme à Antioche à la fin du ie siècle d'après Jean Chrysostome," *Studia Patristica* 17 (Oxford: Pergamon Press, 1982), pp. 1176–1184; D. Trout, *Paulinus of Nola* (Berkeley: University of California Press, 1999), pp. 133–159.

10. H. Bolkestein, *Woltätigkeit und Armenpflege im vorchristlichen Altertum* (Utrecht: A. Oosthoek, 1939), pp. 202–212; P. Veyne, *Le pain et le cirque* (Paris: Le Seuil, 1976), pp. 44–67, trans. *Bread and Circuses* (London: Allen Lane Penguin, 1990), pp. 19–34.

11. Libanius, *Orations* 2.30 and 30.20, ed. A. F. Norman, *Libanius: Select Works*, Loeb Classical Library (Cambridge, Mass.: Harvard University Press, 1977), 2:26 and 118. See also G. W. Bowersock, "Mechanisms of Subversion in the Roman Provinces," *Opposition et résistance à l'empire d'Auguste à Trajan*, Entretiens de la Fondation Hardt 33 (Vandoeuvres: Fondation Hardt, 1987), pp. 291–320, at 304–310.

12. Jerome, *Tractatus in Psalmos* 133.2, ed. G. Morin, Corpus Christianorum 78 (Turnhout: Brepols, 1958), p. 288. The *Vision of Paul*, in its Latin version, speaks of pagans who gave alms. They are seen in Hell, "dressed in splendid robes," but their "eyes were blind," for they "did not know the Lord God": *Visio Pauli* 40, ed. C. Carozzi, *Eschatologie et au-delà: recherches sur l'Apocalypse de Paul* (Aix-en-Provence: Université de Provence, 1994), p. 240.

13. V. Neri, *I marginali nell'Occidente tardoantico* (Bari: Edipuglia, 1998), pp. 127–132; E. Patlagean, *Pauvreté économique et pauvreté sociale à Byzance: 4e–7e siècles* (Paris: Mouton, 1977), p. 386.

14. Felix, *Constitutio de ecclesia Ravennatensi: Patrologia Latina* 65:12C; Patlagean, *Pauvreté économique et pauvreté sociale à Byzance*, p. 398.

15. *Life of Theodore of Sykeon*, 78, trans. E. Dawes and N. H. Baynes, *Three Byzantine Saints* (Oxford: Blackwell, 1948), p. 141.

16. I take the expression from S. Cavallo, *Charity and Power in Early Modern Italy* (Cambridge, U.K.: Cambridge University Press, 1995), p. 257.

17. C. Kelly, "Late Roman Bureaucracy: Going Through the Files," *Literacy and Power in the Ancient World*, ed. A. K. Bowman and G. Woolf (Cambridge, U.K.: Cambridge University Press, 1996), pp. 161–176; and "Emperors, Government and Bureaucracy," *Cambridge Ancient History XIII: The Late Empire* A.D. 337–425, ed. A. Cameron and P. Garnsey (Cambridge, U.K.: Cambridge University Press, 1999), pp. 138–183.

18. P. Brown, "The World of Late Antiquity Revisited," *Symbolae Os-*

loenses 72 (1997): 5–90, at pp. 24–25; and now esp. C. Roueché, "The Functions of the Governors in Late Antiquity: Some Remarks," *Antiquité tardive* 6 (1998): 31–36.

19. *P. Cairo Isid.* 1: see R. Bagnall, *Egypt in Late Antiquity* (Princeton, N.J.: Princeton University Press, 1993), pp. 166–167 and 243. See now J. M. Carrié, "Dioclétien et la fiscalité," *Antiquité Tardive* 2 (1994): 33–64.

20. K. Hopkins, "Conquest by Book," *Literacy in the Roman World*, ed. J. H. Humphrey, Journal of Roman Archaeology Supplement 3 (Ann Arbor, Mich.: Michigan University Press, 1991), pp. 133–158.

21. Bagnall, *Egypt in Late Antiquity*, p. 166.

22. A. Kovelman, "From Logos to Mythos: Egyptian Petitions of the 5th–7th Centuries," *Bulletin of the American Society of Papyrologists* 28 (1991): 135–152, at p. 147; see now J. L. Fournet, "Notes critiques sur les pétitions du Bas-Empire," *Journal of Juristic Papyrology* 28 (1998): 7–18.

23. Nilus of Ancyra, *Letter* 1.102: *Patrologia Graeca* 79:125C.

24. R. MacMullen, *Corruption and the Decline of Rome* (New Haven, Conn.: Yale University Press, 1988).

25. See now P. Garnsey and C. R. Whittaker, "Rural Life in the Later Roman Empire," *Cambridge Ancient History XIII*, pp. 277–311, at 281–285.

26. J. Harries, *Law and Empire in Late Antiquity* (Cambridge, U.K.: Cambridge University Press, 1999), p. 97.

27. Well seen by Kelly, "Emperors, Government and Bureaucracy," pp. 155–156 and 181–182.

28. F. Millar, *The Emperor in the Roman World* (London: Duckworth, 1977), pp. 541–544.

29. D. Feissel and J. Gascou, "Documents d'archives romains inédits du Moyen-Euphrate," *Comptes Rendus de l'Académie des Inscriptions et Belles Lettres 1989*, pp. 547–548; F. Millar, *The Roman Near East 31 BC–AD 337* (Cambridge, Mass.: Harvard University Press, 1993), p. 130.

30. Justinian, *Novellae* 80.1–2 (539), ed. P. Schöll and W. Kroll (Weidmann: Zurich, 1972), pp. 391–392.

31. P. Brown, *Power and Persuasion in Late Antiquity: Towards a Christian Empire* (Madison: University of Wisconsin Press, 1992), pp. 78–79.

32. J. E. Lendon, *Empire of Honour. The Art of Government in the Roman World* (Oxford: Clarendon Press, 1997), p. 7.

33. Brown, *Power and Persuasion*, pp. 35–47.

34. R. Webb, "Imagination and the Arousal of Emotions in Greco-Roman Rhetoric," *The Passions in Roman Thought and Literature*, ed. S. M. Braund and C. Giles (Cambridge, U.K.: Cambridge University Press, 1997), pp. 112–127.

35. Brown, *Power and Persuasion*, pp. 48–61; R. Kaster, "The Shame of the Romans," *Transactions of the American Philological Society* 127 (1997): 1–19.

36. K. Holum, *King Herod's Dream: Caesarea on the Sea* (New York:

W. W. Norton, 1988), p. 170 and fig. 123; and "Inscriptions in the Imperial Revenue Office of Byzantine Caesarea Palaestina," *Journal of Roman Archaeology: Supplement* 14 (1995): 333–345.

37. Dorotheus of Gaza, *Instructions* 2.34, ed. L. Regnault and J. de Préville, *Dorothée de Gaza: Oeuvres spirituelles*, Sources chrétiennes 92 (Paris: Le Cerf, 1963), p. 198.

38. John Chrysostom, *Homily 11 on I Thess.* 30: *Patrologia Graeca* 61:466; trans. J. A. Broadus, *Library of the Nicene and Post-Nicene Fathers* (Grand Rapids, Mich.: Eerdmans, 1979), 13:373; and *Homily 1 on II Tim.: Patrologia Graeca* 62:606, trans. P. W. Schaff, ibid., p. 476.

39. Cecaumenus Catacolon, *Strategicon* 2, ed. B. Wassiliewsky and V. Jernstedt (Amsterdam: Hakkert, 1965), p. 3.

40. H. I. Marrou, "L'origine orientale des diaconies romaines," *Mélanges d'archéologie et d'histoire* 47 (1940): 95–142, at p. 113; now in *Patristique et Humanisme* (Paris: Le Seuil, 1976), pp. 81–117, at 95.

41. M. Jeremić and M. Milinković, "Die byzantinische Festung von Bregovina (Südserbien)," *Antiquité Tardive* 3 (1995): 209–225, at p. 218.

42. T. Sternberg, "Der vermeintliche Ursprung der westlichen Diakonien," *Jahrbuch für Antike und Christentum* 31 (1988): 173–209, at p. 203.

43. L. S. B. MacCoull, "SPP XV.250ab: A Monophysite Trishagion for the Nile Flood," *Journal of Theological Studies*, n.s. 40 (1989): 129–135, at p. 130.

44. *P. Oxy.* XVIII. 2193, *Oxyrhynchus Papyri XVIII*, ed. E. Lobel, C. H. Roberts, E. P. Wagner (London: Egypt Exploration Society, 1941), pp. 153–154, citing Job 30:19, Ecclesiasticus 32:17, and Psalm 19:13.

45. *Pap. Oxy.* XXVII. 2479, *Oxyrhynchus Papyri* 27, ed. E. G. Turner, J. Rea, L. Koenen, J. Fernandez Pomar (London: Egypt Exploration Society, 1962), pp. 177–180, at 178.

46. *Pap. Cairo Masp.* 1. 67020.5–6, ed. J. Maspéro, *Papyrus grecs d'époque byzantine* (Cairo: Institut français d'archéologie orientale, 1911), p. 46.

47. L. Robert, "Épigrammes du Bas-Empire," *Hellenica* 4 (1948): 99–100.

48. R. R. R. Smith, "Late Antique Portraits in a Public Context: Honorific Statuary at Aphrodisias in Caria, A.D. 300–600," *Journal of Roman Studies* 89 (1999): 155–189, at p. 186.

49. Gregory of Tours, *Life of the Fathers* 7.1 and 3, trans. E. James (Liverpool: Liverpool University Press, 1985), pp. 60 and 62.

50. R. Rémondon, "L'Église dans la société égyptienne à l'époque byzantine," *Chronique d'Égypte* 47 (1972): 254–277.

51. *Pap. Abinn.* 19, *The Abinnaeus Archive*, ed. H. I. Bell et al. (Oxford: Clarendon Press, 1962), p. 65.

52. C. Zuckerman, "The Hapless Recruit Psois and the Mighty Anchorite John," *Bulletin of the Society for American Papyrologists* 32 (1995): 183–194.

53. D. Frankfurter, "'Things Unbefitting Christians': Violence and Christianization in Fifth-Century Panopolis," *Journal of Early Christian*

Studies 8 (2000): 272–295, at p. 280. See also S. Emmel, "The Historical Circumstances of Shenute's Sermon *God Is Blessed*," *Themelia. Spätantike und koptologischen Studien Peter Grossmann zum 65. Geburtstag*, eds. M. Krause and S. Schaten (Wiesbaden: Reichert, 1998), pp. 81–95.

54. Besa, *Life of Shenoute* 76, ed. J. Leipoldt and W. E. Crum, *Corpus Scriptorum Christianorum Orientalium* 41, *Scriptores Coptici* 1 (Leipzig: O. Harassowitz, 1906), p. 38; trans. N. Bell, Cistercian Studies 73 (Kalamazoo, Mich.: Cistercian Studies, 1983), p. 64.

55. *Council of Serdica* 7, ed. E. J. Jonkers, *Acta et symbola conciliorum quae saeculo quarto habita sunt*, Textus Minores 19 (Leiden: Brill, 1974), p. 65.

56. A. van Lantschoot, "Allocution de Timothée d'Alexandrie prononcée à l'occasion de la dédicace de l'église de Pachôme à Pboou," *Le Muséon* 47 (1934): 13–56, at p. 42.

57. Cyril of Scythopolis, *Life of Sabas* 51, ed. E. Schwartz, *Kyrillos von Scythopolis*, Texte und Untersuchungen 49:2 (Leipzig: J. C. Hinrichs, 1939), p. 142.

58. K. Barth, *Church Dogmatics, Volume IV, part 2: The Doctrine of Reconciliation*, trans. G. W. Bromley (Edinburgh: T. and T. Clark, 1958), p. 167.

59. *Midrash Rabbah: Leviticus* 34.9, trans. S. M. Lehrman (New York: Soncino Press, 1983), pp. 435–436.

60. *Babylonian Talmud: Baba Bathra* 10a, trans. I. Epstein (London: Soncino, 1935), p. 47.

61. Origen, *Contra Celsum* 1.28, trans. H. E. Chadwick (Cambridge, U.K.: Cambridge University Press, 1965), p. 28.

62. Julian, *Against the Galilaeans* 191D and 206D, ed. W. C. Wright, *The Works of the Emperor Julian*, Loeb Classical Library (London: Heinemann/New York: Putnam, 1953), 3:376.

63. Theodotus of Ancyra, *On the Nativity*, cited at the Council of Ephesus: *Collectio Vaticana* 73.8, ed. E. Schwartz, *Acta Conciliorum Oecumenicorum* [henceforth *ACO*] 1.2 (Berlin: W. de Gruyter, 1927), pp. 85.3–86.7; and J. D. Mansi, *Sacrorum conciliorum nova et amplissima collectio* [henceforth *Collectio*] (Florence, 1762), 5:196BD.

64. Augustine, *Sermon Mayence 61/Dolbeau 61*, 24.495, ed. F. Dolbeau, *Revue des études augustiniennes* 37 (1991): 75, now in F. Dolbeau, *Vingt-Six Sermons au Peuple d'Afrique* (Paris: Institut d'Études augustiniennes, 1996), p. 265, trans. E. Hill, *The Works of Saint Augustine: A Translation for the 21st Century: Sermons III/11* (Hyde Park, N.Y.: New City Press, 1997), p. 381.

65. R. Brändle, *Matth. 25, 31–46 im Werk des Johannes Chrysostomos*, Beiträge zur Geschichte der biblischen Exegese 27 (Tübingen: J. C. B. Mohr, 1979), pp. 311–314.

66. Gregory of Nyssa, *On the Beatitudes: Patrologia Graeca* 44:1201B, cited as an authority at the Council of Ephesus: *Gesta Ephesina* 54.xvi, ed. Schwartz, *ACO* 1.2, p. 44.17.

67. See esp. P. Angstenberger, *Der reiche und der arme Christus. Rezeptionsgeschichte von 2 Kor.8,9 zwischen dem zweiten und dem sechsten Jahrhundert*, Hereditas: Studien zur Alten Kirchengeschichte 12 (Bonn: Börengasser, 1997).

68. *Ptocheia or Odysseus in Disguise (P. Köln inv.VI.245)*, ed. M. G. Parca, American Studies in Papyrology 31 (Atlanta, Ga.: Scholar's Press, 1991).

69. Inscription of Kefr-Haouar, ed. *Bulletin de Correspondance Hellénique* 21 (1897): 60–61. For a similar phenomenon of priests who received alms out of fear of their curse, see J. D. Y. Peel, "Poverty and Sacrifice in 19th-Century Yorubaland," *Journal of African History* 31 (1990): 465–484.

70. John Chrysostom, *Homily 11 on I Thess. 5* 3: *Patrologia Graeca* 62:464.

71. Brändle, *Matth. 25, 31–46 im Werk des Johannes Chrysostomos*, pp. 338–341.

72. John Chrysostom, *Hom. 15 in Rom. 6: Patrologia Graeca* 60:547, trans. J. B. Morris and W. H. Simcox, *Library of the Nicene and Post-Nicene Fathers* (Grand Rapids, Mich.: Eerdmans, 1975), 11:458.

73. John Chrysostom, *Baptismal Catecheses* 1.45 and 4.17, ed. A. Wenger, *Jean Chrysostome: Huit Catéchèses Baptismales*, Sources chrétiennes 50 bis (Paris: Le Cerf, 1970), pp. 131 and 191.

74. F. Van de Paverd, *Zur Geschichte der Messliturgie in Antiochien und Konstantinopel gegen Ende des vierten Jahrhunderts. Analyse der Quellen bei Johannes Chrysostomus*, Orientalia Christiana Analecta 187 (Rome: Institutum Pontificium Studiorum Orientalium, 1970), p. 223.

75. G. G. Blum, *Rabbula von Edessa, Corpus Scriptorum Christianorum Orientalium* 300, Subsidia 34 (Louvain: Corpus Scriptorum Christianorum Orientalium, 1969), pp. 68–69.

76. *Les Sentences des Pères du Désert. Nouveau recueil* 442, trans. L. Regnault (Sablé-sur-Sarthe: Abbaye de Solesmes, 1970), p. 64.

77. For a brief survey of exemplary clarity of the issues dividing the parties, see H. E. Chadwick, Preface, *Actes du Concile de Chalcédoine: Sessions III-VI*, ed. A. J. Festugière, Cahiers d'Orientalisme 4 (Geneva: P. Cramer, 1983), pp. 7–16; with J. A. McGuckin, *St. Cyril of Alexandria: The Christological Controversy, Its History, Theology and Texts* (Leiden: Brill, 1994); and J. M. Hallman, "The Seed of Fire: Divine Suffering in the Christology of Cyril of Alexandria and Nestorius of Constantinople," *Journal of Early Christian Studies* 5 (1997): 369–391. See now N. Russell, *Cyril of Alexandria* (London: Routledge, 2000).

78. Vegetius, *Epitome of Military Science* 2.5, trans. N. P. Milner (Liverpool: Liverpool University Press, 1993), p. 35. See, in general, C. Kelly, "Emperors, Government and Bureaucracy," pp. 139–144; and now "Empire Building," *Late Antiquity: A Guide to the Postclassical World*, ed. G. W. Bowersock, P. Brown, and O. Grabar (Cambridge, Mass.: Harvard University at the Belknap Press, 1999), pp. 170–195.

79. Ambrose, *Expositio in Psalm 118* 8.19.

80. John Matthews, *The Roman Empire of Ammianus Marcellinus* (London: Duckworth, 1989), pp. 244–249.

81. J. Engemann, "The Christianization of Late Antique Art," *The 17th International Congress of Byzantine Studies: Major Papers* (New Rochelle, N.Y.: A. Caratzas, 1986), pp. 83–105.

82. Theodoret, *Ecclesiastical History* 5.19.2–3, ed. J. Parmentier and G. C. Hansen, Die griechischen christlichen Schriftsteller, n.s. 5 (Berlin: Akademie Verlag, 1998), p. 314; trans. B. Jackson, *Library of Nicene and Post-Nicene Fathers* 3 (Oxford: Parker, 1892), p. 145.

83. Gregory of Nyssa, *Funerary Laudation for Flacilla,* ed. A. Spira, *Gregorii Nysseni Opera 9: Sermones 1* (Leiden: Brill, 1960), pp. 487–488.

84. K. Holum, *Theodosian Empresses. Women and Imperial Dominion in Late Antiquity* (Berkeley: University of California Press, 1982), p. 26.

85. Sozomen, *Ecclesiastical History* 9.1.6–8, ed. J. Bidez and G. C. Hansen, Die griechischen christlichen Schriftsteller 50 (Berlin: Akademie Verlag, 1960), p. 391; trans. C. D. Hartranft, *Library of the Nicene and Post-Nicene Fathers* 11 (Grand Rapids, Mich.: Eerdmans, 1979), p. 419.

86. Socrates, *Ecclesiastical History* 7.23.11–12, ed. G. C. Hansen, Die griechischen christlichen Schriftsteller n.s. 1 (Berlin: Akademie Verlag, 1995), p. 372; trans. A. C. Zenos, *Nicene and Post-Nicene Fathers* 11, p. 166.

87. Socrates, *Ecclesiastical History* 7.22.17, p. 370; trans. Zenos, p. 165.

88. Edict on Sanctuary preserved in the documents of the Council of Ephesus: *Collectio Vaticana* 137.3, ed. Schwartz, *ACO* 1.4, p. 64.8; trans. P. R. Coleman Norton, *Roman State and Christian Church* (London: SPCK, 1966), 2:657. I owe this reference, and this view of Theodosius II, to the innovative study of Neil McLynn, "Theodosius II: The Emperor Goes to Church" (forthcoming).

89. John Rufus, *Plerophoriae* 99: *Patrologia Orientalis* 8:173. Similar stories circulated about other rulers at this time: see P'awstos Buzand, *The Epic Histories* 3.10, trans. N. Garsoian (Cambridge, Mass.: Harvard University Press, 1989), p. 79 (a practice ascribed to Constantine); *Life of Peter the Iberian,* ed. T. Raabe, *Petrus der Iberer* (Leipzig: J. C. Hinrichs, 1895), p. 17 [Syriac, p. 7] (a pious queen of Georgia); E. Diehl, *Inscriptiones christianae latinae veteres,* no. 46.7 (Zurich: Weidmann, 1970), 1:13 (Queen Caretene of Burgundy).

90. The best study of this issue is Roberta Chesnut, "The Two Prosopa in Nestorius' *Bazaar of Heracleides,*" *Journal of Theological Studies* n.s. 29 (1978): 392–409, esp. at pp. 407–409.

91. J. McGuckin, "Nestorius and the Political Factions of Fifth-Century Constantinople: Factors in His Personal Downfall," *Bulletin of the John Rylands Library* 78 (1996): 7–21.

92. Nestorius, *The Bazaar of Heracleides,* trans. G. R. Driver and L. Hodgson (Oxford: Clarendon Press, 1925), p. 21.

93. Cyril, *Letter to the Empresses* 8, *Collectio Vaticana* 150.8, ed. Schwartz, *ACO* 1.5, p. 65.5; Mansi, *Collectio* 4:688E.

94. A. Wenger, "Notes inédites sur les empereurs Théodose I, Arcadius, Théodose II et Léon I," *Revue des études byzantines* 10 (1952): 47–59, at pp. 51–54—a sermon ascribed to John Chrysostom.

95. For a nuanced exposition of the thought of Nestorius, see McGuckin, *St. Cyril of Alexandria*, pp. 126–174.

96. The best study remains that of N. H. Baynes, "Alexandria and Constantinople: A Study in Ecclesiastical Diplomacy," *Journal of Egyptian Archaeology* 12 (1926): 145–156; now in *Byzantine Studies and Other Essays* (London: London University Athlone Press, 1955), pp. 97–115, esp. 107–113.

97. D. S. Wallace-Hadrill, *Christian Antioch* (Cambridge, U.K.: Cambridge University Press, 1982), p. 129.

98. Brown, *Power and Persuasion*, pp. 15–17.

99. See esp. L. R. Wickham, *Cyril of Alexandria: Select Letters* (Oxford: Clarendon Press, 1983), pp. xix–xliii. The religious thought of Cyril is best seen in details, such as his distinctive attitude to the Eucharist, on which see H. E. Chadwick, "Eucharist and Christology in the Nestorian Controversy," *Journal of Theological Studies* n.s. 2 (1951): 145–164, and E. Gebremedhin, *Life Giving Blessing: An Enquiry into the Eucharistic Thought of Cyril of Alexandria* (Uppsala: Borgström, 1977). In general, see McGuckin, *St. Cyril of Alexandria*, pp. 175–226. See now Russell, *Cyril of Alexandria*, pp. 31–56.

100. Cyril of Alexandria, *Homily 4* (preached at Ephesus): *Collectio Vaticana* 8, ed. Schwartz, *ACO* 1.2, p. 103.31; Mansi, *Collectio* 4:1256 AC. See now S. Wessel, "Nestorius, Mary and Controversy in Cyril of Alexandria *Homily IV*," *Annnuarium Historiae Conciliorum* 31 (1999): 1–49, at pp. 44–47, with translation.

101. Synesius of Cyrene, *de regno* 10 (14), ed. N. Terzaghi, *Synesii Cyrenensis Hymni et Opuscula* (Rome: Regia Officina Tipografica, 1944), pp. 29–30; trans. A. Fitzgerald, *Essays and Hymns of Synesius* (Oxford, U.K.: Oxford University Press, 1930), p. 124.

102. Cyril of Alexandria, *Letter 3 to Nestorius* 5, *Collectio Vaticana* 6.5, ed. Schwartz, *ACO* 1.1, p. 36.19; Mansi, *Collectio* 4: 1073DE, trans. H. R. Percival, *The Seven Ecumenical Councils of the Undivided Church*, Library of the Nicene and Post-Nicene Fathers 4 (Grand Rapids, Mich.: Eerdmans, 1972), p. 203; and McGuckin, *St. Cyril of Alexandria*, p. 268.

103. Cyril, *Letter 2 to Nestorius*, *Collectio Vaticana* 4.3, ed. Schwartz, *ACO* 1.1, p. 27.13; Mansi, *Collectio* 4:889A, trans. Wickham, *Cyril of Alexandria: Select Letters*, p. 7, and McGuckin, *St. Cyril of Alexandria*, p. 264.

104. Chadwick, "Eucharist and Christology in the Nestorian Controversy," p. 155 n.1.

105. See esp. H. E. Chadwick, review of L. Abramowski, *Untersuchungen zum Liber Heraclidis des Nestorius*, in *Journal of Theological Studies* n.s. 16 (1975): 214–218, at p. 218; and S. Ashbrook Harvey, "The Sense of a Stylite," *Vigiliae Christianae* 42 (1982): 376–394, at pp. 378–381.

106. See K. R. Bradley, "Sexual Reproduction in Nursing Contracts for Roman Egypt," *Klio* 62 (1980): 321–325, at p. 322 n.5.

107. The physiology of breast-feeding is explained at length by Clement of Alexandria, *Paidogogus* 1.6, trans. A. Clark Coxe, *Library of the Ante-Nicene Fathers* 2 (Grand Rapids, Mich.: Eerdmans, 1977), p. 219.

108. J. Horn, *Untersuchungen zur Frömmigkeit und Literatur des christlichen Ägyptens: Das Martyrium des Viktor, Sohn des Romanos,* Diss. Göttingen, 1988, at pp. 214, 217, and 232. See also *Martyrdom of Saint Febronia* 29, trans. S. P. Brock and S. Ashbrook Harvey, *Holy Women of the Syrian Orient* (Berkeley: University of California Press, 1987), p. 169: "Are you not mindful of the day when you were born . . . how you too received nourishment at breasts flowing with milk?"

109. On the Sinai icon, see K. Weitzmann, *The Monastery of St. Catherine at Mount Sinai: The Icons 1* (Princeton, N.J.: Princeton University Press, 1976), B3, at pp. 18–21, with plates IV and V; now also in R. Cormack, *Painting the Soul* (London: Reaktion 1997), fig. 50 at p. 137. On the Cleveland tapestry, see D. G. Shepherd, "An Icon of the Virgin: A Sixth-Century Tapestry Panel from Egypt," *Bulletin of the Cleveland Museum of Art* 59 (1969): 90–120.

110. Chadwick, "Eucharist and Christology in the Nestorian Controversy," pp. 163–164. On the Pantheon icon, see H. Belting, *Bild und Kult. Eine Geschichte des Bildes vor dem Zeitalter der Kunst* (Munich: C. H. Beck, 1990), p. 141; trans. E. Jephcott, *Likeness and Presence* (Chicago: University of Chicago Press, 1994), p. 124.

111. See, in general, W. H. C. Frend, *The Rise of the Monophysite Movement* (Cambridge, U.K.: Cambridge University Press, 1972), pp. 104–295; and now s.v. Monophysites, *Late Antiquity: A Guide,* pp. 586–588.

112. A. H. M. Jones, "Were the Ancient Heresies National or Social Movements in Disguise?" *Journal of Theological Studies* n.s. 10 (1959): 280–298; and E. Wipszycka, "Le nationalisme a-t-il existé dans l'Égypte byzantine?" *Journal of Juristic Papyrology* 22 (1992): 83–128, now in *Études sur le christianisme dans l'Égypte de l'antiquité tardive,* Studia Ephemeridis Augustinianum 52 (Rome: Institutum Pontificium Augustinianum, 1996), pp. 9–61.

113. For the links between Christian Christological thought and Neo-Platonic discussions of mediation, joining, and identity, see Chadwick, "Eucharist and Christology in the Nestorian Controversy," pp. 160–163, and Preface to *Actes du Concile de Chalcédoine,* p. 15.

114. Synod of Ephesus of 447, ed. J. Flemming, *Die Akten der ephesinischen Synode von 447,* Abhandlungen der königlichen Gesellschaft der Wissenschaften zu Göttingen: Philol.-histor. Klasse 15.1 (1917): 118.9–10 (Syriac), 119.8–16 (trans.).

115. M. Van Esbroeck, "The Memra on the Parrot by Isaac of Antioch," *Journal of Theological Studies* n.s. 47 (1996): 464–476. On the chant in question, see s.v. Trisagion, *The Oxford Dictionary of Byzantium,* ed. A. Kazhdan (Oxford, U.K.: Oxford University Press, 1991), 3:2121.

116. Isaac of Antioch, *On the Incarnation,* lines 272–273, ed. G. Bickell, *Isaaci Antiocheni opera omnia* (Giessen: W. Keller, 1873), p. 44; trans. S. Landersdorfer, *Ausgewählte Schriften der syrischen Dichter,* Bibliothek der Kirchenväter (Munich: J. Kosel, 1913), p. 136.

117. Brändle, *Matth. 25, 31–46 im Werk des Johannes Chrysostomos,* pp. 331–338.

118. Severus of Antioch, *Homeliae cathedrales* 81: *Patrologia Orientalis* 20:369.

119. Severus of Antioch, *Homeliae cathedrales* 71: *Patrologia Orientalis* 12:67–68.

120. *Discourse of Demetrius, Archbishop of Antioch*, ed. E. A. W. Budge, *Coptic Texts in the Dialect of Upper Egypt* (London: British Museum, 1915), p. 693.

121. B. Alster, *Proverbs of Ancient Sumer* (Bethesda, Md.: CDL Press, 1997), 1:362.

122. R. Chesnut, *Three Monophysite Christologies* (Oxford, U.K.: Oxford University Press, 1976), p. 55.

123. Severus of Antioch, *Homeliae cathedrales* 28: *Patrologia Orientalis* 36:585–587.

124. See now D. W. Winkler, *Koptische Kirche und Reichskirche* (Innsbruck: Tyrolia, 1997).

125. Shenoute, *Letter* 31, ed. J. Leipoldt and W. E. Crum, *Corpus Scriptorum Christianorum Orientalium* 42: *Scriptores coptici* 3 (Leipzig: O. Harrassowitz, 1989), p. 95; trans. H. Wiessmann, *Corpus Scriptorum Christianorum Orientalium* 96: *Scriptores coptici* 8 (Louvain: L. Durbecq, 1953), p. 38.

126. W. E. Crum, *Der Papyruscodex saec.vi–vii der Phillippsbibliothek in Cheltenham*, Schriften der Wissenschaftlichen Gesellschaft in Strassburg 18 (Strassburg: K. J. Trübner, 1915), p. 44.9–22 (Coptic) 100 (trans.).

Index

Abinnaeus, Flavius, 89
Abraham (bishop of Hermonthis), 66
Advocacy revolution, 81, 83, 84
Aerius, 37–38
Africa: Carthage, 24–25, 27, 70–71; Cirta, 25–26, 120n.87; Cyrene, 103–4; Fussala, 65; Hippo, 55–56, 63, 64–65, 75; shortage of clergy in, 57; Thagaste, 55, 71
Against the Rich (Basil of Caesarea), 40–41
Alexander of Abonouteichos, 119n.73
Alexandria, 12–13, 30, 65
Alms. *See* Charity
Amasya (Amaseia), 12
Ambrose (bishop of Milan), 70, 71, 75, 98
Amiens, 12
Anastasioupolis, 78
Anastasius (emperor), 91
Ancyra, 11–12
Annona system, 27–28, 32
Antioch: amnesty after tax revolt in, 70; beggars outside the church in, 94; dole for the clergy in, 32; John Chrysostom on the poor in, 14; Monophysite notions of solidarity in, 108–10; widows and orphans on poor lists in, 65
Antiochene School, 100, 105
Antoninus (bishop of Fussala), 64–65, 71
Apamea (Abamiya), 52

Aphrodisias, 54
Apostles, 92, 93
Arcadius (emperor), 97, 101–2
Arian heresy, 30, 38
Aristides, Aelius, 85
Armenia, 42–43
Arsacius, 2, 33
Artisans, 21, 54, 57
Asceticism, 36, 37
Asclepius, 34
Asterius (bishop of Amaseia), 12
Athanasius of Alexandria, 30, 32
Augustine of Hippo, Saint: and amnesty for Carthaginian tax revolt, 70–71; *defensor civitatis* established by, 57; *The Didache* cited by, 56; and Honoratus, 71; immigrants welcomed into clergy by, 63, 75; as judge, 67–68; on Melania and Pinianus, 55–56; *On the Work of Monks*, 68; and the poor, 63–64; on poverty of the Apostles, 93; sermons and letters of, 63; and slavery, 61–62, 63; as stranger in Milan, 75
Augustine of Hippo: A Biography (Brown), viii
Augustus (emperor), 4, 98

Barbarian invasions, 61
Barth, Karl, 91
Basil (bishop of Ancyra), 68
Basileias, 35, 36, 39, 40, 46, 125n.150
Basil of Caesarea, Saint: *Against the Rich*, 40–41; Basileias of,

Basil of Caesarea *(continued)*
35, 36, 39, 40, 46, 125n.150; in
Cappadocian famine relief, 35–
36, 39–41; *chorepiscopi* system
of, 51; on euergetism, 28; on
monks not behaving like the
poor, 53; Nersês compared with,
43; tax relief sought by, 57
Bassianus (bishop of Ephesus),
126n.155
Beggars: begging as way of earning
money, 77; believers compared
with, 86; Christ as, 94, 97; commended to charity of the believers, 65; in late Roman empire,
12, 13–14; licenses for, 66; religious begging, 24, 119n.73; Severus on ignoring, 110
Besa, 90
Bet Shean (Scythopolis), 4, 12
Bishops, 45–73; and advocacy revolution, 83, 84; annual amount of
money dispensed to the poor by,
78; care for the poor as primary
duty of, 45; *chorepiscopi*, 51;
episcopalis audientia, 67–70;
freeing persons in danger of enslavement, 63; as governors of
the poor, 45, 79; to imperial
court, 90–91; increasing prominence in late Roman society, 1;
language of claims used by, 80,
111; laudatory epitaphs for, 72;
lay pressure on, 32; love-of-the-
poor notion developed by, 8–9;
as lovers of the poor, 1; as protectors of the weak, 89; schis-
matic, 30; social background of,
48, 49; on society as divided
between rich and poor, 80; as
stewards of wealth of the
church, 24–26; support of, 20;
tax exemption for, 29–30; widows and orphans protected by,
58–60; *xenodocheia* associated
with, 35
Bishop's court (*episcopalis audientia*), 67–70

Body and Society, The (Brown), ix
Bolkestein, Hendrik, 6–7, 16
Booth, William, 14
Bostra, 67
Bread and Circuses (Veyne), 7
Breast-feeding, 106
Bregovina, 87
Brown, Peter, vii–ix
Burial, 76, 109–10, 126n.160

Caesarea Cappadociae, 35–36, 39–
40, 41, 57
Caesarea Maritima, 52
Cannadine, David, 14
Cappadocia: Basil seeking tax relief
for, 57; Caesarea Cappadociae,
35–36, 39–40, 41, 57; *chorepiscopi* system in, 51; famine in,
35–36, 39–40, 41–42; poverty
and wealth contrasted in, 46
Cappadocian Fathers, 35
Care of the poor: acquisition of resources for, 56–57; by Basil of
Caesarea, 35–36, 39–41, 43; as
bishops' primary duty, 45;
Christians taking for granted,
19–20; Constantine charging
the church with, 32; direct charity as absent in late antiquity, 3;
downward extension of, 78–79;
Eustathius's program for, 38; by
Flacilla, 98–99; by Gregory the
Great, 60; and *humanitas*, 1; in
Judaism, 2, 113n.4; for middling
people, 49–50, 79; and
monotheism, 87; by Nersês, 42–
43; and novel forms of poverty
in late Roman empire, 7–8; performed in return for privileges,
31; public giving before rise of
Christianity, 3–6, 10–11; and
self-understanding in late classical society, 2–3, 74; and slavery, 61–63, 79; for widows and
orphans, 58–60; *xenodocheia
(ptôchotropheia)* for, 33–35
Carthage, 24–25, 27, 70–71
Chadwick, Henry, 106

Chalcedon, council of, 97, 107, 108, 109

Charity: Christianity on the cheerful giver, 3, 18; dole, 5, 32; as increasing in late antiquity, 77–78; as obligatory for Christians and Jews, 56; public giving before rise of Christianity, 3–6, 10–11; as public service, 31. *See also* Care of the poor; *Euergetai*

Chesnut, Roberta, 110

Chorepiscopi, 51

Christ. *See* Jesus of Nazareth

Christianity: alms as obligatory for, 56; Apostles, 92, 93; Arian heresy, 30, 38; care for the poor and novel forms of poverty in late Roman empire, 7–8; care for the poor taken for granted by, 19–20; charity of as new departure, 6; on the cheerful giver, 3, 18; clergy and bishops supported in, 20–26; Constantine charging church with care of the poor, 32; Constantine's giving to, 26–27; Donatist schism, 30, 55; Eucharist, 96; euergetism Christianized, 77–78; evolution from Saint Paul to Constantine, 16–19; finding place for outsiders of all classes, 74–75; images of the poor in, 11–14, 45–46; lay pressure for poor relief on, 32–33; middling persons as principal constituency of, 48–58; model of society of, 46–47, 79, 80, 86, 89, 111; monasticism, 36–37, 39, 80; Monophysites, 87, 107, 108–11; Paul, 17–18, 21, 86, 94; as percentage of Roman population in 312, 17; petitions employing language of, 89–91; poverty as moral challenge to, 16; Roman emperors humanized by, 98–100; solidarity of Christian community, 95–97; tax exemption for, 29–31; upper classes giving to 31; clergy and the poor, 28–29; wealth of the churches, 54–55. *See also* Clergy; Councils; Jesus of Nazareth (Christ); Scriptures

Christological controversies, 97–98, 100–108

Chronicon Paschale, 123n.121

Chrysostom, John. *See* John Chrysostom

Church, the. *See* Christianity

Cimitille, 34

Circus factions, 13

Cirta, 25–26, 120n.87

Civic model of society, 5, 11, 27, 32–33, 79, 84–85, 111

Claims, language of, 80, 111

Clarke, Graeme, 25

Class structure: Christian model of, 79, 80, 86, 111; of late Roman society, 15, 46–47, 74. *See also* Poor, the; Rich, the

Clergy: accountability of, 31; and advocacy revolution, 84; African shortage of, 57; allying with artisan guilds, 57; as closer to the poor than to the rich, 31; Constantine's levies for, 32; immigrants welcomed into, 63, 75; and slavery, 79; social background of, 48, 49–50, 54; on society as divided between rich and poor, 80; struggles against impoverishment of, 64–65; as successors to pagan priesthoods, 31; support of, 20–22; tax exemption for, 29–31. *See also* Bishops

Constantine (emperor): bishop's courts authorized by, 67; burial system of, 76; Christianity at time of conversion of, 16–17; donations to the church of, 26–27; levies to the clergy of, 32; tax exemptions granted by, 29–30

Constantinople: all roads leading to, 97; Constantine's burial system in, 76; Hagia Sophia, 99;

Constantinople *(continued)*
Hippodrome, 98, 99, 100; Nestorius as patriarch of, 100; peasant petitioners to, 84; poor relief in, 38; Theodosius I and, 99
Constantius II (emperor), 30, 34, 38, 43
Cornelius (bishop of Rome), 25
Corpora, 54
Councils: Chalcedon, 97, 107, 108, 109; Ephesus, 97, 110; Gangra, 36–37, 124n.130; Serdica, 91
Court, bishop's *(episcopalis audientia)*, 67–70
Cyprian (bishop of Carthage), 24–25, 58
Cyrene, 103–4
Cyril (bishop of Jerusalem), 40
Cyril (patriarch of Alexandria), 45, 72, 103–6, 110, 111, 144n.99

Defensor civitatis, 57
Demographic change, 7–8, 10, 75–76
Didache, The, 56
Dioscoros of Aphrodito, 88
Dole, 5, 32
Domitian (emperor), 21
Domnus (bishop of Antioch), 108–9
Donatianus of Suppa, 64
Donatist schism, 30, 55

Early modern Europe, demographic change in, 75–76
Eastern empire: Ancyra, 11–12; Armenia, 42–43; Caesarea Maritima, 52; Phrygia, 41, 126n.154; Pontus, 37; poverty and solidarity in the, 74–112; Scythopolis (Bet Shean), 4, 12; *xenodocheia* in, 34. *See also* Antioch; Cappadocia; Constantinople; Egypt
Ecclesiasticus (Wisdom of Ben Sira), 20
Egypt: Alexandria, 12–13, 30, 65; Aurelius Isidore's archive, 81; Christian language in petitions

in, 89–91; as Monophysite, 110; Oxyrhynchus, 12, 62, 114n.13
Elderly, the, 62
Elias (governor of Cappadocia), 40
Eliezer, 56
Emperors. *See* Roman emperors
Ephesus, council of, 97, 110
Ephraim of Nisibis, 41
Epidaurus, 34
Epiphanius of Salamis, 37
Episcopalis audientia (bishop's court), 67–70
Eraclius (bishop of Hippo), 126n.155
Eucharist, 96
Euergesia, 4
Euergetai: Basil of Caesarea appealing to, 39, 40, 42; Christianization of euergetism, 77–78; in Roman civic model of community, 4–5, 10–11; Roman emperors as, 4, 27–28; upper class Christians as, 28–29; *xenodocheia* built by, 35
Eusebius of Caesarea, 21, 120n.85
Eustathius of Sebasteia, 36–38, 39, 43

Farmers (peasants), 21, 84, 118n.64
Febronia, Saint, 145n.108
Felix, Saint, 34
Firmus (bishop of Thagaste), 71
Flacilla (wife of Theodosius I), 98–99
Flavian (bishop of Antioch), 70, 71
Fussala, 65

Gain, B., 132n.56
Gallicanus, 123n.121
Gangra, council of, 36–37, 124n.130
Garnsey, Peter, 47
Gaul: Bacaudic revolts in, 13; care for the poor in, 50; laudatory epitaphs for bishops, 72
Gaza, 65, 86
Gender studies, viii–ix
Gerasa (Jerash), 87

Gesios, 90
Gospels, 17
Governors, 88–89
Grammatici, 48–49
Greek and Latin Authors on Jews and Judaism (Stern), 2
Gregory of Langres, 89
Gregory of Nazianze, 35, 40, 76, 125n.142
Gregory of Nyssa, 35, 41, 93–94, 125n.142
Gregory of Tours, 72–73
Gregory the Great (pope), 60, 63
Gribomont, J., 39
Gutton, Jean-Pierre, 15

Hagia Sophia, 99
Hammurabi, 69
Harnack, Adolf von, 3
Hebrew Scriptures: on the pauper, 70, 80; petitions using language of, 87; Psalms, 70, 84, 87, 97
Heriêous, 58
Hermits, 51, 129n.22
Hesiod, 21, 88
Hippo, 55–56, 63, 64–65, 75
Hippodrome (Constantinople), 98, 99, 100
Honestiores, 52–53
Honoratus (bishop of Caesarea), 71–72
Hopkins, Keith, 49
Horden, Peregrine, 9
Hospitals, 33–34
Humanitas, 1
Humfress, Caroline, 47
Humiliores, 53

Impoverishment: fear of, 14–15. *See also* Poverty
Incarnation, 92, 110, 111
Isaac of Antioch, 109
Isidore, Aurelius, 81
Isotés, 18

Jerash (Gerasa), 87
Jerome, Saint, 70, 78, 128n.12

Jesus of Nazareth (Christ): as beggar, 94, 97; calling his disciples to life of poverty, 17; Christological controversies, 97–98, 100–108; Incarnation, 92, 110, 111; "My God, my God, why have you forsaken me," 82; Paul contrasted with, 19; poverty of, 91–95, and the rich, 17
John (patriarch of Alexandria), 12–13
John Chrysostom: Augustine of Hippo compared with, 63–64; believers compared with the poor by, 86; on charity of average Christians, 65–66; and Christological controversies, 106, 109, 110; on church support of widows, 59; on class structure in Antioch, 14; Eucharist and sermons of, 96; on euergetism, 28; leper house near Constantinople, 34; on poverty of Christ, 95; Theophilus in overthrow of, 103
John of Lycopolis, 90
Judaism: alms as obligatory for Jews, 56; care of the poor in, 2, 113n.4; charity of as new departure, 6; love of the poor praised in, 2; *Midrash*, 92; Pharisees, 21; rabbis, 22, 31, 60, 119n.67; slaves redeemed in, 62; support of clergy in, 20, 22; synagogues, 55. *See also* Hebrew Scriptures
Julian the Apostate (emperor), 2, 32, 33, 34, 67, 92
Justin II (emperor), 88
Justinian (emperor), 59–60, 84

Kaster, Robert, 48
Kayseri (Caesarea Cappadociae), 35–36, 39–40, 41, 57
Khorenac'i, Movsês, 43
Kiss of Peace, 96
Kissufim, 28, 55, 121n.95
Kovelman, Arkady, 82
Krt, 69

Laodike (wife of Antiochus III), 114n.14
Last Judgment, 95, 111
Lepers, 33–34, 40
Leporius, 65
Letter to the Romans (Saint Paul), 86
Linen burial shrouds, 126n.160
Love of the poor: and almsgiving in ancient Mediterranean, 77–78; bishops as lovers of the poor, 1; bishops in development of notion of, 8–9; and civic sense of community, 5–6; the emperor associated with, 1, 89; and governors, 88; lay pressure on church for, 32–33; and novel forms of poverty in late Roman empire, 8; as public virtue, 1, 3, 74; Scriptures on, 17–18
Lucian, 21, 26
Lucilla, 26–27, 120n.87

Ma'ale Adummim, 33
Ma'arat an-Numan, 35
Marathonius, 38
Marcian (emperor), 1
Marcus Aurelius (emperor), 85
Marshall, John, 29
Martin of Tours, Saint, 12, 50–51
Martyrius, Saint, 33
Mary, as *Theotokos*, 101, 104–6
Maternus, Firmicus, 64
Matricula, 65
Matthew, 95
Maurilio (bishop of Cahors), 72–73
Meeks, Wayne, 19
Melania the Younger, Saint, 55–56
Midrash, 92
Migne, Jacques Paul, 48
Miôs, 89–90
Mission and Expansion of Christianity, The (von Harnack), 3
Models of society, 9; Christian model, 46–47, 79, 80, 86, 89, 111; civic model, 5, 11, 27, 32–33, 79, 84–85, 111
Modestus, 57

Monasticism, 36–37, 39, 80
Monophysites, 87, 107, 108–11
Monotheism, 87, 97
Mosaics, 55

Neoclaudiopolis, 35
Neo-Platonism, 107, 145n.113
Nersès (patriarch of Armenia), 42–43, 126n.160
Nestorius (patriarch of Constantinople), 100–107
Nicetius of Lyon, 66
Nilus of Ancyra, 82

Old people's homes, 62
Olympian Zeus, 88
On the Love of the Poor (Gregory of Nazianze), 76
On the Work of Monks (Augustine of Hippo), 68
Order of widows, 59
Orphans, 32, 58–59, 65, 69
Oxyrhynchus, 12, 62, 114n.13

Paideia, 53, 85
Pamonthios, 58, 62
Panapolis, 90
Patlagean, Evelyne, 7, 8, 9, 10
Patrologia Graeca (Migne), 48
Patrologia Latina (Migne), 48
Paul, Saint, 17–18, 21, 86, 94
Paulinus of Nola, 34
Pauvreté économique et pauvreté sociale à Byzance: 4–7e siècles (Patlagean), 7
P'awstos Buzand, 42, 43, 143n.89
Pbow, monastery of, 91
Peasants (farmers), 21, 84, 118n.64
Pelagius I (pope), 60
Peter the Fuller, 109
Petitions, 81–84, 88, 89–91
Pharisees, 21
Philanthropia, 34
Philopatris, 5
Philotimos, 4
Phrygia, 41, 126n.154
Piioutios, 88
Pinianus, 55–56

Pliny the Younger, 115n.26
Ponos, 21
Pontus, 37
Poor, the: Augustine of Hippo and,
63–64; believers compared
with, 86–88; bishops as governors of, 45, 79; bishops as invent-
ing, 8, 10; Christian images of,
11–14, 45 46, clergy associated
with, 31; clergy sharing wealth
of the church with, 24–26; in
Cyril's Christology, 104; fear of,
13, 116n.40; Hebrew Scriptures
on, 70, 80; *humiliores*, 53; impoverished members of upper
classes, 60; Jesus on, 17; as judicial category, 69–70; justice for,
69–70; number of, 14; Paul on
equalizing resources, 18; poor of
the church, 65; Roman
emperors' gifts to, 4, 5; society
seen as divided between the
wealthy and, 6, 15, 46–47, 51,
74, 79, 80, 111; *tenuiores*, 53,
78; uprisings by, 13, 53; upward
slippage in notion of, 71–72. *See
also* Beggars; Care of the poor;
Love of the poor; Poverty
Poorhouses, 34, 35, 38, 50
Population growth, 7–8, 10, 75–76
Potentiores, 53
Poverty: of Christ, 91–95; deep and
shallow, 15, 16; fear of impoverishment, 14–15; Jesus calling
his disciples to life of, 17; of
monks, 36; as moral challenge
to Christianity, 16; novel forms
in late Roman empire, 7–8; and
solidarity in the Eastern Empire, 74–112. *See also* Poor, the
*Power and Persuasion in Late An-
tiquity: Towards a Christian
Empire* (Brown), 84
Pozzuoli, 32
Procopius, 59
Prosopographie chrétienne, 48
Psalis, 66
Psalms, 70, 84, 87, 97

Psois, 90
Ptôchotropheia (xenodocheia), 33–
35, 38, 43, 50, 65
Pulcheria (sister of Theodosius II),
101
Purcell, Nicholas, 10

Questions and Answers (Coptic
collection), 45, 72, 111

Rabbis, 22, 31, 60, 119n.67
Rabbula (bishop of Edessa), 96
Ravenna, 78
Religious expertise, democratization of, 20–22
Rich, the: Basil of Caesarea's
Against the Rich, 40–41; in cities, 52; in Cyril's Christology,
104; Eustathius redistributing
wealth of, 38; impoverished
members of upper classes, 60;
Jesus associating with, 17; Paul
on equalizing resources, 18;
praising generosity of, 77; public giving before rise of Christianity, 3–6; society seen as divided between the poor and, 6,
15, 46–47, 51, 74, 79, 80, 111.
See also *Euergetai*
Riots, urban, 53
Robert, Louis, 28, 125n.146
Roman emperors: Anastasius, 91;
annona system, 27–28; Arcadius, 97, 101–2; Augustus, 4,
98; Christian ritual humaniz-
ing, 98–100; Christological controversies and, 98, 102–3; Constantius II, 30, 34, 38, 43;
Domitian, 21; as *euergetai*, 4,
27–28; exaltation of, 98; fear of,
86; Julian the Apostate, 2, 32,
33, 34, 67, 92; Justin II, 88; Justinian, 59–60, 84; love of the
poor associated with, 1, 89;
Marcian, 1; and *paideia*, 85; personal generosity of, 4; petitions
invited by, 83; representatives
of, 83–84; Theodosius I, 70, 71,

Roman emperors *(continued)*
90, 97, 98; Theodosius II, 97,
99–105; Valens, 41–42,
126n.157; Valentinian III, 1. *See
also* Constantine
Roman state: governors, 88–89; increasing closeness to its subjects, 81–86. *See also* Roman
emperors; Taxation
Rome: *annona civica,* 27;
emperors' gifts of free food in, 4,
5; *xenodocheion* in, 123n.121

Sabas, Saint, 12, 91
"Safety-net," social, 50
Scriptures: in Augustine's judicial
decisions, 68–69; Gospels, 17;
on love of the poor, 17–18; Mat-
thew, 95; Paul's *Letter to the
Romans,* 86; Paul's *Second Let-
ter to the Corinthians,* 94. *See
also* Hebrew Scriptures
Scythopolis (Bet Shean), 4, 12
Sebasteia, 37–38
Second Letter to the Corinthians
(Saint Paul), 94
Serdica, council of, 91
Severus of Antioch, 109–10
Shakespeare, William, 22
Shenoute of Atripe, 90–91, 110
Silthous, 28, 55
Slaves, 61–63, 79
Smyrna, 85
Social "safety-net," 50
Sportulae, 26
State, the. *See* Roman state
Stern, Menahem, vii, 2
Stratonikeia, 72
Symeon Stylites, 105
Synagogues, 55
Synesius (bishop of Ptolemais),
103–4

Tarragona, 52
Taxation: bishops seeking relief
from, 57; church exemption
from, 29–31; petitions regard-
ing, 81, 83; *philanthropia,* 34;
revolts against, 70; *xenodocheia
(ptôchotropheia)* as exempt
from, 34, 35
Tenuiores, 53, 78
Tesserae, 5
Thagaste, 55, 71
Theissen, Gerd, 19
Theodoret of Cyrrhus, 105
Theodosius I (emperor), 70, 71, 90,
97, 98
Theodosius II (emperor), 97, 99–
105
Theophilus, 103
Thessalonica, 70
Town councilors, 53
Trier, 35
Tyre, 12

Urban riots, 53
Urukagina of Lagish, 69

Valens (emperor), 41–42, 126n.157
Valentinian III (emperor), 1
Valetudinaria, 34
Veyne, Paul, 7, 8, 9
Virgin Mary, as *Theotokos,* 101,
104–6

Wallace-Hadrill, Andrew, 47
Wealthy, the. *See* Rich, the
White Monastery of Shenoute, 90
Widows, 32, 58–60, 65, 69
Wild-beast shows, 96
*Wisdom of Ben Sira (Ecclesiasti-
cus),* 20

Xenodocheia (ptôchotropheia), 33–
35, 38, 43, 50, 65

Z'daqah, 70
Ze'aqah, 70
Zeus, Olympian, 88

Index of Authors

Abramowski, L., 144n.105
Alster, B., 146n.121
Ambrose of Milan, 142n.79
Anderson, J. G. C., 123n.124
Angstenberger, P., 142n.67
Ashbrook Harvey, S., 144n.105,
    145n.108
Asterius of Amaseia, 116n.29
Athanasius of Alexandria, 122n.113
Augustine of Hippo, Saint,
    131nn.41, 44, 46, 133n.72,
    136n.110, 137n.130, 137n.2
Avemarie, F., 119n.67
Avi-Yonah, M., 123n.119

Bagnall, R., 121n.100
Barkan, Ömer, 123n.118
Barnes, T. D., 121n.98, 124n.133,
    136n.114
Barnish, S., 120n.90
Barth, K., 141n.58
Basil of Caesarea, Saint, 119n.72,
    124n.142, 125nn.146, 147, 149,
    130n.34, 131n.47, 132n.56
Baynes, N. H., 116n.35, 138n.15,
    144n.96
Bell, H. I., 132n.50, 140n.51
Bell, N., 141n.54
Belting, H., 145n.110
Bernardi, J., 125n.142
Besa, 141n.54
Bickell, G., 145n.116
Bidez, J., 122n.111
Billerbeck, P., 113n.4
Blum, G. G., 142n.75
Bolkestein, H., 115n.18

Bonnardière, A. M. de la, 128n.14
Bonnassie, P., 133n.69
Booth, William, 117n.45
Bosworth, C. E., 117n.41
Botterweck, G. J., 118n.56
Bowersock, G. W., 116n.38,
    123n.126, 138n.11
Bowman, A. K., 138n.17
Bradley, K. R., 144n.106
Bram, J. R., 134n.89
Brändle, R., 141n.65
Braund, S. M., 139n.34
Bremmer, J., 132n.54
Brennecke, H. C., 124n.138,
    126n.157
Broadus, J. A., 140n.38
Brock, S. P., 145n.108
Bromley, G. W., 141n.58
Brown, Peter, 114n.12, 116n.38,
    138n.18
Browne, C. G., 125n.142
Bruck, E., 118n.54
Budge, E. A. W., 146n.120

Caillet, J. P., 131n.38
Cameron, A., 116n.38, 121n.97,
    128n.13
Cannadine, David, 117n.43
Carozzi, C., 138n.12
Carrié, J. M., 120n.89, 135n.105,
    139n.119
Catacolon, Cecaumenus, 140n.39
Cavallo, G., 115n.20
Cavallo, S., 125n.150
Cecconi, A., 129n.14, 131n.41
Çetin Şahin, M., 137n.134

Chadwick, H. E., 141n.61, 142n.77,
    144nn.99, 105
Champlin, E., 115n.27
Chastagnol, A., 115n.25
Chekalova, A. A., 116n.38
Chesnut, Roberta, 143n.90,
    146n.122
Christie, N., 129n.19
Clark, E., 131n.40
Clark Cox, A., 144n.107
Clarke, Graeme, 119n.75
Clement of Alexandria, 144n.107
Coleman Norton, P. R., 143n.88
Cormack, R., 145n.109
Cowgill, G. C., 136n.121
Cracco-Ruggini, L., 127n.1,
    130n.35, 132n.48
Crum, W. E., 113n.1, 127n.1,
    135n.97, 141n.54
Cumont, F., 123n.124
Cyprian of Carthage, 119n.75
Cyril of Alexandria, 143n.83,
    144nn.100, 102
Cyril of Scythopolis, 116n.31,
    141n.57

Dagron, G., 124n.136, 130n.31,
    132n.58, 138n.7
Daley, B. E., 125n.145
Datema, C., 116n.29
Davis, N. Z., 137n.6
Dawes, E., 116n.35, 138n.15
Deferrari, R. J., 119n.72
Delmaire, R., 122n.110, 137n.127
Demosthenes, 126n.156
Demougin, S., 115n.25
Déroche, V., 116n.35
de Ste Croix, G. E. M., 128n.8
Dewing, H. B., 132n.59
Diehl, E., 113n.3
Dihle, A., 121n.99
Dolbeau, F., 133n.72
Dorotheus of Gaza, 140n.37
Drake, H. A., 136n.105
Draper, J. A., 118n.57
Drinkwater, J., 133n.69
Driver, G. R., 143n.82

Ducloux, M., 133n.74
Duncan-Jones, R., 115n.26
Durliat, Jean, 120n.89
Duval, Y., 120n.87
Dyers, H. J., 127n.7

Edwards, M., 120n.84
Eleonksaia, A. S., 137n.6
Elton, H., 133n.69
Emmel, S., 141n.53
Engemann, J., 143n.81
Eno, R., 131n.46
Ephraim of Nisibis, 125n.153
Epiphanius of Salamis, 123n.116
Epstein, I., 119n.67
Esmonde-Cleary, A. S., 128n.11
Eusebius of Caesarea, 118n.63,
    122n.111

Faroqhi, S., 125n.144
Feissel, D., 139n.29
Felix, 138n.14
Fensham, F. C., 136n.118
Fernandez Pomar, J., 140n.45
Ferrandus, 127n.3
Festugière, A. J., 142n.77
Fitschen, K., 124n.133
Fitzgerald, A., 137n.132
Flemming, J., 135n.96
Flusser, D., 117n.52
Foerster, G., 114n.11
Foss, C., 128n.13
Fournet, J. L., 139n.22
Fox, M. M., 128n.9
Frankfurter, D., 140n.53
Frend, W. H. C., 124n.140,
    145n.111
Friedman, F. D., 135n.97
Furlani, J., 129n.15

Gain, B., 125n.150
Gallant, T. W., 114n.9
Garnsey, P., 114n.7, 115n.16,
    121n.97, 128nn.12, 13, 131n.35,
    133n.67
Garsoian, N., 126nn.158, 159, 160
Gascou, J., 139n.29

Gatier, P.-L., 128n.13
Gebremedhin, E., 144n.99
Geremek, B., 117n.44
Giardina, A., 129n.18, 130n.24
Giles, C., 139n.34
Gorce, D., 131n.40
Gordon, D., 118n.61
Grabar, Oleg, 116n.38
Grant, R. M., 121n.104
Gray, J., 136n.122
Grégoire, H., 123n.124, 135n.94
Gregory Nazianzen, 125n.142
Gregory of Nyssa, 125n.142,
    130n.22, 141n.66, 143n.83
Gregory of Tours, 127n.2, 129n.22
Gregory the Great, 133n.60
Greiser, H., 133n.69
Gribomont, J., 123n.128
Grodzynski, D., 130n.33
Gruszka, P., 128n.9
Gutton, J.-P., 117n.40

Hallman, J. M., 142n.77
Hansen, G. C., 122n.111, 124n.137,
    126n.157
Harmon, A. M., 118n.65
Harnack, A. von, 114n.6
Harries, J., 139n.26
Harris, W. V., 133n.71
Hartel, W., 119n.75
Hartranft, C. D., 122n.111
Hauschild, W. D., 123n.129,
    125n.142
Henderson, John, 117n.44
Hermas, 119n.67
Hesiod, 118n.64
Hezser, C., 119n.67
Hill, E., 133n.72
Himmelfarb, G., 127nn.4, 7
Hinrichs, J. C., 143n.89
Hirschfeld, Y., 128n.13
Hoare, F. R., 129n.21
Hock, R. E., 119n.68
Hodgson, L., 143n.82
Hollerich, M. J., 122n.111
Holman, S., 124n.142
Holum, K., 139n.36, 143n.84

Holum, K. G., 130n.28
Hopkins, K., 117n.51, 139n.20
Hörander, W., 122n.114
Horden, Peregrine, 115n.24,
    134n.93
Horn, J., 145n.108
Hufton, O., 133n.70
Humbert, M., 134n.81
Humfress, C., 128n.12
Humphrey, J. H., 139n.20
Hunt, A. S., 134n.78

Iliffe, J., 137n.4
Isaac of Antioch, 145n.116
Israeli, Y., 121n.95

Jackson, B., 126n.157
Jacobs, M., 122n.107
Jacques, F., 114n.11, 131n.46
Jaeger, W., 125n.142
James, E., 130n.22
Jephcott, E., 145n.110
Jeremić, M., 140n.41
Jernstedt, V., 140n.39
Jerome, Saint, 132n.55, 136n.124,
    138n.12
John Chrysostom, 117n.42,
    134n.94, 140n.38, 142nn.72, 73
John the Deacon, 133n.63
Joly, R., 119n.67
Jones, A. H. M., 121n.100,
    126n.156, 131n.37, 145n.112
Jonkers, E. J., 141n.55
Julian the Apostate, 113n.5,
    141n.62
Justinian, 139n.30

Kamlin, R., 119n.67
Kaplan, M., 128n.13
Kaster, R., 129n.16, 139n.35
Kazhdan, A., 145n.115
Keay, S., 130n.27
Keck, L., 118n.54
Kelly, C., 121n.97, 138n.17,
    142n.78
Kennedy, H., 129n.19, 130n.24
King, G. R. D., 128n.13

Kislinger, E., 122n.114
Kittel, G., 118n.52
Klingshirn, W., 134n.79
Koenen, L., 140n.45
Kovelman, A., 139n.22
Kramer, S. N., 136n.119
Krause, J. U., 132n.52
Krause, M., 141n.53
Kravari, V., 138n.7
Kroll, W., 139n.30
Krüger, P., 113n.2
Kugener, M.-A., 135n.94

Lamoreaux, J., 135n.103
Lane-Fox, R., 117n.51
Langenfeld, H., 133n.73
Laniado, A., 130n.29
Lantschoot, A. van, 141n.56
Le Blant, G., 113n.3
Lehrman, S. M., 141n.59
Leipoldt, J., 141n.54
Lendon, J. E., 139n.32
Lenski, N., 126n.154
Leontius, 116n.35
Lepelley, C., 115n.25, 120n.92,
    137n.127
Leporius, 134n.92
Le Vaillant de Florival, 126n.161
Levine, David, 116n.36
Levine, L., 119n.67
Libanius, 138n.11
Lifshitz, F., 131n.39
Lightfoot, J. B., 131n.43
Linder, A., 122n.107
Lizzi, R., 121n.101, 137n.125
Lobel, E., 140n.44
Loseby, T., 129n.19
Lucian, 118n.65

Ma, John, 114n.8
MacCoull, L. S. B., 140n.43
MacMullen, R., 120n.92, 133n.68
Magen, Y., 122n.115
Mahé, A., 126n.160
Mahé, J.-P., 126n.160
Mandouze, A., 128n.14
Manning, C. E., 115n.26

Mansi, J. D., 124n.131, 135n.96
Maraval, P., 130n.22
Marazzi, F., 129n.18
Mark the Deacon, 135n.94
Markus, R. A., 133n.60
Marrou, H. I., 140n.40
Martin, A., 113n.1
Martindale, J. R., 126n.156
Martz, Linda, 123n.118
Maspéro, J., 140n.46
Maternus, Firmicus, 134n.89
Mathews, T., 120n.85
Matthews, John, 142n.80
Mazzarino, Santo, 120n.89
McGiffert, A. C., 118n.63
McGinn, T. A. J., 132n.52
McGuckin, J. A., 142n.77, 143n.91
McLynn, Neil, 137n.126, 143n.88
Meeks, Wayne A., 118n.58
Melinkoff, Ruth, 117n.40
Mentzou-Meimari, K., 122n.114
Mevorah, D., 121n.95
Meyer, R. T., 115n.28
Milinković, M., 140n.41
Millar, F., 139n.28
Miller, T. S., 123n.117
Milner, N. P., 142n.78
Moffat, J., 114n.6
Morin, G., 138n.12
Morris, J., 126n.156
Morris, J. B., 142n.72
Movsês Khorenac'i, 126n.161
Mucznik, S., 121n.95

Natali, A., 138n.9
Nau, F., 116n.33
Naveh, J., 131n.39
Neri, Valerio, 116n.37
Nestorius, 143n.82
Nilus of Ancyra, 139n.23
Noethlichs, K. L., 121n.99
Norberg, D., 133n.60
Norman, A. F., 138n.11
Noy, D., 113n.4

Olivár, A., 127n.5
Optatus of Milevis, 120n.84

Origen, 141n.61
Ovadiah, A., 121n.95

Palladius, 115n.28, 132n.55
Parca, M. G., 142n.68
Parker, T., 134n.76
Parmentier, L., 126n.157
Pascal, P., 137n.6
Patkanean, K., 126n.159
Patlagean, E., 115n.20, 129n.18
Patrich, J., 130n.28
Paulinus of Nola, 123n.122
P'awstos Buzand, 126n.159
Peel, J. D. Y., 142n.68
Pelagius, 133n.66
Percival, H. R., 124n.131
Petrus Chrysologus, 127n.5
Pharr, C., 122n.105
Picard, J. C., 136n.111
Pietri, Charles, 123n.121, 127n.6,
    128n.14, 130n.23
Pietri, Luce, 123n.121, 128n.14
Pigulevskaia, N., 127n.161
Polley, M. E., 136n.116
Possidius, 136n.110
Préville, J. de, 140n.37
Prevost, G., 134n.94
Price, R. M., 116n.31
Procopius of Caesarea, 132n.59
Pseudo-Athanasius, 113n.1
Purcell, Nicholas, 115n.24,
    120n.90

Raabe, T., 143n.89
Raban, A., 130n.28
Rajak, T., 113n.4
Rawson, B., 134n.76
Rea, J., 140n.45
Rebillard, E., 113n.1, 129n.14,
    138n.7
Redgate, A. E., 127n.165
Regnault, L., 140n.37, 142n.76
Reidel, W., 113n.1
Rémondon, R., 140n.50
Renoux, C., 125n.153
Reynolds, J., 113n.4
Riccobono, S., 121n.98

Ringgren, H., 118n.56
Robert, L., 121n.93
Roberts, C. H., 140n.44
Robinson, A. N., 137n.6
Rosenzweig, R., 118n.53
Roth-Gerson, L., 131n.39
Rouche, M., 135n.94
Roueché, C., 116n.38, 121n.93,
    134n.76, 135n.105
Rougé, J., 116n.40
Rousseau, P., 124n.129
Rowland, R. J., 114n.13
Rubin, Z., 116n.38
Rufus, John, 143n.89
Russell, J., 126n.160
Russell, N., 142n.77
Russell-Wood, J. R., 133n.75
Rutgers, L. V., 113n.3

Sá, I. dos Guimarâes, 133n.75
Saffrai, Ze'ev, 113n.4
Samson, R., 133nn.68, 69
Sanders, E. P., 118n.61
Schaff, P. W., 140n.38
Schaten, S., 141n.53
Scheidel, W., 115n.16
Schiavone, Aldo, 117n.49
Schimmel, Anne Marie, 116n.30
Schöll, P., 139n.30
Schöllgen, G., 118n.59, 120n.81,
    132n.52
Scholten, G., 130n.23
Schwab, M., 122n.106
Schwartz, E., 141nn.57, 63, 66
Selb, W., 135n.104
Severus of Antioch, 146n.118
Shakespeare, W., 119n.66
Shanin, T., 134n.86
Shaw, Brent, 116n.38, 128n.8
Shenoute of Atripe, 146n.125
Shepherd, D. G., 145n.109
Simcox, W. H., 142n.72
Slack, P., 117n.40
Slavinetskii, Epifanii, 137n.6
Smith, J. M. H., 129n.18
Smith, R., 134n.93
Smith, R. R. R., 140n.48

Socrates, 124n.137
Soden, H. von, 120n.84
Sotinel, C., 113n.1, 128n.14
Sozomen, 122n.111
Spira, A., 143n.83
Stark, R., 117n.51
Stern, Menahem, 114n.5
Sternberg, T., 122n.114, 134n.79,
    140n.42
Strack, H. L., 113n.4
Strubbe, J., 114n.14
Sulpicius Severus, 116n.32,
    129n.21, 136n.112
Swallow, J. E., 125n.142
Synesius of Cyrene, 137n.132,
    144n.101

Tabbernee, W., 121n.96
Tannenbaum, R., 113n.4
Teja, R., 128n.9
Terzhagi, N., 144n.101
Theissen, G., 118nn.57, 58,
    119n.68
Theodoret of Cyrrhus, 126n.157
Theodotus of Ancyra, 141n.63
Theophilus of Alexandria, 132n.55
Thomas, C., 131n.38
Thomas, J. P., 122n.114
Thompson, E. A., 116n.39, 134n.79
Thompson, R. W., 127n.161
Thorpe, L., 127n.2
Tomlin, R. S. O., 115n.15
Trombley, F. R., 130n.24
Trout, D., 138n.9
Tsafrir, Y., 114n.11
Turner, E. G., 140n.45

Van Dam, R., 125n.142
van den Bosch, L., 132n.54
Van de Paverd, F., 142n.74
Van Esbroeck, M., 145n.115
Van Ommeslaeghe, F., 123n.119
Vaporis, N. M., 130n.24

Vegetius, 142n.78
Veyne, P., 114n.7
Virlouvet, C., 115n.17
Vittinghoff, F., 121n.99
Volpe, G., 118n.64

Wagner, E. P., 140n.44
Walker, J., 135n.95
Wallace-Hadrill, A., 128n.10,
    144n.97
Walsh, P. G., 123n.122
Wassiliewsky, B., 140n.39
Weaver, P., 134n.76
Webb, R., 139n.34
Weinfeld, M., 122n.104
Weitzmann, K., 145n.109
Wenger, A., 142n.73, 143n.84
Wessel, W., 144n.100
Whitby, M. and M., 123n.121
Whittaker, C. R., 128n.13, 131n.35
Whittow, M., 129n.19
Wickham, L. R., 144n.99
Wiessmann, H., 146n.125
Williams, F., 123n.116
Williams, M. H., 113n.4
Willis, J. T., 118n.56
Wimbush, V. L., 124n.131
Winkler, D. W., 146n.124
Wipszycka, E., 130n.25, 131n.37,
    145n.112
Wischmeyer, O., 118n.60
Wolff, M., 127n.7
Woolf, G., 115n.15, 138n.17
Wright, W. C., 113n.5
Wrightson, Keith, 116n.36

Yarborough, O. L., 124n.131
Yoffee, N., 136n.121

Zenos, A. C., 124n.137
Ziegler, J., 122n.111
Ziwsa, J., 120n.84
Zuckerman, C., 140n.52